THE OUTSKIRTS OF REDEMPTION

CLAYTON TRIER

THE OUTSKIRTS OF REDEMPTION

Copyright © 2023 Clayton Trier

First Edition: 2023

All rights reserved. No part of this publication may be reproduced, distributed, or transmitted in any form or by any means, including photocopying, recording, or other electronic or mechanical methods, without the prior written permission of the publisher, except in the case of brief quotations embodied in critical reviews and certain other noncommercial uses permitted by copyright law.

This book is a work of fiction. Names, characters, places, and incidents are either products of the author's imagination or are used fictitiously. Any resemblance to actual persons, living or dead, or locales is entirely coincidental.

ISBN-13: 978-1-955937-48-1 (Paperback)
ISBN-13: 978-1-955937-47-4 (eBook)

Published by Defiance Press & Publishing, LLC

Bulk orders of this book may be obtained by contacting Defiance Press & Publishing, LLC. www.defiancepress.com.

Public Relations Dept. – Defiance Press & Publishing, LLC
281-581-9300
pr@defiancepress.com

Defiance Press & Publishing, LLC
281-581-9300
info@defiancepress.com

To my dearest **KELLEY**

Contents

CONFESSIONAL: June 1974

Chapter 1: I'M ONLY DOING THIS BECAUSE I LOVE HER 7

PART ONE: Monday, January 11, 1965

Chapter 2: 7:00 a.m. 11
Chapter 3: 7:05 a.m. 21
Chapter 4: 7:07 a.m. 27
Chapter 5: 7:10 a.m. 39
Chapter 6: 12:00 noon 53
Chapter 7: 12:30 p.m. 63
Chapter 8: 12:40 p.m. 75
Chapter 9: 2:40 p.m. 87
Chapter 10: 3:40 p.m. 103
Chapter 11: 4:25 p.m. 108
Chapter 12: 4:30 p.m. 112
Chapter 13: 5:00 p.m. 123
Chapter 14: 5:40 p.m. 139
Chapter 15: 6:00 p.m. 148
Chapter 16: 6:30 p.m. 160
Chapter 17: 7:30 p.m. 162
Chapter 18: 8:00 p.m. 175
Chapter 19: 8:20 p.m. 189
Chapter 20: 9:00 p.m. 199
Chapter 21: 9:30 p.m. 208
Chapter 22: 10:20 p.m. 225
Chapter 23: 11:00 p.m. 242
Chapter 24: 11:55 p.m. 248
Chapter 25: BE SOMEBODY 253

CONTENTS

PART TWO: 1973-74 The Aftermath

Chapter 26: LARRY 257
Chapter 27: MARTY 267
Chapter 28: ALLIE 295
Chapter 29: BAD GUYS 311
Chapter 30: BEST FRIENDS 334
Chapter 31: DAD 359

POSTSCRIPT 379
AUTHOR'S NOTE 380

CONFESSIONAL

June 1974

Chapter 1

I'M ONLY DOING THIS BECAUSE I LOVE HER

Everything came crashing down on January 11, 1965. It was the day they told me about my best friend, Daniel—that he was suddenly gone, that he had killed himself. Like me, he was 12 years old back then.

They tell you that the pain will go away over time. But when you're only 12, "over time" is incomprehensible. I was certain that the anguish raging within my young soul would burn for the rest of my life. That's because I carried a secret that none of them knew—not my parents, my dead friend's parents, our teachers, the nuns, the policeman investigating the case, nor the beautiful young psychologist they brought in. None of them knew the role I had played in this tragedy. None of them knew that it could not have happened without my complicity, at least not on the particular day and in the particular way it occurred. No matter how I've tried to rationalize it over the nine years that have followed, I still reach the same inescapable conclusion: I was the one responsible for Daniel's suicide.

I recently broke down and spilled my guts to Allie. She's my psychologist friend, who also happens to be the most amazing woman on this planet. I've been infatuated with her since I first laid eyes on her on that January day nine years ago. Now that she finally knows everything, she's convinced me that telling this story will be a cleansing experience. Allie says that human beings are dented cans. We all make mistakes from time to time, sometimes gigantic ones that make big dents. We can't expect to be perfect. It's the same thing my father often says, especially on mornings when he's had too much to drink the night before.

She knows all the right buttons to push with me. She plays on my Catholic upbringing by saying that it will be just like going to confession. In catechism classes, they filled our heads with platitudes like, "Confession is good for the soul." They quoted from the Book of John: "If we confess our sins, He who is faithful and just will forgive us our sins and cleanse us from all unrighteousness."

I don't know about all that religious stuff anymore. I'm only doing this because I love her, and I know that she loves me as well and wants to see me get better. Allie and I have been through a lot together, and I trust her implicitly.

But deep down, I'm not so sure. If I confess, maybe God will forgive me. Maybe the people who hear this story will forgive me. Or maybe they won't. But I'm ready to take that chance because if I can be forgiven, then maybe I'll be able to forgive myself. And that's what Allie says it's going to take for me to escape from the little corner of purgatory where I've resided for the past nine years. It's a desolate and lonely place located this side of Hell but firmly outside the tall white gates of Redemption.

So, bless me, Father, for I have sinned. It is the summer of 1974, and I am 21 years old. It has been over nine years since my last confession, or at least since my last truthful confession, before I came to have a friend's blood on my hands.

PART ONE

Monday, January 11, 1965

Chapter 2

7:00 a.m.

My folks told me after breakfast. I always had cereal before leaving for school. It was fast and, best of all, was the one time I didn't have to depend on either of my doting parents to do anything for me. I could feed and take care of myself, and the feeling of independence, brief as it may have been, was exhilarating.

Breakfast required just four simple items: bowl, spoon, milk, and cereal from a choice of two or three varieties that my mother kept stocked in a small pantry. The cereal selection was the only thing that took any deliberation. I thought the Kellogg Company had to be run by very smart people since they named their cereals *Sugar* Frosted Flakes, *Sugar* Smacks, and *Sugar* Pops. That was brilliant. That way, parents could easily see which cereals were best for their kids—which ones the kids would enjoy the most. On that Monday morning, I chose Sugar Frosted Flakes. I had just slurped the last spoonful, picturing Tony the Tiger in my mind and thinking they were *Grrreat!* That was the kind of idiot childlike stuff I used to think about before that day, before they told me.

"Sit down, please," my father said with a strange softness in his voice.

"But Dad, I need to—"

"I'll get your bowl." My mother's voice also was soft like tiptoeing over a creaking floor. So was her hand on my shoulder, tenderly urging me back into my seat across from Dad.

Oh, Lord, help me! What have I done now? My mind raced as I struggled to void my face of any emotion, especially that telltale look that screamed, *Yes, I did it!* Masking that guilty look was difficult at 12, but I had been practicing. By the end of that day, I would have it down pat.

My father didn't seem interested in my look. He licked his lips, and there was a tightness in his face and his voice. "Lawrence, I need to tell you something, and I don't know any other way than to just come out with it."

Now I knew something was terribly wrong. Dad always called me "Buddy" or "Son." When he used my formal name, it meant that he required my complete attention. Looking over Dad's shoulder, I saw my mother staring into the metal sink where she'd set my empty bowl so gently that it never made a sound. A tear rolled slowly down her cheek.

That unsettling scene brought back memories from two years before. I was ten years old, and it was a Sunday morning about two weeks before Christmas. It was the day I found out for sure that there was no Santa Claus. Oh, I had strongly suspected that he was a fairy tale, but my parents always made such a huge fuss over Santa at Christmas time. Having no siblings to confer with about my skepticism, I still had a slight degree of uncertainty. And I wasn't about to officially proclaim Santa to be a myth without 100 percent corroboration on the off chance that I might be wrong and therefore receive no presents for the rest of my faithless childhood.

We had just returned from Mass at St. Christopher, the beautiful cathedral for the Roman Catholic Diocese of Beaumont, Texas, where our family worshiped on Sunday mornings. I was dying to get out of my stiff white shirt, slacks, and loafers that made me look "so grown up," according to my mother. I climbed the concrete steps and opened the door to the trailer home we lived in back then, my shirt already unbuttoned.

Dad grabbed my arm. "Hold on there," he said. "Let's sit down at the table, Lawrence. We need to have a conversation with our little man."

My anxiety spiked as I took my usual seat at the little round table where we ate all our meals, followed by both parents.

My father, a reserved and unemotional man of few words, spoke with a deep, commanding baritone voice that always seemed odd coming from his compact frame. That morning, he started a full octave lower than normal, which was not a good sign. He explained that we were going to discuss a very serious subject: *money*. Or rather, the lack of it. He'd been out of work for two months, and the meager salary my mother received from her secretarial job wasn't enough to cover the bills. The bottom line was that there weren't going to be any Christmas presents that year. There would be no Daisy BB rifle under the tree, and I would have to make do for a little while longer with my old bicycle. I looked down at the fake-wood design on our plastic table as he spoke.

"Will I get anything from Santa Claus?" I asked, looking up, holding out the faintest of hopes.

"No, I'm afraid there'll be no Santa this year," he said. My mother turned her eyes away as Dad continued with his solemn report, trying to reassure me that this was a temporary situation.

But I tuned out. I was devastated. I had dreamed about that Daisy rifle since the start of school in September, ever since Dad had agreed that ten years of age was old enough and I had acted responsible enough to have one. Miraculously, I think with help from the Blessed Mary and all the angels, he'd astounded me by convincing Mom. Sure, that was back when he had a job, but so what? Isn't a promise supposed to mean something?

And not getting a new bicycle was preposterous. I was riding a bike that was three years old and two sizes too small. It was so badly rusted that you couldn't tell it was supposed to be green, not brown. For the past two months, I had been leaving early for school, telling my folks I wanted to get a head start on the day. The truth was that I wanted to get there before any other kids saw me ride up, crouched over that squeaking, miniature rust bucket with my knees smacking me in the chin.

It was all so disappointing and confusing. Dad had changed jobs a couple of times since we moved to Texas four years earlier, and we had never canceled Christmas before. He was the hardest-working man in the world. Wasn't it just a matter of time before he'd be able to get a new job?

He finally quit talking, and I felt the weight of their stares as they waited for me to say something. My first instinct was to tell them how I really felt—to complain loudly and bitterly about the unfairness of it all. But even a ten-year-old could see that the situation was hopeless. Nothing I could say was going to change anything. So, I made a fateful decision.

I shrugged my shoulders and told them that it was no big deal. I said that I knew they were making sacrifices and pinching pennies, and it wouldn't be right to splurge on things that weren't essential. I wanted to cry out and explain how essential a new bike was and how I richly deserved the BB rifle after being so good for months. Instead, I added in a slow, deliberate voice how, even though they had taught me that *a promise is supposed to be a sacred thing,* I figured it was okay to break that promise if there was *no possible way on earth* to keep it, even if *someone you truly loved* was counting on that sacred promise. As I spoke, I hung my head, but I glanced up enough to know that I was scoring some great points. I added that I suspected *I wasn't good enough this year* and that was probably why Santa wouldn't be coming to see me.

That really got to them. As they scrambled for reassuring words, I was stunned to see the effect of my remarks. By demonstrating self-sacrifice and not whining, I was exhibiting the maturity that they continually nagged about, and I was making them feel anxious and horrible in the process, much worse than when we first sat down for this little chat. I felt so encouraged by their reaction that I decided to press even deeper into this uncharted territory. I went for the Oscar. With my head bowed, not daring to look at them, I added some flowery words like, "Besides, Christmas should be about the birth of Jesus, and that should be enough of a gift for all of us."

My mother exploded in tears like a volcano erupting. She wept uncontrollably despite the bear hug that my dad, later joined by me, put on her. Dad tried to console her, but she continued sobbing in this awkward embrace for a solid five minutes, which seems like five hours when you're ten years old.

As I sat holding my mother, I replayed the conversation in my mind to try to make sense out of what had transpired. I had never imagined that I could somehow take control of a tense situation and exert power over these adults, who seemed to have all the power in the world over me. I tried to conjure up situations where I could use this newfound skill again.

During the latter stage of that hugfest ordeal, my father made direct eye contact with me. Dad's cobalt blue eyes are his most prominent physical feature. Staring at me, his eyes were daggers and the look on his face was void of any expression except intensity. It was the first of several such eyeball to eyeball experiences I was to have with my father over the years, where he wasn't just looking at me; he was looking *into* me. That morning, as we clung to my sobbing mother, his eyes held me hypnotized in a trance-like state for a full second or two before I was finally able to pull away. My heart raced inside my chest. I knew instinctively what he was doing, what he was searching for. I wondered if, in my eyes, he had found the sincerity he was hoping for or if he'd seen through me.

That question was answered in a roundabout way that evening after my parents tucked me into bed and we finished our nightly prayers. My father lingered at my bedside as Mom shuffled slowly down the narrow trailer hallway leading back to their bedroom.

He leaned over, and I felt his warm breath on my cheek as he whispered in my ear, "I want you to know I appreciate your attitude 'bout this Christmas thing, Buddy. But let's try not to overdo it. This is a tough time for your mother. Getting womenfolk all worked up . . . Well, that's not the kinda thing that *men* do. Do we understand each other?"

"Yes, sir."

"Good. Good night, Son."

"Good night, Dad."

He patted me on the back, stood, and then walked down the hallway to join my mother. She had started crying again.

*****

My parents are very different. I'm not like either one of them and yet I'm much like both of them.

Several months after the thing with Daniel—when I was so messed up and we had to move to the country—Simon & Garfunkel's "I Am a Rock" was climbing the pop charts, and I asked my father to listen to the song with me. It ended with the singers saying that rocks feel no pain and islands never cry. Dad said that was correct; men needed to be strong like rocks and shouldn't outwardly show their emotions. That way, you could become a good poker player and a better negotiator with used car salesmen. I nodded my head and grunted in agreement. He seemed pleased that we had that intimate moment together.

A few minutes later, alone in my room, I played the record again and listened closely to Paul Simon's lyrics. I heard the bitterness as he sang about not needing friends, that friendship just causes pain. I felt the isolation and loneliness when he sang about hiding in his room where it felt safe, never touching anyone and never having anyone touch him. It was so depressing and real for me that I wanted to cry. I fought back the tears like a man is supposed to do, biting my lower lip so hard I eventually broke the skin and tasted warm blood inside my mouth.

When my mother walked by and saw me sitting on the bed, she instinctively knew that something was wrong and came into my room. That's when I lost it. Mom closed the bedroom door, sat beside me, and wrapped me in her loving arms. "It's okay. It's okay," she kept repeating as she gently rocked me from side to side. She didn't mind that I wouldn't tell her why I was crying. To her, crying was a natural part of life, like laughing or breathing. Afterward, when I asked her not to tell Dad, she gave me a hurt look that said, *Don't you know me?* She, the one whose love I never had to earn, would never expose my soft underbelly to the one I wanted so desperately to please, the one who was constantly trying to mold me in his own highly controlled and dispassionate image.

* * * * *

Mom was born and raised in Honolulu. Her mother was a *kama'āina*, a mix of Portuguese and Hawaiian. Her father was an Irish merchant seaman, a *haole* who jumped ship in Waikiki. Mom was 12 years old, the youngest of three children, when Pearl Harbor was attacked. Her family was living less than a mile away on that infamous Sunday morning, and they all cowered under a four-poster bed during the bombardment. They held their ears to protect them from the deafening sounds as the concussion from exploding bombs raised the bedposts off the floor.

She said it was chaotic after that. Inhabitants of Hawaii lived under strict curfews and martial law. The civilian populace was continually drilled on how to respond during a Japanese invasion, which they were told could come at any time, just like the sneak attack on Pearl Harbor. Mom and her older sister had heard about the Rape of Nanking, and they went through the first part of the war agonizing over the likelihood that they would suffer a similar fate on the front lines in Hawaii.

Mom's brother, Patrick O'Conner, immediately enlisted and officially joined the Navy after he graduated from high school in May of 1942. He was killed in one of the early South Pacific battles. Mom never went into details about how he died, so I improvised. When I was young, I used to pretend I was him, bravely defending my battleship from Japanese bombers. I would shout, "Ak, ak! Ak, ak!" while rotating and shooting my imaginary anti-aircraft gun with precision accuracy. Then we would get broadsided by a wave of kamikazes and had to abandon ship. Thrashing around in the water, oblivious to my own wounds, I would rescue scores of shipmates. Finally, exhausted and unable to defend myself or protect my wounded, I'd be devoured by sharks that were attracted by the huge amount of blood I was losing into the ocean. My death throes, flopping around on my bed and the floor as I lost various limbs to the hungry predators, were Oscar-worthy, I'm sure.

When World War II finally ended without Hawaiian citizens

ever having to come face to face with the Japanese—not even the local Japanese Americans, who had all been rounded up and interned in camps—it's no wonder my mother became a devoted Roosevelt Democrat. Franklin Roosevelt had guided our country to victory in the war and saved Hawaiian womanhood from the sex-mad Japanese soldiers. After she became eligible to vote, Mom tried to repay President Roosevelt by pulling the Democrat lever in every election.

When I was growing up, we weren't allowed to engage in political debates nor talk about controversial political figures in the Torrence household. It was one of Dad's rules, and he said it also applied to guests, although we never had any guests. I think it was one of the reasons why my parents' marriage stayed so strong since his political views were quite different from Mom's. Dad thought the Democrats were way out of line pushing social giveaways and integration of the schools so rapidly. He lamented to me on several occasions that he didn't know whether our country was going to make it, whether it could hold together during the unprecedented turbulent times we were living in.

My dad is a hard-working man who believes there's a right way and a wrong way to do things, and by God, if you're his only son, you'd better learn to do it the right way. Dad was born in Chicago and lived there for the first eight years of his life. His father, my Grandpa Torrence, was a mechanical engineer. He had been born and raised in Glasgow, Scotland and immigrated to the United States as a young man. He spoke with a sing-song accent that was hard for me to understand, and he liked to quote from the Bible, working it into the conversation so it seemed natural.

But Grandpa Torrence was no saint. He was a burly, fun-loving man with a weakness for Scotch whiskey and Kentucky bourbon, and they cost him his marriage when Dad was eight. Dad never talked much about his mother. He was the oldest of three children, and his mother remarried and took custody of the youngsters—my Uncle Robert and Aunt Bonnie—while Grandpa Torrence took my dad. That seemed strange to me, splitting the kids like that, but Dad said it wasn't uncommon in the Great Depression.

Grandpa Torrence and my father moved around after the divorce. The big construction company my grandpa worked for would assign him to a project for a year or two, and then they'd move on to the next project in a different town. Most of his jobs were in Alabama and Tennessee, where Dad picked up a slight Southern drawl and his simple, down-home way of describing things. They moved to Honolulu in the summer of 1945, where Grandpa worked on an expansion of the port. Dad was 16 and that's how he and Mom met. They were high school sweethearts.

My parents looked so young in the pictures in their high school yearbook. Dad had closely cropped hair and a devilish grin. Mom had long, flowing hair and a beautiful open-mouth smile. I have brown hair and eyes like Mom. When I was growing up, Dad would tell anyone who would listen that I looked just like my mother. Why do parents say things like that? I spent much of my youth in front of a mirror worrying that I looked feminine.

Neither of my parents are particularly tall, and when I was 12, I worried that I'd be short when I grew up. I think that's something that all boys with short parents spend a lot of time worrying about, especially the ones who look like their mother.

Mom is five feet, four inches tall, and I was an inch shorter than her when I was 12. Although I never thought she was the least bit overweight, Mom was always talking about going on a diet. Dad has a workingman's build—a strong back and muscular arms and legs with oversized hands and feet. He's five-eight and a little on the skinny side.

After high school, Dad worked repairing cars in a garage in Honolulu. He said the money wasn't very good and he grew restless and bored. So, he joined the Air Force to learn how to work on aircraft engines. He got to see a lot of the country during his service, stationed at Biloxi, San Antonio, and then later, back to Honolulu.

Dad was a great mechanic. He was constantly tinkering with our car and fixing things that broke down in our trailer home.

During those times, he would call me over and demonstrate why something was no longer functioning properly and explain in painstaking detail what would be required to fix it. I was fascinated with mechanical things, and I hung on every word and ran to fetch tools and help however he asked. But that was back before Daniel. After he came into my life and then suddenly left—well, it was different.

Chapter 3

7:05 a.m.

"Lawrence, Daniel Carter is dead," my father said.

It caught me like a sucker punch, crashing into my chest so hard that I couldn't breathe.

"I'm sorry, Son."

As I stared at him, my head moved involuntarily from side to side. I wanted him to be mistaken. But deep down in that place where reality resides, I knew it was true.

"How—?" I couldn't finish the question. I felt lightheaded.

He leaned forward and his words echoed incoherently in my ears. An inner voice told me to find an anchor, something that I could lock onto to get my bearings. The first thing that came into sight was the round clock hanging on the wall over the kitchen sink.

There are certain scenes from our past, snippets in time from a key event that each of us can remember vividly. In my case, it's that damned clock, as though time stopped for me at that moment. I can close my eyes—at any time, in any place—and clearly see the straight line that the black, knife-like hands cut across the clock's white face. How those hands pointed ominously at the Roman numerals—I and VII—just beyond their reach on the peripheral of that simple face. I have since come to measure my life in two distinct segments: before 7:05 on that morning and after that time—when my father uttered those words and my childhood ended.

"I know this is a shock. Now, I want you to take some deep breaths and we'll tell you what we know. Is that okay? Buddy? Are you okay?"

I continued to stare at the clock as he spoke. Out of the corner of my eye, I saw Mom reach for a chair and take a seat at the little kitchen table. She did it in slow motion like she was afraid that any sudden movement would shatter the fragile moment. When I looked in her direction, she covered her open mouth with her hands.

There was an uncomfortable silence as they waited for a response. "Yes, sir," I said instinctively. I said it because that was the way young boys must address their fathers, although I couldn't remember the question. I looked down at the table.

"Good," Dad said. "Now, he . . . Buddy, look at me. Son? Look up, please. Lawrence?"

I could barely breathe as I said, "I'm okay. Just go ahead with it." But I didn't dare look up from the table. There was no way I could go eyeball to eyeball with him, not with what was whirling through my mind.

"Okay," he said. "Daniel died on Saturday at Baptist Hospital. Last night, folks from the school called 'round. They wanted to reach the parents of Daniel's best friends in seventh grade, so they could get the news before school today. We decided to break it to you this morning. I'm just . . . I'm so sorry."

"They didn't have too many calls to make," I muttered under my breath. I don't know why I said it. It just came out.

"What's that?" Dad asked.

I mumbled the words numbly, mindlessly. "I said that they couldn't have had too many calls to make. Marty and me, we're the only friends Daniel has."

My mother must have felt obligated to come to Daniel's assistance since he wasn't going to be able to defend himself. "Now, I can't believe that's true," she said. "Daniel was such an intelligent, delightful young man. He must have had many friends, lots of *hoalohas*, yah?"

I lifted my head, irritated by her cheerful Hawaiian pidgin slang at a serious time like this. I wasn't afraid to lock eyes with her. Giving her one of those icy stares my father was world-famous for, I said in my most condescending tone, "Well, that shows how ignorant you are." It melted her smile.

My father intervened or I'm sure I could have made her cry. "Look, it doesn't matter," he said. "Let me tell you what we know."

My head went back down. Why did I say that to my mother? Why did I say anything? What time was it? I glanced up at the big round clock only to find its striking black hands in the same position they were less than a minute ago, a lifetime ago when the whole ordeal began. I lowered my head. As my father continued speaking, I panicked and looked up again. I couldn't recall what time it was.

"On Friday after school," Dad said, "Daniel's mother was out with his little sister. He was home alone."

I looked down and focused on two small drops of milk that must have spilled onto the table while I was slurping my cereal.

"Somehow, Daniel got his father's handgun. They don't know how he got it, but he did. And this is the part that's still a little sketchy. He either had an accident playing with the gun or he deliberately shot himself."

With those words, wave after wave of indescribable emotion pulsed through my body like currents of electricity. I couldn't move, speak, or think clearly. I could only stare helplessly at the drops of milk.

"When Daniel's father came home from work, he found him and rushed him to the hospital. The doctors fought to save him and were able to keep him alive through the night, but—" Dad cleared his throat. "The wound was in the head, and they said he never regained consciousness. Are you listening, Son? Can you hear me?"

I forced some saliva into my dry mouth. "Did he leave a note—you know, explaining everything?" I muttered at the two drops of milk, my voice quivering.

"No, no note," Dad said.

I closed my eyes and gave a silent prayer of thanks.

"That's why they're not completely sure if it was intentional," he said. "I'm sorry, Buddy. Buddy? Talk to me, please."

I felt him leaning closer, though I dared not look up. I gave an exaggerated shrug, hoping to extricate myself from his hand which now rested on my shoulder, and I hunched over the table even lower. If I stuck out my tongue, I could lap up the milk.

"I'm okay." They were obviously expecting more, so I spoke in short phrases, halting between them to catch my breath. "It's just a surprise. It's like, it hasn't sunk in yet. I don't know what I feel. I think it hurts."

I suddenly jerked my head up from the table, frantic to see the clock, to know what time it was.

Dad's romance with the lovely Leilani O'Conner, my mother-to-be, heated up again when he was stationed back in Honolulu. He proposed to her on the day he was discharged from the Air Force. My parents were fond of saying, "We were married in June of 1951, and Lawrence was born in July." With a mortified glance at each other, they'd hurriedly add in unison, "—of the following year!" I had seen this routine a hundred times, and they always broke out in hysterical laughter. I failed to grasp the humor.

In 1955, just after my third birthday, Dad convinced Mom that our family's future was on the mainland, not in laid-back Hawaii. My Uncle Robert had said he could get Dad a job where he worked, at one of the huge shipyards near Chicago where they built oceangoing tankers and large cargo ships. It was tough, outdoor work under grueling conditions. It would be bitter cold in winter and stifling heat in summer, but Uncle Robert said the money was good. He also said it would be interesting work, even fun because the two brothers would be able to work together on one of the crews that sprayed asbestos insulation throughout the interior of the ships. We left Hawaii that year and we've never been back.

We measured time in Chicago by the winters; we only lasted three. It was a miserable time for me because of the earaches I got each winter. When you're a small child with an earache, your entire world becomes centered in that ear. Nothing else matters—not toys, games, desserts, or anything. The pain was excruciating for me and exasperating for my parents. Each winter, a large part of their savings, which they worked so hard to accumulate, went to doctors and pharmacies to treat my ear problems.

The third winter we spent there was godawful. My parents had enrolled me in a half-day kindergarten class in September, but once winter rolled around, I missed about as much as I attended with recurring ear infections.

Dad worked long hours at the shipyard. My mother, who was an outstanding typist, had a secretarial job at minimum wage. I spent my days, when I wasn't in kindergarten, being looked after by Mrs. French, a war widow who lived in the same apartment building as us. After Christmas, Mrs. French told Mom that she would only be able to take me when I was healthy. She couldn't take my crying any longer. Neither could our neighbors. They filed numerous complaints, and the landlord responded with letters threatening eviction if my folks didn't keep me quiet. Mom eventually got fired from her job because she kept taking time off to stay home with me. She said it was unfair, but Dad told her that corporations had to have the right to hire and fire as they pleased, or we'd end up being Communists or something.

The pain was worst at night. I tried to stifle my sobs and be "a brave little man" like my father asked, but it was impossible. As that long winter dragged on, my folks began talking about moving south. "Wouldn't you like to live where it's always warm and green, Buddy? Where it doesn't snow?" Mom would ask.

"Uh-huh. That would be good," I would respond weakly. The earaches had worn me down, and I was intolerably bored being cooped up in that apartment. What good was snow if you couldn't play in it because your parents were paranoid that exposure to the elements would cause another ear infection?

Near the end of that insufferable winter, Uncle Johnny, Dad's best buddy from his Air Force days, came to visit us in Chicago. He told my father that he was sure he could get Dad a job where he worked—at the big Mobil Oil refinery in Beaumont, Texas. It was manual labor, but Dad said that didn't matter to him. He told Mom and me that once he got established there, he would be able to either work himself up through the ranks or find a better job.

"What do you think?" my father asked.

"I think we should go, my *ku'uipo*," Mom said as she leaned forward to embrace him.

"Me, too!" I chimed in, not sure what it all meant, except that something new and exciting lay ahead. We were going to Texas.

Chapter 4

7:07 a.m.

My hands were clutched together under the table. My neck muscles were tense. As soon as my father began speaking again, I lowered my eyes from the clock on the wall, and my head commenced a slow descent until it was parallel with the table. I was once again face to face with the two drops of spilled milk.

I'm sure that Dad was trying to say something comforting. He knew how close Daniel and I were. But his words reverberated in my head without clarity. I think he talked about how he knew I was in pain, although he admitted he couldn't begin to comprehend the depths of that pain since he had never personally experienced anything like this. He went on about how the pain would probably get worse before it got better and how I needed to be brave. He added that Mom and he were there to help me get through this pain. It seemed like every other word he said was "pain," but I wasn't sure. I was floating in a catatonic state, an involuntary defense mechanism triggered to keep my fears at bay while I struggled to comprehend the ramifications of my situation.

He seemed to be wrapping up when I heard, "Now, when you go to school this morning—"

"School?" I blurted out. My body tensed and I looked up—not too far—just enough to stare into his chest.

"They're gonna have an assembly first thing this morning and tell all the junior high students 'bout Daniel," he said.

"Oh," I replied, my head still reeling.

"The school has arranged for some professional counselors—psychiatrists, I guess—to be there to help with something they're calling 'grief counseling.' They wanta meet privately, one-on-one, with the seventh graders who were especially close to Daniel and with any of the children who seem like they're . . . disturbed."

My concern increased with each word he said. "Marty and you were best friends with him. So, they asked if a parent could accompany you two boys in these meetings today, and I've arranged to take the day off to be with you. Mrs. Shannon will be there with Marty."

Tiny beads of sweat formed at my hairline. If I understood the situation, not only would I have to face all the other kids and the teachers at school, but also some shrink who wanted to question me, who would want information about Daniel and me. All this, with my father's hyper-perceptive blue eyes seeing everything, burning a hole through me, searching for clues in my body language. All this, with his ears perked up, hearing everything I said. To ease the trembling in my hands, I squeezed them between my knees.

All the things that Marty had told me about shrinks ran through my brain. He said that his uncle in Dallas had studied and trained for ten years to become a shrink. He said that's how long it takes to learn all their tricks and develop control over their mental powers.

Marty explained that a shrink's power field is strong but only extends for a limited range—a few yards or so. That's why they try to make you lie on a couch right next to them. When you relax, that's when you're most vulnerable and come under their power. Marty called it a "double whammy." On the couch, close to the shrink, they can force you to talk about your mother and reveal your innermost secrets. And *you can't tell lies.* That's because they could hypnotize you. Marty said that once a shrink had you hypnotized, he could make you do whatever he commanded, no matter how much of an idiot you might look like. He could make you act like a chicken, just for his amusement. Or worse, he could make you wet the bed every night for the rest of your life, so you'd be too embarrassed to ever get married. Marty had heard of a shrink who hypnotized priests and made them kill for the U.S. government. They were like James Bond secret agents, except they weren't cool with the ladies like 007. Nobody suspected them because they were real priests.

Marty wasn't the brightest kid on the block, and he was prone to exaggeration. Some of the stuff he would come up with was absurd, way off the wall. *But not this.* I'd seen it a hundred times on television shows where villains, victims, and witnesses were put under a shrink's hypnotic power to make them recall what they'd seen or done at some gruesome event and then blab about it to the cops and everybody. Two months earlier, at Thanksgiving, Marty's shrink uncle was in town for the holiday, and I had to shake hands with him. He was tall and thin, so much so that he looked like a skeleton with a thin layer of skin pulled tightly over his bones. He had cold hands with long fingernails, stringy black hair, and black eyes. At least, Marty swore his eyes were black. I never checked because Marty had cautioned in his most serious manner that Daniel and I should never look directly into those black eyes. If you did, *he had you!*

Shrinks were powerful people, to be avoided at all costs. And they would be at St. Christopher School this morning—at my school, waiting for me.

Beaumont is in the southeast corner of Texas near its border with Louisiana, and the terrain is a boring coastal plain, flat as a pancake. When we moved there, it was a sleepy, blue-collar town of about 100,000 inhabitants. The refining and petrochemical industry had taken root along the Neches River as it meandered through Beaumont and Port Arthur just before spilling into the Gulf of Mexico. In June of 1958, my father had joined the abundant supply of cheap labor in the region that kept the plants running for Texaco, Gulf Oil, American Petrofina, DuPont, Mobil Oil, and others. He sent for Mom and me in early August.

The two-day bus trip wasn't the fun adventure that Mom had promised and certainly not the one Greyhound promoted in their flashy brochure. Our bus, the cheaper "local service," stopped at every town and village in its southward path—dropping passengers and picking up new ones. They made us get off every couple of hours so we could use the smelly bus terminal bathrooms, eat tasteless food, and wait, sometimes hours, for our appointed departure time. We slept overnight on hard benches in terminals in Nashville and Baton Rouge and finally arrived in Beaumont on a Saturday morning. I was dog-tired from our Greyhound odyssey, but the confinement and boredom of the prior two days evaporated when I felt my father's arms wrap around Mom and me as we stepped off the bus.

Uncle Johnny also was there. Even though we weren't really related, he was Dad's best friend, and I was supposed to call him "Uncle," just like Uncle Robert. I didn't mind. I liked Uncle Johnny.

I was also thankful to see our big blue Pontiac again. It was a huge car, about the size of a sperm whale. Dad had driven it to Texas, and that morning, I rode in the back seat with Uncle Johnny as the Pontiac pulled out of the bus station, its massive trunk filled with our suitcases and boxes. Mom and Dad snuggled close together on the big bench seat in front.

"Oh, Dad, please, can I?" I begged. He knew what I wanted.

"Okay, just don't you make faces at the cars behind us. Don't be distracting any drivers. That wouldn't be safe," he said.

I leaped up and scrambled over the back seat to curl into that long, flat area under the rear window. Lying there, I could feel the warmth of the sun penetrating through the window. It made me feel safe and secure, pressed tightly under the sloping glass.

But after half a minute, I began to feel very warm and climbed down onto the seat beside Uncle Johnny. All the windows were rolled down, and I stuck my head out like a dog. I wanted to take in all the sensations our new hometown was offering.

"You know, Buddy," Uncle Johnny said, "we have five seasons here in Beaumont."

I pulled in my head and stared at him. "Oh yeah?" I said.

"Yeah, we have fall, winter, spring, summer, and *August*. It gets so damn hot and humid 'round here in August that it's a whole different season. Get it?"

I continued to stare at him. No, I didn't get it, but I was about to. The morning sun was shining brightly, and the temperature was on its way to 100 degrees that day.

"Yeah, but you won't freeze your ass off in winter," Dad said. "And hopefully, no more earaches and no more breathing in all that asbestos crap. I think that shit's killin' poor Robert."

Mom slapped him hard on the shoulder, and the car swerved to the left. "You watch that language, Mac Torrence! Bless my soul! You leave me for six weeks and you talk story like a sailor."

"Sorry, Lon."

Looking into the rear-view mirror, he shot a sheepish grin at Uncle Johnny. Although her formal name was Leilani, after some Hawaiian princess, he called her "Lonnie" or "Lon."

Dad adjusted the mirror so he could see me sitting behind him. "Buddy, let me tell you 'bout our new home. Your mom and I have been talkin' on the telephone, and we decided to buy something here rather than just throwin' away good money on rent. Don't that sound like a good idea?"

I looked at his face in the mirror without offering a reply. He turned onto a gravel road into what appeared to be a trailer park. *It must be a shortcut to our new home*, I thought.

"You see, we wanted something that's gonna be ours, that we could sink some equity into. We couldn't afford a two-bedroom house with a yard and all. So, we came up with a great idea—*a trailer home*. Isn't that neat?"

He stopped the car in front of a blue trailer with wide white stripes. NEW MOON was stenciled in block letters on the front. It looked huge, but everything looks huge when you're six years old. All the excitement of the morning vanished, and I felt a knot forming in my stomach.

Dad continued talking to my reflection in the mirror. "You see, a trailer home is perfect for us. We own it instead of renting. Well, technically, the bank owns it for now, but it's ours free and clear after the last payment—in just ten years." It must have dawned on him that he was speaking to a six-year-old, and he shrugged before continuing. "Look, those are just details. The thing is, Buddy, the trailer is ours. And if we don't hanker to livin' in this place—Beaumont, you know—we can take our trailer down off the blocks and go to the next town." He turned around and grinned at me, looking for my reaction.

Now I was feeling ill. Before we left Chicago, hadn't he talked about Texas like some promised land? Hadn't he talked about me starting first grade and having lots of friends? Hah! *Trailer rats* didn't have friends, except maybe other trailer rats. That's what the other kids had called Jimmy Green at kindergarten in Chicago—a worthless trailer rat. They would taunt the poor little boy every day until he cried. He became the outcast of our kindergarten class, like he had cooties or something, all because he lived in a trailer. And now I was on the verge of sinking into the same subhuman category. It was too scary and depressing for words.

We got out of the car. Since I had not responded, my father felt compelled to keep selling.

"There's a playground down this road and a swimming pool. And there's lots of other kids here," Dad said.

Oh, great! A whole nest of trailer rats.

Mom had walked around the car while he was speaking. She did a slow 360 degrees, taking in the entire trailer park. She seemed uncertain. "Is this place safe?" she whispered to my father, but I heard every word. "It looks, you know, *seedy.*"

Suddenly, a ray of hope. One of my parents was coming to their senses.

He gave her a hurt look. "I obviously think it's safe or I wouldn't have chosen it for us. Oh, you'll wanta be careful when you're alone here, but that's like anywhere."

When she didn't respond, he took her hands in his. He had it all worked out and spoke with confidence. "Buddy's school is just six blocks away. I can drop him off in the mornings on my way to the plant. Or, if you want, you can walk with him. It'll only take ten minutes. I met a fifth-grade teacher that lives up the street, and she walks home in the afternoons with kids from the trailer park. And there's two teenage girls that live on the far side of the park. They said they could watch after Buddy for a couple hours after school for 25 cents an hour. That is, if you decide you wanta get a job."

He looked into her eyes. "Lonnie, this is gonna be home for us. It's gonna be just fine. We'll be a real family here. Trust me."

* * * * *

Uncle Johnny was right about August. That summer, the last three weeks of August were particularly oppressive, even by Beaumont standards. The temperature soared over 90 degrees each afternoon, several times making it over 100. The humidity went over 90 percent on a regular basis. Mom and I had never experienced anything like this. We spent a large part of those August days sitting inside the trailer with all the windows open to catch the soft breezes that fan the Texas Gulf Coast. We would sip cold drinks near one of the four little plug-in fans that went full throttle inside our trailer for 24 hours a day. The trailer was well insulated to protect its inhabitants from cold in the winter, but it would turn into an oven in the hot Texas sun without constant air circulation inside.

The trailer park's swimming pool provided a welcome reprieve on those hot days. When Dad was at work, we could only go to the pool after Mom had thoroughly scouted the area and determined that it was free from any *undesirables*. As best I could determine, undesirables were men who didn't work during the day. Most of these men worked the graveyard shift in the refineries and chemical plants. They slept during the day or wandered around in their undershirts looking bored and yawning a lot.

Mom never wore her bathing suit when she and I went to the pool on weekdays. She would sit on one of the lounge chairs in knee-length shorts and a sleeveless blouse, reading and sweating. Every few seconds, she'd glance up from her reading material to make certain I wasn't drowning. She also would scan the horizon like a lioness ever alert to protect her cub, gazing at the other trailers and up and down the gravel roads. If an undesirable emerged from his den while we were at the pool, they received Mom's full attention until their intentions were determined. If one emerged wearing swim trunks or ventured too close to the pool, she calmly and as discreetly as possible brought me a towel and announced that it was time to go—*now*!

As evening approached and it got close to the time when Dad came home from work, I held vigil near the door to the trailer. From there, I could hear our Pontiac braking on the gravel, and I always ran out to greet my father as he stepped from the car. His forearms would be streaked with black smudges and his clothes soaked with perspiration, but it didn't matter to me. I would hug him around the waist as hard as I could while he tousled my hair and asked, "How's my little man today?"

Mom, who was usually behind me wearing an apron, would give him a quick kiss before instructing him to hurry inside to clean up. After his shower, we had dinner at the fake-wood plastic table in the middle of the trailer. Mom stuck to the basics at dinnertime—a simple beef or pork, potatoes or rice, and a vegetable like sweet corn or black-eyed peas that I would willingly eat.

I always cleaned my plate—it was a rule—and then dutifully carried my dirty dishes and silverware to the sink. With a smile, I repeated the nine words that Dad had taught me that I must say at the conclusion of every meal—it was another rule—to my mother or whoever had prepared the food: "Thank you for the dinner; it was very good." Even if it wasn't.

Over dinner those first few weeks in our new trailer home, Mom talked about how hot it was, Dad talked about his day at work, and I talked about my exploits at the pool. At bedtime, Dad would move one of the fans to the top of the built-in drawers that held all my clothes. It blew air across the narrow hallway onto my bed, and its gentle hum helped me sleep. I was learning to cope with the heat and starting to settle into this new life in Texas. But the start of school was approaching. As a result, my nights grew increasingly restless, filled with apprehensive dreams of life without friends, as an outcast first-grade trailer rat.

* * * * *

My fears about school proved unfounded. On a muggy September morning, the Tuesday after the Labor Day holiday, I found myself with about 60 other first graders, wide-eyed and nervous on our first day at Robert E. Lee Elementary School. After a brief orientation in the school cafeteria, they called each student's name and told us the teacher we'd been assigned to. The first graders got either a frumpy, middle-aged lady with a beehive hairdo or a short, slumped-over, elderly lady with wild white hair who looked like Lon Chaney. I got the Hunchback of Notre Dame, and we were made to shuffle off in single file to her classroom to commence our journey into learned bliss. The only other trailer rat in my class was Jeremy Larkin, a mousy little guy who was afraid to go head-first off the diving board at the pool.

Either the other kids didn't know about Jeremy and me—about our shameful living accommodations—or, more likely, they didn't care. The kids who lived in south Beaumont in the blue-collar neighborhood surrounding Lee Elementary came from families that struggled to pay the bills, just like mine. The breadwinners in these families mostly worked in low-skilled positions in the refineries and petrochemical plants, on assembly lines in oilfield equipment manufacturing factories, or in transportation or construction. Some relied on undependable contract work to get by.

Our trailer park was on Eleventh Street, the western boundary for our school district. The one-story houses along my route to school had been erected before the Great Depression—close together and just a few yards off the street for maximum density. They were small, rectangular wooden boxes resting on cinder blocks, bricks, or rotting piers. Under the houses, you could generally find odd collections of broken furniture, bicycles, toys, appliances, and other rusted or rotted things that the inhabitants couldn't bear to part with. Many had oversized porches or folding chairs in the yards. Residents sat outside in the evenings to converse with neighbors while they watched their children playing in the street.

A busy set of railroad tracks ran just beyond and parallel

with First Street, and they delineated the eastern boundary of the school district. On the proverbial "other side of the tracks" was one of Beaumont's largest and poorest black neighborhoods. They had their own school, and I often wondered what it was like. Did the first graders have cheerful-looking teachers like Aunt Jemima on the box of pancake mix, or was there a black version of my teacher—Quasimodo? I wondered what streets came after First Street. Was it Zero Street or did they start over with negative numbers? I was curious about what lay on the other side of those tracks, but Dad had warned me in the strictest terms that it was dangerous over there and I could never venture past First Street into "Colored Town." Another of his rules.

I attended Robert E. Lee Elementary for first-through-sixth grade. During those six years, I never had any close friends. Oh, I got along fine with the other kids at school, but I never wanted to get too chummy. I didn't want any of my classmates to expect an invitation to come home to play after school or spend the night on weekends. I was shy, self-conscious, and hopelessly afflicted with the trailer-rat complex.

I got off to a slow start academically. I made okay, but not great, grades in first grade. Then, at the beginning of second grade, a miracle happened.

Mrs. Applebee, my second-grade teacher, must've been a hundred years old and had a reputation for being mean as a witch. She made all the kids in her class sit in an assigned seat in alphabetical order. That put me, Torrence, at the back of the room next to Carol Trotter. She was okay for a girl, so that part was tolerable, but I couldn't read what was on the chalkboard from my remote location. On the third day of school, Mrs. Applebee caught me peeking at Carol's paper to copy the addition and subtraction problems on the board. What happened next was a blur.

Mrs. Applebee marched to my desk, squealing that she would not tolerate cheating in her class. She stood over me as I tried to melt into my desk chair. Whispering to her so the others wouldn't hear, I explained that I couldn't see the chalkboard. I pleaded that I wasn't copying Carol's answers, just the problems. That must have sounded like the worst story she'd ever heard, and it infuriated her. She made big waving motions with her arms in the general direction of the chalkboard, proclaiming that it was as big as the side of a barn and that I was not only a copycat cheat but a despicable liar as well.

The old biddy announced that she was going to make an example of me, so everyone could see what happened to those who dared to lie and cheat in her classroom. At that point, I broke down, losing all dignity and crying profusely in front of her and my classmates. When I had been sufficiently humiliated to suit her purpose, Mrs. Applebee marched me to "the office," that dreaded place where juvenile delinquents went to be punished for their transgressions. After explaining my version of the story through muffled sobs to Mrs. Gilliam, the hard-as-nails vice principal, she sent me to see Miss Simms, the school nurse.

Miss Simms covered one of my eyes with a piece of cardboard and pointed to a chart hanging at the end of a hallway outside her office.

"Now, Buddy, I want you to relax and read the farthest line down that you can see clearly," she said.

"E," I replied.

She waited a few seconds. "And what else?"

"That's it."

Thirty minutes later, my father picked me up from the nurse's office, and I was off to meet my first optometrist. His diagnosis was that I was severely nearsighted. The eyeglasses that he prescribed were Coke-bottle thick, but I didn't care. They opened a whole new world. I saw birds flying in the sky, baseballs being thrown to me, and other everyday things that had previously been invisible or indistinguishable shapes. My hand-eye coordination quickly developed, and in short order I became a decent athlete and an outstanding student.

Old Mrs. Applebee apologized to me in front of the entire class the next morning after meeting with my father in the vice principal's office. One of Dad's rules was to always be respectful of other people. Another was to never assume bad things about someone without first listening carefully to their side of the story. Mrs. Applebee had broken two rules. I'm sure he enlightened her with his piercing eyes and deep voice.

Mom acted weird the first few days after I got glasses. She talked to herself, or maybe she was talking to God or to the wall. Cooking dinner or cleaning dishes, she would stare straight ahead and blurt out something like, "How could I be so stupid?" or "I must be the worst mother in the world." Or she'd say, "I should've known when we had to keep telling him to move away from the television set."

It was highly disconcerting to me. I wondered if I had done something wrong. But after a week had passed, she stopped verbally flogging herself, and our lives returned to normal, except that normal for me included 20/20 vision.

It's clear to me now that Mom was being hard on herself for not recognizing earlier that I needed glasses. Both of my parents had enjoyed near-perfect vision for all their 30 years up to that time, and they simply were not alert for this type of imperfection in their child. From my perspective, and it may sound screwy to people with good eyesight, I thought that everyone saw things far away just like I did—fuzzy, indistinct, blurred. So, I never made a big deal about it.

My father was fond of saying that each of us lives at the center of our own little universe. He would explain how we're each a product of our own unique life experiences that take place as people and things revolve around us. We tend to assess our environment, evaluate people, contemplate choices, and make decisions within those individual frames of reference.

But that can be extraordinarily limiting. Sometimes it can be downright unhealthy or even dangerous, particularly when we don't know how, or don't even try, to view things through someone else's eyes, to see past our own blurs to understand their point of view, their pain, their fears. A narrow outlook and self-absorbed focus can cause you to miss something right in front of your face. I know that now.

# Chapter 5

7:10 a.m.

"Oh, one other thing," Dad said. "The Beaumont police will be at your school today. I understand they'll wanta ask you some questions."

"What?" I asked. I could barely say the word as my mind went spinning. *Police? Questions? No way! This is getting completely out of control.*

"It's routine, something the police have to do when there's a death under mysterious circumstances."

I forced myself to swallow hard. "Mys . . . terious?" I said slowly and then there was an intense, dull pain as my throat tried to contract. Now, not just my hands, but my whole body began to quiver. A bead of sweat on my brow broke free and rolled down the length of my face. I felt cold and clammy and could taste that morning's cereal and milk rising into my throat.

"Look, this is too much! I can't do this." My voice shook as I forced out the words, "You want me to talk to cops, shrinks, and God knows who else." My eyes darted from one parent to another. I gulped for air and then said, "Don't you see? They all want, you know . . . They all want inside me. Well, I'm telling you, I can't do this. Now, *leave me alone*!" I leaped from my seat.

* * * * *

After that infamous Christmas of 1962, the one with no presents, things improved for the Torrence clan. My father landed a job in January with the Pest-Off Chemical Company in Port Neches, a redneck refinery town southeast of Beaumont. They blended chemicals at their plant to form a compound that was lethal to fire ants and just about anything else that lived or grew outdoors. I wasn't sure what part Dad played in this important process, but I overheard Mom refer to it as steady work and steady hours—at last.

Dad got regular promotions over the next two years: 1963 and 1964. Being a modest man, he didn't talk much about them, but Mom lit up with pride when he made these periodic announcements to us. For a solid week afterward, she would fix his favorite dinners like pork chops or meatloaf with ketchup.

My father periodically did work at home now—paperwork. That was unsettling at first. I had never pictured him as one of those paperwork-type dads. To me, he was the dirt-under-the-fingernails type. But every three months, he would sit at the plastic table in our trailer and struggle with quarterly evaluation forms for each of the crew who worked for him—"the men," as he called them. He would stare at the ceiling for inspiration and often hold his chin in his hands or rub his eyes. He seemed to spend as much time erasing and rewriting as he did writing in the first place.

I made the mistake one Monday evening, during a commercial on *The Andy Griffith Show*, of asking my father why this paperwork required so much time. He launched into a long dissertation about the importance of accurate and candid job performance evaluations. He said that the men needed to know when they were falling short of the mark and when they were hitting it. He compared it to the report cards I got from school.

"But they're grown men. Can't they tell without you having to spell it all out for them?" I asked.

Now, believing that I was deeply interested in these evaluations instead of just trying to satisfy some idle curiosity during a commercial break, he carried on about how some people deserved recognition for their good work, and he was pleased to provide it. But others tried to overlook or minimize their own shortcomings. According to my father, they were the ones who needed honest feedback the most. He said it was his responsibility as their leader to weed out the slackers and to inspire all the men in his crew to become more productive workers. If not, he was breaking a good-faith bargain with the company and could even jeopardize lives in a volatile chemical plant. I wondered if he'd seen *The Bridge on the River Kwai* too many times. But that was my father, the way he saw things in black-or-white, right-or-wrong terms.

The commercial break had ended, and I was anxious to get back to the tube where Barney Fife was expounding to little Opie about the meaning of life. I didn't want to miss that important lesson, but I felt compelled to challenge my father on this point.

"But what if one of those guys who's not cutting it has a family? You wouldn't fire him, would you? You wouldn't put him in a position like we were in two Christmases ago, would you?"

He gave a heavy sigh. "Son, there are rules and standards that apply to each of us—in our jobs and in our lives. We must resist the temptation to bend those rules or lower our standards. If we do, the whole system collapses. We should never lose compassion for our fellow man, but we can't let that cause us to make exceptions or turn our heads when that man cannot do the job that we rely on him to do."

"So, you would fire him?" I asked.

"Yes, I'd have to or I wouldn't be doing *my* job."

"You'd fire him, even if he had a family depending on him?"

"Yes."

"Even if he was a good friend or a member of your own family?"

"Yes."

"Even if he was me?"

"Yes, *especially* if it was you."

His cold stare made me shiver.

About that same time, Dad started getting after Mom that she should give up her second job, the one she had taken after he was laid off by that construction company. In addition to her regular day job as a receptionist and secretary for Dr. Holland, Mom worked two nights a week and Saturdays doing medical transcription at St. Elizabeth Hospital. Dad was like a broken record. He said that she was only making $2.00 an hour at her second job, barely more than the legal minimum wage of $1.25. After taxes and everything, Dad didn't think it was worth it.

I knew he was wasting his breath. My mother, as our family breadwinner during that stressful time, had kept us afloat financially. In my mother's mind, the second job was a necessity then and a safety valve now. It didn't matter that Dad finally had a good, steady job or that they'd tucked away a little money in savings for the proverbial rainy day. It didn't matter that Mom had good skills and worked hard for low wages. Being a woman, that was to be expected, she had said. What mattered was that my mother hated insecurity and uncertainty, particularly when it came to family finances.

Knowing that she wasn't going to change her position about working two jobs, my father did something that surprised me. On a Saturday afternoon, a beautiful spring day in 1964, I was lounging around reading a comic book as The Beatles' "Can't Buy Me Love" drifted through the trailer from my transistor radio. The sound of a car braking on the gravel aroused my curiosity, and I got up to investigate. Peering out the long, narrow window on the side of the trailer, I watched as my father stepped out of a maroon station wagon. He had parked it behind the white Ford Falcon he'd bought the previous year when our old Pontiac belched black smoke and Dad had been unable to resuscitate it. The flashy station wagon dwarfed the little Falcon.

Dad stood beside the wagon, a huge grin filling his face as he stared toward our trailer door. I moved to the other side of the window to see what he was looking at. There, on the lowest of the three concrete steps that led up to our trailer entrance, my mother sat finishing a smoke. She was staring back at him with the intensity of an approaching storm. After a few seconds, she flicked the cigarette away, stood, and crossed her arms over her chest.

"*Maaac*," she said warily, dragging out his name, "whose car is that?"

I turned my head to watch him stride toward her, the smirky

PART ONE: 7:10 a.m.

grin still on his face. When he reached the concrete steps, he glanced back at the station wagon and said, "It's yours, Lon! I got it for you. I've—"

"What?" she exclaimed, but he kept right on speaking and grinning.

"—checked it out from top to bottom. I got a great deal on it from Honest Motors, that used car place down the street. It was just $350 down and only—"

"Mac, we don't need another car and, more importantly, we can't afford it. Have you been drinking, or have you just lost your mind?"

This could be interesting, I thought. My parents were fanatical about one thing: They never argued or raised their voices at each other in front of me. A strained, "Can I please see you in the bedroom, honey?" or, if the weather was nice, "Can you please join me outside, dear?" was their signal to meet in private to thrash out the dispute of the day. They hadn't spotted me at the window, which was open that afternoon to catch the pleasant spring breeze.

"No, I haven't been drinking, not *really* drinking," he said. "But I thought we might celebrate tonight, if you get my drift," he added in a strange voice that I think was supposed to be sexy, ending with an exaggerated wink of his right eye.

"Are you that stupid? Do you think I can't tell?"

"Okay, so I had a beer on the way back from the car lot. But this car, it—"

"Just a beer? Just one?" she mocked him.

"Look, get off the beer, please. You said you were gonna let up on that. Let's talk 'bout your car, okay?"

"My car? This is not funny, Mac. I don't know what—"

"It's not a joke. I got a great deal on it, and we need this car, Lonnie."

"I'm sure that's what you think." She frowned at the big maroon wagon and then asked, "And just what is this . . . this *thing*, anyway?"

"It's a Rambler, and it's got—"

"A *Rambler!*" She covered her heart with her hand and took

a small step backward. "My God, is it one of those Japanese cars?"

"No, no, of course not! For heaven's sake, Lon. C'mon now, gimme a little credit here. You don't think I'd be caught dead buying one of those shoddy foreign cars, do you? This car is made by American Motors, and they build great automobiles—great *American* cars. Pretty soon they'll be talkin' 'bout the Big Four instead of the Big Three automakers, with AMC right in there. Did you know that Rambler was the Car of the Year last year? And I've checked—"

Mom was clearly underwhelmed. "We don't need another car," she interrupted, "and that's the end of this discussion. You need to just—" She paused and then flicked her wrist at him as she completed the sentence, "—take it back. Right now!"

Instead of responding with a harsh comment of his own, he stared at her with those blue eyes and a puppy-dog-needs-love expression. After a long silence during which their eyes were locked, she'd had enough. She turned her back to him and started up the steps. He stepped forward, grabbed her arm, and pleaded in a desperate tone, "Hey, wait a minute! Can we talk—*please*?"

My mother whipped her head around and glared at his hand on her arm until he released his grip.

"Well, can we have a little conversation here?" he pleaded again.

She made him wait several seconds before fully turning to face him, and she replied with a single syllable. "Go," she said. I took it as a signal that he'd been granted the privilege of speaking, but he should not expect her to change her mind.

He reached up and this time gently took her arm to assist her down the porch steps. She shook off his hand and again folded her arms over her chest. She held the high ground on the top step and wasn't about to yield it. He would have to plead his case looking up to her. My father was facing an uphill battle.

"Okay," he said, "but first you have to understand that this car is not a *want*; it's a *need*. We need this car for three very logical reasons."

Oh, no, I thought. The poor man couldn't help himself. He had thought this through (over a couple of beers) in his analytical fashion and reached the obvious (to him) conclusion that had driven up five minutes ago. The problem, as I saw it, was that my mother didn't approach decision-making the same way. She was much more cautious and conservative and didn't like to take risks, even when the odds were greatly in her favor. She was compassionate and emotional, governed by her feelings and intuition to the same extreme that Dad's life was governed by his adherence to rules. She was clearly not impressed by his initiative, and if he now intended to sway her with his *one, two, three* logic, I didn't give him much of a chance.

"First," my father began, "this station wagon will be great for family vacations."

"Vacations?" she shrieked.

Strike one on the batter, I thought.

"Yes, *vacations*," he said. "Not for us, Lonnie—for the boy. Buddy needs to see this great country of ours. He's smart, but he can only get so much education sitting in a schoolroom. Pictures in textbooks are no substitute for seeing the real thing. He needs to experience the Grand Canyon, the Gettysburg Battlefield, Washington, D.C. He needs to stare up at the Statue of Liberty and walk through Ellis Island, where his grandfather first entered this country. That's how he'll develop pride in his country and that'll translate to pride in himself.

"He'll go off to college someday," my father continued, "and just think of the terrible wrong we'll have done him if the only thing he's seen and experienced is this backwoods town. The summer vacations are not for me and they're not for you. They're for Buddy! And they're not optional. They are required for his education and this wagon is big and roomy, the ideal way to go."

"What else?" she said calmly, but I detected a quiver in her voice.

"Second, we need it for flexibility. Remember last month—when the Falcon had to go in the garage for a whole week?"

"Yeah, so what? You got a rental car," Mom said.

"And we paid a small fortune for it! Plus, what 'bout those

couple of days last winter when I couldn't get the Falcon to crank over and couldn't get to work?"

"So? You got Ames Boudreaux to drive out from the plant and pick you up," Mom said flippantly.

Mr. Boudreaux was one of "the men" who worked for Dad. Dad seemed to like him, and my parents and the Boudreauxs had become friends. I was uneasy around Mr. Boudreaux. I couldn't help it. I worried that my father might have to give him a bad evaluation, fire him, and ruin his life.

"And that wasn't good," Dad responded. "I had to take Ames off the clock to come get me, so I had to make up for his lost wages."

"And I told you that you were a fool to do that. You should've left him on the clock. What's one hour of his time to that big company?"

He sighed, shook his head at her, and tried another approach. "Look, Buddy'll be in junior high next year—playing sports and participating in school programs. You know how he loves baseball. He'll have practice after school and games during the weeknights when you have the car. And he keeps askin' 'bout a Saturday bowling league, but you need the car to get to your hospital job on Saturdays."

"You know good and well you can drop me off and then pick me up on Saturdays if you need the car. That goes for Monday and Thursday nights as well."

"I know," Dad said, "but think how much more flexibility a second car gives us. There's gonna be all those social events in junior high. You know what Tom and Dolores say, how they feel like professional chauffeurs since Billy started junior high, what with spirit parties, dances, and the like."

"What else?" She cut him off.

"Strike two," I whispered to myself.

"Well, third, we need it for safety and peace of mind."

Her forehead wrinkled and her eyes shot a dart at him. This was the one I sensed she was waiting for. Dad took the Falcon to work each morning, and Mom walked a mile or so each way to and from Dr. Holland's office. She had to go down Eleventh

Street through one of the less desirable parts of town. If his final point was about defenseless females walking alone, my father's cause was lost. It looked like strike three to me.

He ignored her cold stare and said, "It's for *Buddy's* safety and *my* peace of mind."

She cocked her head to one side, uncertain of his meaning. I caught myself doing the same.

"You owe that to us," he said.

"Come again?" she said.

"I know you try to be careful, Lon. But that neighborhood you walk through is getting so bad with lowlifes moving in and all the crime. You walk right past Triangle Grocery, and they got robbed at gunpoint last month—*again*! And the traffic is murder along there, so many cars zipping up and down Eleventh Street, all those people with things on their minds other than driving. I know, deep down, you're concerned too. You're just too tough to admit it, and you won't let me drive you in, drop you off on my way to the plant."

"An hour early? And who'd make sure Buddy gets his breakfast and gets off to school?"

"I know! That's what I'm talkin' 'bout. That's why you need your own car—for Buddy. If something happens to you walkin' out there, you'll never forgive yourself for being so reckless in your regard for Buddy's future. He needs his mother. And he needs her whole and able to take care of him. This car keeps you safe—for Buddy."

His voice was softer now. "And I have needs too." He paused to let her digest this strange vulnerability. "My first hour at work is spent worried sick that the phone's gonna ring and it's the police saying you've been taken to the hospital. Why do you think I call you at work so often, first thing in the morning, to remind you of something or ask some stupid question? I need to hear your voice and know that my girl is okay.

"And do you have any idea how fast I drive home in the evening to get here and make sure you've made it home safe and sound? All the while, I'm thinking maybe there's a police car waiting for me instead of you getting supper started.

"I love you, Lon," he said, "but you need to understand that the big hug you get when I pop in that door at 5:30 has as much to do with relief as, you know, affection." He had lowered his head when he said that last word. When she didn't reply, he added, "It's just $65 a month; that's all."

"How much?" she asked.

"Sixty-five bucks a month. Heck, we've been saving twice that much each month since I got the promotion last year. And I'm due for a raise in June. I've worked it out, and I can show you the figures if you just let me. In fact, when you think 'bout Buddy's summer vacations, the flexibility that a second car provides, and the need for safety and peace of mind—all those things—I think you'll agree that *we can't afford not to buy this car.*"

He was finished. That last line was a tidy conclusion just like they taught us in sixth-grade composition class. *Not bad*, I thought. My father was full of surprises. Maybe I had underestimated him.

Mom had turned her body away from him during that final soliloquy. I couldn't get a clear view of her face, but she seemed tense near the end and raised her hand once to wipe her cheek. After a long silence, she spun her head around toward my father. "I hate maroon!" she said in a loud voice. She cocked her right index finger and pointed it down into his face, waving it up and down and shouting, "You have no right to pick a color without asking me first! Do you understand me?"

His head nodded.

"Good!" she said.

Mom wheeled around, opened the door, and entered the trailer. I scrambled away from the window and tried to look busy as she slammed the door behind her, rushed to their bedroom at the back of the trailer, and shut the sliding door behind her. She never acknowledged my presence, or perhaps she never noticed.

I looked back out the window. Dad was sitting on the concrete steps. He'd lit a cigarette, and he slowly smoked it to the end. I think that's how he measured the right amount of time to give my mother to come to grips with her feelings, but not so long that she would think him insensitive.

Dad stubbed out his cigarette and stood up, and I flopped onto the sofa and turned up my radio to appear less conspicuous. He opened the door and entered the trailer. He looked at me without speaking, but he flashed that boyish grin and then nodded his head at me—just once. I held my breath, suddenly wondering, *Did he know all along that I was listening? Was that performance for my benefit? A lesson?*

He turned and walked down the narrow hallway. He slid the bedroom door open, sat next to my mother on the bed, and took her into his arms. She returned his embrace. Looking over Mom's shoulder, my father's eyes met mine. He nodded again and maintained eye contact with me for just a second before he slid the door shut.

Of all the cars we owned when I was growing up, that Rambler station wagon was by far the most memorable. No contest. In addition to providing reliable transportation for my mother to go to and from work and run her errands, the station wagon was our *family* car. We owned it for four years and took it on successive summer vacations to Michigan, California, Florida, and New York. We always took it to go to Mass on Sundays.

It was the car that Mom used on Saturday mornings to chauffeur Marty, Daniel, and me to the Gaylynn Theatre to see the kids' movies, on her way to work. We would lie all scrunched together in the back of the station wagon, and Mom would frown at us through the rear-view mirror if we got too rowdy. It was the car that took the three of us to junior high parties and football games.

In 1968, I passed my driving test in that car. Later that summer, Dad amazingly secured two tickets for us to go to the All-Star baseball game in Houston—indoors, in the Astrodome. I got to see Mays, Yastrzemski, and all the other great players. He let me drive the station wagon to the game and home that evening, one and a half hours each way. On the way there,

Dad taught me how to tell a Chevy from a Ford or a Chrysler and about all the different makes and models of cars. On the way home, we talked nonstop about baseball. It's one of the few pleasant memories from my teenage years.

It was also the last time I ever drove that car. The week after the All-Star Game, I announced to my parents that they could no longer force me to go on summer vacations with them. I told them I didn't want to go anywhere or do anything, not this year or any year, especially not with them. I was 16 and it was just another phase in my messed up teenage years, but I was a real asshole about it. Dad wasn't pleased, but he didn't argue or try to debate the issue with me. The next day, without consulting me, my folks went to the American Motors dealership and traded in our station wagon for a brand-new green (Mom's favorite color) Rambler Marlin coupe. I pretended that I didn't care.

But my most vivid memory of that station wagon is a cold and dreary January morning in 1965. I rode to Daniel Carter's funeral service that day, alone in the back seat of that car, my head filled with confused thoughts. On the way home, my mother sat next to me in the back seat as I cried into her bosom. She held me tightly as my father drove us in silence.

* * * * *

I bolted from the kitchen table as my parents were rising to reach out to me. I couldn't take any more talk about Daniel and what was likely to happen to me if I went to school that morning. I knocked away their arms, raced through the kitchen, slammed my bedroom door behind me, and dove onto the bed.

I curled into a fetal position and gently rocked back and forth on the small bed. Rocking seemed to reduce and eventually calm the shaking in my limbs, but it was replaced by a cold chill pulsing through my stomach and diaphragm as I contemplated a series of unpleasant scenarios involving cops, shrinks, teachers, parents, and schoolmates.

A couple of minutes passed. I figured that Dad had convinced Mom to give me some time to myself. I removed my glasses and placed them on the nightstand. Then I went back to my curled position on the bed, silent and motionless except for my rhythmic, slow rocking. There was a knock on the door that was firm enough to tell me that it belonged to my father. He was respecting the rule about knocking first—my rule.

* * * * *

My parents had sold the trailer after I finished sixth grade in the summer of 1964. Mom talked constantly about how we were now "middle-class" people and how "nice" that was—to be able to rent a nice two-bedroom house in a nice middle-class neighborhood with nice middle-class neighbors. I wasn't sure how we got the promotion or what that made us before the promotion. I know for certain that it wasn't "low class" because I specifically asked Mom about that, and she set me straight that I shouldn't ever use that term to describe our family.

After thinking about it, however, I reached the conclusion that less-than-middle-class kids lived in trailers, apartments with noisy neighbors, or small shacks that passed as houses. They shared a single bathroom with their parents and siblings. They had no privacy because, if they were like me when I was less-than-middle-class, their bedroom was actually a hallway in a trailer with a small built-in bed on one side and built-in drawers on the other.

Middle-class kids, on the other hand, had their own private bedroom, even if it was small, and their own bathroom. Best of all, the room belonged to the middle-class kid. Therefore, the kid was able to have a rule for the parents whereby a parent could only enter the room if he or she knocked first and was then granted permission to come in. It was good to be middle class.

* * * * *

Dad asked calmly without opening the door to my room, "Buddy, are you okay?"

Silence from my side.

"Buddy, answer me," he commanded.

"I'm okay! Just leave me alone!" I cried at the door, but then I added, "For a little while, okay? Please?"

"But school will be—"

"I ain't going to school!" I shrieked, lifting my head and breaking the fetal position so I could see the closed door that separated us. I prayed that my father would know better than to push me before I had a chance to be alone, to digest what he'd said and evaluate my situation. Over the sound of my heavy breathing, I heard them whispering in the hallway. After a few seconds, my prayers were answered.

Dad opened the door, just slightly, so he could see me as he stood in the hall and said, "Okay, listen up."

I nodded and he continued, "Everything's gonna be okay. Just stay put, stay calm for a minute, and let me make a phone call. Your mother's gotta go to work now, but I'll be in the next room if you need me. I'll be making that phone call, all right?"

"Yeah. Thanks," I said.

He shut the door, and I heard their footsteps walking away. I turned to resume my position—to think.

Chapter 6

12:00 noon

I didn't go to school that day. Dad and I got that settled with another conversation around 7:30 after he insisted that I grant him entry into my room. He checked on me every 30 minutes over the next four hours, each time going through the required protocol to knock first and then gain permission to open the door and observe me curled on the bed in my little sanctuary. We would exchange a sentence or two, and he'd remind me that he was in the living room if I needed anything. Then he would close the door and leave me to the privacy of my own thoughts and schemes.

At noon, he arrived with lunch. Even though I told him I wasn't hungry, he insisted on bringing it in.

"Mind if I eat with you?" he asked, although it wasn't really a question, more like a comment. Frankly, I didn't mind. It was going to be tricky, but I needed to get more information from him.

"Yeah, that's fine," I said.

He was carrying a tray, which he set on my desk. Looking at the tray as I sat up, I had to blink to clear my vision and make sure I wasn't seeing double. There were two white napkins, each with a silver soup spoon resting on them. Steam was rising from two identical bowls that I assumed contained soup. Chicken noodle was my guess, since everyone knew that was my favorite. On two identical little plates sat grilled cheese sandwiches, each sliced diagonally and complimented with a dill pickle spear. The two pickles were the same size. There was milk to drink, served of course in two identical clear plastic glasses. When I saw that the level of liquid in each glass was exactly the same, I looked away and shook my head.

"What?" he asked.

"Nothing. Just talking to myself."

He placed my half of this feast on my nightstand, arranging each piece in a certain order that I knew had some deep significance to him. The soup bowl was the centerpiece of the banquet. Spoon and napkin were placed to the right of the bowl. The milk glass guarded the soup's left flank, and the sandwich and pickle sat ready in reserve to the rear and right of the soup. With everything in place, he cocked his head for a better view of the nightstand and then moved the glass up an inch. I wasn't about to ask.

"There you go," he said. He then removed each of his items from the serving tray and placed them one by one on the left side of my desktop. When he was finished, they were, of course, in the exact same arrangement as mine, to the centimeter. It was like we had two equally matched forces placed into position and poised to be devoured with maximum efficiency.

"Say the blessing, please," he said as he set the serving tray on the floor.

He was seated in my desk chair with the chair pulled to the side of the desk so he could face me. I sat on the edge of my bed, the same angle to my lunch as he was to his. We were in perfect symmetry.

I bowed my head and placed my hands together. He did the same. I said softly, "Bless us, oh Lord, for these thy gifts, which we are about to receive from thy bounty, through Christ, our Lord. Amen."

"Amen," he whispered with me and then raised his head and smiled.

I watched to see what he would do first. He placed the little napkin in his lap, picked up his spoon, and took a sip of the soup broth. He looked at me.

"It's chicken noodle," he said. What a surprise.

Without answering, I picked up one of the sandwich halves and took a small bite. He frowned. I chewed slowly while he returned to his soup bowl. He took a couple of quick spoonfuls, this time slurping the noodles with great satisfaction on his face like he was thoroughly enjoying it.

"This soup is really good and just the right temperature," he said.

Without responding, I took another bite of grilled cheese, this time a large one. After staring at my inflated cheeks, he let out a soft sigh and looked away. Head down, he settled into a slow, silent rhythm with his soup.

Two more bites finished off my first sandwich half. It was becoming evident that he had decided not to comment on my priorities in food selection. That was disappointing, so I tried another tactic. With my chewing not quite complete, I picked up the glass and took a sip, allowing the milk to mix with the partially chewed sandwich in my mouth. He saw what I was doing.

"Buddy," he said in a firm voice, "you know we never drink with our mouths full. It's rude. You know that's a rule."

"Yes, sir," I mumbled after a big swallow. While he was looking at me, I set the glass down—as far from its assigned spot as I could get it—precariously close to the nightstand's edge. My milk was now in danger of falling victim to a careless hand or a sliding dish later in the meal and winding up as another stain on the cheap carpet in my room. My father cringed.

"And put your napkin on your lap. You know that's the way we always begin our meals."

I stared at him, unafraid. After all, he was supposed to be nice to me today. Didn't my best friend just die, as in dead and gone forever? In my most sarcastic voice, I replied, "Well, it may be that I forgot because I've got a few other things on my mind right now."

"Yes," he responded sharply, "and we need to talk 'bout that. But first, I want you to eat your lunch—properly." He reached over and slid my glass a few inches back into the more secure interior of the luncheon formation.

"I'm not hungry."

"You seemed hungry enough when you were taking those big mouthfuls and washing 'em down with your milk."

"Yeah, well, I'm not hungry now," I said.

There was a firmness in his voice as he said, "You will eat the rest of your lunch, young man. That is not negotiable." He leaned forward, only an arm's length from me. "Do you understand?"

I hesitated, to not appear totally compliant, but only for a second. "I'll try," I said slowly, in a pained voice.

"Good. Thank you."

It was clear that I would receive no quarter, no special dispensation, even on this solemn day. In my father's world, order must always be maintained. All his rules were to remain in place, no matter the graveness of the situation. I was hurt. I had hoped for some relief, a little slack from him. However, my father's reaction to my experimental probing was precisely what I had been conditioned after 12 years to expect from him.

He went back to his soup, and I slowly attacked the pickle spear, inspired to try a new tactic. I would drag out the lunch, saving my soup for last. I would complain that it was cold, and I didn't want to eat it. It wasn't likely that he would excuse me from the soup, but I also knew my father well enough to know that he wasn't going to force me to eat cold soup. Instead, he would have to go back into the kitchen, relight the stove, pour my cold soup into the heating pan, and deal with all that inconvenience—just so his little prince could have warm soup at the end of his meal.

My plan worked to perfection. Surprisingly, he didn't appear displeased, and he didn't say a word in reply to my complaint about the cold soup. He just picked up my bowl and headed for the kitchen. It took him six minutes and ten seconds before returning with steam coming from the bowl. I know because I timed him.

I picked up the spoon and went for my first bite. At the same time, he commenced lecturing. He began with the proper order to eat your food. He went into excruciating detail to demonstrate with irrefutable facts how I had made a grave error in judgment by first going for the sandwich. When he had exhausted that topic, he proceeded to enlighten me with an essential tidbit of culinary knowledge: the history and significance of the

PART ONE: 12:00 noon   57

appetizer-salad-entree-dessert-coffee batting order. With that discussion came the complimentary, although mildly repulsive, discourse on how stomach acids break down the various food groups.

I tried to ignore him, but it was hopeless. There was nowhere to hide. I was trapped in my own room, forced to hear about proteins being devoured in the deep recesses of my gut. Halfway through the soup, I couldn't bear it any longer.

"Dad, please, I don't care."

"You be quiet and eat." He shook his index finger at me. "Your behavior shows that you clearly need to understand these things. I'm perfectly happy to educate you so that, in the future, you won't *accidentally* inconvenience someone 'cause of your ignorance. Now, since I forgot where I was, I'll start over with the starch food group."

I ate quickly.

* * * * *

Before lunch, while I was alone in my room for four hours, I had thought a lot about my friend, Marty Shannon. Daniel, Marty, and I were close, just like those guys in *The Three Musketeers*. Marty must have been devastated and bewildered by the news—like me, except he was probably at school with teachers, shrinks and cops prying at him. I worried about what he might be telling them.

Our rental house was on Hazel Street, and Marty and his mom lived directly behind us in a similar-sized house that faced North Street. A white picket fence that was only three feet high separated the two back yards.

My parents met Mrs. Shannon over the Memorial Day weekend, when they were walking around the back yard of the Hazel Street house with the rental agent and me in tow. They had enrolled me at St. Christopher Junior High for the coming school year and were trying to determine whether we could afford to move to a better neighborhood.

Mrs. Shannon was in her back yard hanging clothes to dry. She gave us a smile and started chatting with my folks over the little fence. They instantly took a liking to her. She told them that she also had a boy who would be in seventh grade at St. Christopher. She made her son, Martin, come out of the house to put him on display. I fidgeted around and didn't say much past the opening introductions, but Marty blabbed on about school, the neighborhood, other kids he knew. My parents took the whole experience like some divine sign—an omen. They put the trailer up for sale and signed the rental agreement that afternoon. We moved in a week later.

Since both of my parents worked and Mrs. Shannon didn't, she volunteered to watch after me during the summer break. I enjoyed spending time in her house and with her. She was a joyful lady who gave Marty, Daniel, and me a great deal of freedom to be rambunctious 12-year-old boys during those lazy days. Daniel was Marty's good friend, and on most afternoons that summer, he rode his bike to Marty's house to join us after lunch.

Mrs. Shannon didn't say much, but she knew just when to jump in and add something interesting to our conversations. She also had a knack for being able to mediate any argument that the three of us were having and, at the same time, change the subject on us without ever having to declare winners and losers.

When I arrived in the morning, Mrs. Shannon always had the sports pages of *The Beaumont Enterprise* placed on her living room coffee table. She knew a lot about Major League Baseball and was pleased to discuss the stories and box scores, or she would let me read in silence if that was my preference. Like Marty and me, she was a big fan of our struggling Colt .45s, the new expansion team in Houston. Their uniforms proudly displayed a gigantic gun stretched across each player's chest. What could be a more fitting mascot for a Texas team and more inspiring for its players?

We speculated about the domed stadium they were building for the Colt .45s in Houston and what idiots had come up with that idea. Baseball was supposed to be played in the fresh air and sunshine. Besides, how could they expect to air-condition an entire ballpark? It was ridiculous. Neither of us had air-conditioning in our homes, and we couldn't see the point. It seemed like a monumental waste of money. How could any structure anywhere justify spending $35 million, the domed stadium's colossal price tag?

I had serious concerns that such a huge domed roof would cave in during a game and kill our heroes, not to mention the fans in the stands. I came up with a new moniker—the "doomed" stadium—and started referring to it by that name. Mrs. Shannon thought it was a clever play on words and congratulated me for being so witty. I wanted to write a letter to Hal "Woody" Woodeshick, my favorite player, to warn him. However, Mrs. Shannon convinced me that it would be better to keep these concerns to myself for the time being or at least until the new stadium was completed.

The Shannons had a color television, the first I'd seen. It was a Motorola, a high-precision marvel, the kind of complex electronic device that Americans are world-famous for manufacturing. On most nights that summer, after scarfing dinner with my parents, I would rush to the Shannons' house to sit transfixed in front of their TV and watch our favorite programs as the announcer proudly proclaimed, "In living color."

Marty was the most outgoing, extroverted kid that I'd ever met. When we were alone, he was always talking about girls. My father had not had a birds-and-bees chat with me, and much of what Marty said made little sense, which was both frustrating and unsettling. Not wanting to draw attention to my lack of firsthand knowledge, I would nod or grunt in agreement as he offered opinions on a wide range of topics concerning the female sex and confessed about various indiscretions with the many girls in his life. To hear him talk, you'd think he was a regular Don Juan. However, once school began, the girls at St. Christopher, for the most part, acted highly indifferent toward Marty and his frequent advances.

There were a few boys and girls at school who reportedly "liked" each other. Some were even going steady. Every few weeks, Marty got it in his head that one of the seventh-grade belles at St. Christopher thought I was cute or something or could be persuaded to like me. I put on airs about not wanting to restrict myself to just one babe. Despite my protests, Marty was undeterred and kept insisting, "Don't worry, man. I got this. I'll fix you up."

During those times, my anxiety level reached new highs. I didn't understand what responsibilities and obligations getting fixed up might force upon me, nor could Marty concisely define it in terms that made sense. My hormones were making me curious, but that curiosity was kept firmly in check by an overwhelming desire to avoid humiliation because of my ignorance. I finally had to put my foot down, even though I knew it hurt his feelings. Marty was my friend, but he was not the person I wanted in charge of such a delicate aspect of my development.

Marty was one of the tallest boys in seventh grade and one of the better athletes in the sports that didn't require too much concentration or finesse. We both liked sports, but I couldn't have what I considered an intelligent and objective analysis of teams or players with him. For example, who was better: Mantle or Mays? Ford or Koufax? Most of the compelling statistics that I had memorized and could quote with machine-like accuracy—like batting averages, home runs, RBIs, ERAs, and games won/lost—either flew over his head or he just refused to acknowledge them. Marty was more likely to base his assessments on brute force. It drove me crazy. According to Marty, Mantle was better than Mays because he could hit the ball farther. Sandy Koufax was better than Whitey Ford because he could throw harder. Marty Shannon was not likely to become a debate champion.

Marty had an Irish surname like my mother's maiden name, but he didn't look Irish. He had a dark olive complexion, and his eyes were a twinkly warm shade of brown. His hair was black, and it rose and fell in tight little curls on his oversized head. It was curious that his mother was fair-skinned and slightly built at just five feet tall. She seemed much older than most of the kids' moms, more like a grandmother. Wrinkles had cut deeply into her face and hands. The lines spoke not just of age but also of a hard life. There was no Mr. Shannon.

I asked my father about the extreme difference in their looks and age. I went on about how I thought kids were supposed to look a lot like their parents. Also, I had calculated that Mrs. Shannon was probably in her 40s when Marty was born. Wasn't that old to be having babies?

Dad agreed that this was a perplexing situation that Mrs. Shannon had not shed any light upon. He added that it was also odd that there were no pictures of Marty's father around their house. Dad told me that he had discreetly inquired a couple of times about "Mister" Shannon, but she always changed the subject and made it clear in a polite way that she didn't want to talk about him.

"Sometimes there's a story inside folks that's just too painful or too personal to tell," he said. He gave me a half-smile and added, "I think we can all relate to that. There's probably things that've happened to you, things that you'd prefer not to get into, even 'round close friends or your own family. That's not at all uncommon."

I thought about my experience as a trailer rat. I could see his point.

"You're naturally observant and curious," he continued, "and you're right. There's something unusual 'bout havin' a boy that young at her age. And havin' a boy that looks so different from a physical standpoint. And owning her house outright and havin' a steady source of income when she doesn't have a job. But that's *their* business. Do you understand?"

"Yes, sir. I think so. You're saying some people may have family secrets, and it's none of our business to pry into them."

"That's exactly what I'm saying," he said with a satisfied nod. "Listen, there's probably a simple explanation 'bout their family, but we don't need to waste time speculating on it. The Shannons are good people, and that's all that matters." After a short pause, he asked, "You like spending time with Marty?"

"Yes, sir," I said.

Looking into my eyes, he said, "A *really good friend*, now that's a special gift, a blessing. It's someone you don't have to pretend with. You can just be yourself, be at ease, and they'll like you anyway. You don't get to have many of them, and lord knows, we all desperately need at least one."

I gave him a nod.

"You know, I think Marty Shannon could be that one for you," he added. "But don't prematurely jeopardize the friendship by pressing him or his mother on issues they're not ready to talk 'bout. You agree?"

"Yes, sir. But Dad?"

"Yeah?"

"Why don't we get to have many really good friends?"

"'Cause it's gotta be somebody who's compatible, who's just right—for you. And 'cause it takes a whole lotta effort to develop a close friendship with somebody. You gotta take the time to get to know each other deep down, not just on the surface. But that's okay, 'cause you enjoy each other's company doin' just 'bout anything and everything. And," he added, "doin' absolutely nothing." He grinned. "They're the people in your life that you truly enjoy bein' 'round and vice versa. Time passes quickly—too quickly—when you're with your really good friends."

He seemed pleased that he had my full attention, that I was listening closely like a sponge trying to soak up the message he casually dispensed like so many droplets of water. It encouraged him to continue.

"You'll have lots of acquaintances and pals in life, Buddy, but only a precious few really good friends. It's like your Uncle Johnny and me. We've been through a lot and we'll be friends for life. We both know it. I can call on him for anything. Anything! And I know he'll be there. And he knows I'd do the same for him. That's a comforting feeling."

What he said made a lot of sense. As that summer melted into autumn and autumn changed into winter, it helped me to define and appreciate my relationship with Marty Shannon and my very special relationship with Daniel Carter. That part was good. Unfortunately, my father failed to prepare me for the grief, the disorientation, and the agonizing emotional toll that gets extracted when you suddenly lose that really good friend because he decides he'd rather be dead than continue life as your best friend.

Chapter 7

12:30 p.m.

Dad stopped lecturing as soon as I finished the chicken noodle soup. He picked up our dishes and glasses and placed everything back onto the serving tray while I sat quietly on my bed. When he was finished, he reseated himself in my desk chair and asked, "How're you doin'?" He leaned forward to size me up, his keen eyes at the same level as mine.

"I'm okay. And Dad?"

"Yes?"

"You can quit asking that, please. If I'm not okay, I'll tell you. All right?"

He slowly nodded his head before responding. "All right then," he said.

Then he was silent as he stared out the window for a few seconds like he was organizing his thoughts. When he was ready, he turned his head to face me. "I've been on the phone with your school this morning. Let me tell you what I found out and what I've set up for today."

I tensed slightly and involuntarily leaned toward him.

"First, Sister Mary Margaret was very understanding of your not being in school today," he said.

I had figured as much.

* * * * *

St. Christopher had an elementary school (first-through-sixth grade) and a junior high (seventh and eighth). Sister Mary Margaret was the principal for St. Christopher Junior High School, and she seemed exceptionally young to have so much responsibility. At least, I figured she was younger than most of the other nuns, although it wasn't easy to tell in those billowy tents and matching bonnets they always wore. She was full of energy and emotion and quick with a big smile. She wasn't at all like the nuns who taught my classes and were in a constant frump and so serious about everything.

Sister Mary Margaret loved kids. It was obvious. She attended all the football games and other after-school events, where she'd float among us like a perpetual motion machine. If she didn't recognize a student, she thought nothing of stopping the kid and saying, "Hello, my child. I'm Sister Mary Margaret, and who might you be?" She made you feel special when she talked to you, even if it was only to say your name as you passed in the halls or the cafeteria. "Hi, Dick; hi, Jane; hi, Buddy." Yes, she knew my name.

This was her first year at St. Christopher, just like me. On the first day of school, I was sitting in the auditorium with the entire junior high student body, about 120 seventh and eighth graders, when she came onto the stage to introduce herself. She loosened a microphone from its stand beside an official-looking podium. With the mic in her hand, she walked toward us to the edge of the stage. She said she'd forgotten to bring her soapbox to stand on, so she had to come out from behind that big podium to see us. Sister Mary Margaret was at least a couple of inches less than five feet tall.

She said that she'd just moved to Beaumont, and the mother superior in her new convent home had been punishing her since she'd arrived here. Apparently, she was mad because she thought Sister Mary Margaret was sitting during the blessing of their evening meal instead of standing like all the nuns were supposed to do. "Didn't she know? *I was standing!*" she said.

"But our mother superior here in Beaumont is not nearly as tough as the one in my last convent. Now, *she* was really strict."

She told us that was the signal for our part. She wouldn't go on until we all shouted in unison, "How strict was she?"

"Well, she was so strict that she allowed no talking whatsoever in her convent. She said we should always be working or praying—silently. However, she did let us say one sentence—just one sentence—but only at the end of each year."

She had our complete attention as she continued pacing in front of us, making sweeping gestures with her free arm as she spoke into the microphone. "My first year there finally came to an end. I walked into her office for my one sentence, and I said, 'Mother Superior, the bed is hard,' and she just nodded at me. So, I walked away. At the end of my second year, I walked in and said, 'Mother Superior, the bed is hard and the food is bad,' but she just stared at me. I went back and worked and prayed in silence for another year. At the end of my third year, which was this past summer, nothing had changed. So, I marched into her office and said, 'Mother Superior, the bed is hard, the food is bad, and I want a transfer!' She stared right at me and said, 'Well, that's fine because all you ever do is complain.' And that's how I ended up here at St. Christopher School."

We howled. She went on to tell a few more jokes, mostly poking fun at herself, laced cleverly into her welcoming remarks. She was extraordinary, a nun doing a Bob Hope routine. With my new friends, Marty and Daniel, laughing in the seats on either side of me, she dissolved my new-school anxieties.

* * * * *

"Sister Mary Margaret said the assembly this morning was difficult, very emotional," Dad said.

I nodded to show that he had my full attention. I sat erect and tried not to appear too tense.

Dad looked uncomfortable. He was slouched over, elbows resting on his thighs with his fingers interlocked between his knees. He spoke slowly like he needed to tactfully choose the appropriate words to convey some ominous message. I didn't like it. It reminded me of TV shows where the doctor puts on a brave face and uses his best bedside manner to tell the patient that he has a terminal illness.

"There's a lot of confusion right now, Buddy. Sister said some of the students are taking this pretty hard. I don't cotton much to psychiatrists and such, but there's two of them—counselors, she called 'em—at school today and they're meeting with the ones who seem to be the most . . . ah, shook up."

I smiled. I couldn't help it. I had a brief flash of Elvis Presley wiggling his hips on the auditorium stage at St. Christopher, wailing, "I'm in luv; I'm all shook up." The King is then assailed by two shrinks who carry him off to a couch to hypnotize him and probe further into his mysterious muscle-control problem.

I shook it off. I wanted to get to the important issue, the only one I cared about. "Dad?" I interrupted.

"Yes?"

"Do they know why he did it?"

"Well, Sister said that the police haven't made a formal determination as to whether it was an accident or a suicide. They're being somewhat tight-lipped, although she did tell me that—"

"Dad?"

He paused, annoyed by another interruption, and waited for me to speak.

"Dad, do they know why he did it?" He stared at me and I returned his gaze. I had aroused his curiosity, but I didn't care. Four hours alone in that room had dulled my judgment and sense of caution, and I wanted him to cut the crap and answer the question. What did he know?

"No, they don't know." He leaned forward even more as he raised his eyebrows and asked, "Do you?"

How I came to be a seventh-grade student at a parochial school is another story. I had anticipated that, after completing sixth grade at Robert E. Lee Elementary, I would go to South Beaumont Junior High. It was a large public school where all the Lee kids ended up after sixth grade as well as graduates from some other adjacent elementary school districts. At least, that's the way it was before racial integration.

Integration of public schools, although mandated by the federal government and the courts, was a controversial hot potato throughout the South and a no-win issue that the white politicos in Beaumont were not eager to address. However, a chain reaction was set off in May of 1963, as I was completing my fifth-grade school year, after a section of the dilapidated all-black school across the First Street railroad tracks collapsed without warning. Several children and a teacher were injured. That evening, all three local TV networks made it their feature story. They were each critical of the neglectful school board and uncaring city politicians.

Over the ensuing days, the TV news continued to report on the story, and Dad read to us at dinnertime from emotional articles and editorials in the newspaper. There were threats of lawsuits from parents of the black children who were hurt, which brought an angry response and counter-threats from the local chapter of the Ku Klux Klan. With all the negative publicity, the mayor and city council had to do something. So, the old school was closed, condemned by the City of Beaumont as an unsafe structure.

Arrangements had to be made on short notice for the education of about 500 displaced Negro children. The bureaucrats who ran the Beaumont Independent School District debated the issue that entire summer. Out of time and with no funds available to rebuild or replace the all-black school, they finally decided that redistributing these black students to the white schools in the area was a much more progressive and better economic answer.

Dad gave Mom and me a daily account of the controversy. He said that politicians and school boards throughout the South were runnin' scared, especially after President Kennedy and his brother called out 30,000 troops to put down the riots at Ole Miss the prior year and then backed down Governor Wallace in Alabama in June. Dad said he came from "the old school" and thought things were fine the way they were. He referred to South Beaumont's hasty foray into school integration as an experiment, and he seemed disturbed by it all.

I just listened. I didn't admit it to my father, but I liked the president. He was young, had a cool accent, didn't take any crap off the Russians or the Cubans, and didn't sweat like the other guy. Most of all, I liked his plan to put a man on the moon by the end of the decade. *Far out!* I thought. Dad called him a dreamer, but I couldn't see anything wrong with that.

About 70 black children showed up that first week of September in 1963 to begin the new school year at Robert E. Lee Elementary. A dozen of them joined the 60-or-so white kids, including me, enrolled for sixth-grade classes. The first day was wild. The local television and newspaper reporters darted about trying to corner the frightened black children and their apprehensive parents for interviews. Everywhere you turned, there were television cameras with floodlights. The distraught black kids couldn't go pee without some idiot following them into the bathroom with a camera asking what it was like.

Our school was unprepared for integration. Class sizes were 20 percent larger and there weren't enough desks. Even though the black kids rarely spoke in class, there were more students for the teachers to keep up with and more papers to grade. Lunch lines were longer, and after you got your food, most times there were no empty chairs in the cafeteria, especially at the beginning of the school year when the white kids wouldn't sit at a table inhabited by any blacks.

Fifth and sixth graders were assigned lockers at the beginning of each school year, but now there weren't enough lockers. They made the kids at the end of the alphabet do without a locker until some new ones could be requisitioned. I was one of those and was furious. The new kids were the ones causing the problem. They should go without, not me. Some of us threatened to start a protest, but Vice Principal Gilliam got word of it and quickly took control of the situation. She was a tenacious bulldog of a woman who was not to be trifled with. She confronted the "S" through "Z" insurrectionists, asking each of us in the sternest possible manner whether managing without a locker for a few days was going to be a problem. "Of course not, Mrs. Gilliam," I responded with a forced smile. It took three months for the new lockers to arrive.

The administrators and faculty for Lee Elementary weren't trained or prepared to handle the angry parents. The white parents complained that no formal notice had been given that *their* school was about to be integrated, and no meetings had been held to allow them to vent their concerns. The black parents complained about the terse form letters they received a few days before the start of school stating where their child was to report with no further explanation. The educators claimed that the subject was adequately covered in the newspapers, but they apparently didn't focus on the fact that the breadwinners in these families rarely got past the comics and sports pages. The uproar lasted about a month with parents pointing fingers, making threats, and basically acting like little kids.

Two of my sixth-grade teachers resigned during the first month of school. I hated to see Mrs. Carlson leave. She was young, energetic, and tried hard to make history interesting. She was there on a Friday and gone without explanation the following Monday. Between classes I cornered Mr. Howard, who taught math and was really cool, and I asked if he knew why she left. He said that Mrs. Carlson was recently married and wanted to have children, but her husband had been acting distant toward her since she started teaching and interacting daily with black children. For the sake of her marriage, Mrs. Carlson had said that she had to quit. I told Mr. Howard that I didn't understand, and he said that he agreed with me.

Coach Wilson, who taught boys' P.E. and often smelled like one of my dad's whiskey drinks, left for a job at an all-white school in Arkansas, where he'd grown up. He made a point on his last day to tell some of the black kids that they didn't belong in a white school, and they should go back to Africa. One of the little guys started crying. I never liked Coach Wilson and thought that comment showed what an insensitive idiot he was. Most of the black families couldn't afford bicycles or milk money for their kids, much less transportation to a foreign country.

From the students' perspective, there was a lot of curiosity at first. But the novelty soon wore off, and we settled into a familiar daily routine that differed little from pre-integration years if you didn't count the locker and lunch problems. The black kids pretty much kept to themselves and us white kids did the same. There was little interaction on a voluntary basis, and teachers didn't force the issue in the classroom. For example, there were four-to-eight black students in each of my classes, and they always sat together. When teachers assigned groups for study projects, the black kids got paired up together, never mixed with the whites. That made logical sense to everyone.

I don't mean to imply that there were no issues or incidents within our student body. There were a few white kids, real idiots, who played mean tricks on the black ones and called them names, mostly behind their backs but sometimes right to their faces. The offenders were typically the older kids with loud-mouth parents who had picketed outside our classrooms and made such a fuss the first two weeks of school. Mrs. Gilliam initially tried talking to the uncivil students, explaining why such behavior was unacceptable and telling them that they had to be respectful of our new classmates. When that didn't work, she declared that any student overheard saying "nigger" or any other racial slur on a list she published would receive an after-school detention of 20 minutes. No exceptions. After the fifth infraction, the detention became a half-day on Saturday. Eight infractions and you were suspended for a day. Gradually, as the teachers and administrators began enforcing this harsh policy, things calmed down.

By October, the pickets had disappeared, and by November, we pretty much stopped seeing angry parents—white or black—lurking outside the school offices or in the hall waiting to ambush one of the teachers. A half-dozen white kids and two of the blacks had left, transferred by parents who preferred to move their family to a different district rather than have their children go to an integrated school.

My parents adopted a "wait and see" approach. During the first few weeks of school, they required a full report each evening on how I was coping with these monumental changes in my life. When they saw that the whole thing was pretty much a nonevent from my perspective, other than not having a locker, they quit asking me about it. Life at the home front—our ongoing trailer park existence—gradually returned to status quo.

That all changed on November 22, 1963. It was a defining

moment for our newly integrated school, just as it was for the entire nation. I remember a white girl in my class, Bonnie Anderson, putting her arms around a weeping black girl, Londa Walker (she had no locker), to comfort her after they told us. It didn't seem at all unusual under the circumstances. It's hard to describe how much President Kennedy meant to us kids—black and white—and the hope that he gave us for a better country *for everyone*. Now he was suddenly gone, and we each felt an individual as well as a collective sense of loss that we talked openly about over the passing days. I commiserated with new classmates Leroy Barnes and Willie Edwards and discovered that they had doubts, fears, and a host of other confusing adolescent feelings about school, life, and what it means to be an American—just like me—but from a different perspective that my trailer-rat anxiety could relate to.

They also had a keen sense of humor that made them fun and interesting to be around. I wanted to spend more time with these new friends, but when I did, I was intimidated by stares from a sizeable group of white kids and by their threats to beat me up and brand me as a traitor to my race. As a result, I was cordial that sixth-grade year but never close with Leroy, Willie, or any of the other black kids. I should have had more courage, but it was all so complicated back then.

Near the end of that sixth-grade school year, I did something incredibly stupid. Norma Washington was a tall and razor-thin black girl. She was incredibly shy and never spoke in class or anywhere else as far as I could tell. Every single day, Norma wore a freshly pressed white blouse to school. Never green or blue, always white. It drove us crazy. We often speculated on whether she had just one shirt to her name that her mamma washed and pressed each night.

During the first week of May, after this white-blouse thing had been going on for eight months, Jamie Richmond came up with a brilliant idea, or so it seemed at the time. Jamie was a total idiot who worked hard at being the class clown. He pointed out that I sat in the back row in math, our last class of the day, with Norma and her white blouse right in front of me. Jamie figured I could flick a few blobs of black ink from my fountain pen, causing them to splatter on the back of the girl's blouse just before the bell dismissed us for the day. Norma wouldn't feel it and we could see the next day if the stains were there on the same shirt. So, I did it.

The next day, we couldn't make out any stain marks, so Jamie convinced me that I should do it again. I was such an idiot. When there were still no stain marks the following day, I did it again. As I rushed out of math class that third day, I was confronted by Luther Washington, a big black kid who was only in the fifth grade, but rumor had it he'd been held back at least four or five times. It was also widely reported that he could drive a car and buy booze without a fake ID.

Big Luther pushed me hard in the chest. "Ya do this ta my sista?" He pointed to Norma and then spun her around, so I could see the black ink stains on her blouse. Poor Norma started crying. I felt terrible, not just from fear and apprehension, but from shame. They were misinterpreting my action as a sign of bigotry. I needed to let them know that I didn't have anything against Norma, to tell them it was just a little prank, nothing more. I was about to ask Norma to please forgive me when that idiot Jamie Richmond stepped forward.

"So what if he did?" Jamie shouted at Luther.

"Then I'll kick his ass, rightch 'er and now!"

I pushed Jamie aside and told him to shut up and mind his own business. "I can fight my own battles," I said, figuratively of course. But that got Big Luther's juices flowing. His eyes went from my head to my feet, sizing me up as I tried to amend my previous statement. Then it got all out of control. I decided to show no fear of Big Luther, although he terrified me. I said things that came out all wrong like, "Hey, it's just a little black spot." Big Luther was getting madder and madder as a crowd of kids gathered around us, both blacks and whites.

I couldn't believe that I was causing such a scene. I wanted to apologize, but with the whole school standing there, I didn't want to be branded a yellow coward for the rest of eternity. Everything I said to Big Luther to try to calm him down came out backward and pissed him off even more. It was awful, like a whirlpool going round and round, sucking me in deeper and deeper. And all the while, Norma Washington—who wore white blouses every day, never spoke in class, and never did anything to harm anyone—continued to cry in front of everybody.

I never dreamed that Big Luther would hit me. I wore glasses. Dad had made a big deal out of the fact that you couldn't hit a man with glasses on. He said it was a rule. I even heard them say it on TV shows. I thought of my glasses as a shield against any physical assault while I pontificated in Big Luther's face. Apparently, Big Luther's father had forgotten this important part of his education.

I didn't see the punch. I was standing there talking one second and flat on my butt the next. I lay immobile on the ground, trying to determine what had just happened, struggling to clear the cobwebs and ascertain the cause for the sudden intense pain in my mouth. Big Luther was on me before I could sit up, pummeling my face with his big fists. The whole fight lasted about ten seconds before Mr. Howard came running over and pulled Big Luther off before he killed me.

When Dad came home that evening, my face was swollen and red from the beating. I removed the bag of ice cubes that Mom had given me so he could get the full picture. I showed him the tooth dangling loosely in my upper jaw. Mom and I began explaining what had transpired at school as he stared at my shattered glasses on the table.

He looked up with narrowed eyes when Mom said, "The boy, the one who hit him, he was Negro."

"What's his name?" Dad asked.

"Luther Washington," I replied.

"And he threw the first punch?"

"Well, yes, but—"

"And you were wearing those glasses?"

"Yeah, but—"

He didn't wait for any further details. He spun around,

picked up the printed school directory that we kept by the phone, stuffed it in his shirt pocket, and slammed the trailer door behind him. Mom was confused and slow to react. By the time she opened the door and we ran outside, he was already in the Falcon. I screamed to him that it was my fault, but he couldn't hear as he peeled out on the gravel road.

When Dad finally returned, he was breathing hard, panting. His complexion was chalky, almost white, and I saw the muscles in his cheek twitching nervously. He made a beeline for their bedroom. When he returned, he carried a large pistol and box of ammunition. His hands were shaking as he pulled six cartridges from the box and began jamming them into the gun's empty chambers. Mom and I looked at each other in panic.

"What the hell are you doing, Mac?" she shouted.

"That crazy Old Man Washington pulled a shotgun on me. That's what I'm doing," he said. His movements were abrupt and hurried, and there was a wild look in his eyes as he loaded the gun.

I never thought I would see it, but there in front of me, my father was a madman. A madman is very different from an idiot. That's because an idiot is stupid, but he's not crazy. There are idiots everywhere you turn, but they're generally harmless as long as you don't let them get to you too bad. A madman, on the other hand, is extremely dangerous. Madmen don't think about the consequences of their actions; they just do whatever they think needs doing. That night, my father was a madman.

"No nigger's gonna do that to me, by God!" he said. "I went over there to explain some things in a rational manner, to tell him that's not how you teach your children to behave in a civilized world. I told him he owed me for a dentist and a new set of glasses. Goddamnit, you don't hit someone with glasses on! But that old man, he just laughed at me, and then he pulled out his shotgun. His whole nigger family laughed at me!" Dad waved the loaded revolver in the air and said, "Well, he owes me! Let's see how they laugh at this .38 special!"

Mom reached out to stop him as he stepped toward the door, but the madman pushed her aside and she collided into a chair.

Chapter 8

12:40 p.m.

"Daniel was always different. That's what made him so much fun to be around. But he—" I paused. I needed to be careful what I said. I'd been talking too much. I needed my father to give me information, not the other way around.

"But what?" he asked.

"I guess he was sort of like, a bit strange over the past month or so."

"In what way?"

"Oh, you know Daniel. He was smart and always trying to play tricks on us. But here lately, he'd get all moody and start talking about things, you know, like dying and stuff like that."

"And what would he say?" Dad asked.

"He'd just make wisecracks."

"Like what?"

My voice trembled slightly. "Like, you know," I forced myself to mumble the words, "about killing himself."

"And how often did this happen? How often did he talk like that? About—" Now Dad was having difficulty saying the words. He lowered his chin as he added, "About killing himself?"

"Quite a bit lately."

"Like how much?"

"Like all the time."

He frowned at me.

"Well, maybe a couple of times a day here recently," I said. "He'd just come out with something like, 'I don't know what I'm living for.' Sometimes he'd say it for no reason."

"And what did you do? Who did you tell?" he asked.

"I didn't do anything. Most of the time, I just ignored him, like you told me. 'Ignore it and it'll go away.' Remember how you told me to do that?"

"Buddy, c'mon now. That applies when someone is saying mean things to you or acting silly, times like that. You don't ignore something serious like this."

"Hey, I didn't know it was serious! At least—"

"It's okay. I'm—"

"—not at the time. You think I knew it was serious?"

"—sorry I used that word. It's okay. It's okay," he said.

"I'd try to change the subject, you know, whenever I could."

"That's good. That's good." He nodded to encourage me to say more.

I raised my right hand to my head and began nervously pulling at the hair on the back of my head. "Marty, he'd get tired of it," I said. "He'd punch Daniel in the arm and tell him to shut up about all that dying stuff. Daniel told us we'd be sorry someday. But then, after he'd say that, he'd grin like it was a big joke or something, and we'd go back to whatever we were doing." I felt a wave of emotion rising inside me. "I don't get it. I know he did it. But why would he—?" I couldn't finish the sentence.

My hand moved from my hair to reach under my glasses. I squeezed the bridge of my nose and rubbed my eyes with my thumb and index finger, back and forth. For the first time that day, I felt tears forming. I thought about that morning, how weird it had been alone in my room for so long with my mind drifting between two extremes.

I had spent much of that morning motionless on my bed in a semiconscious state. My eyes were closed, but I felt the room and everything in it revolving around me in an eerie, surrealistic slow motion. I couldn't concentrate on any of the details my father had provided. I couldn't pull up any memories of Daniel Carter. Instead, I became hypersensitive to what was going on inside my body. I could hear my breathing and feel the beating of my heart and the blood pulsing through my neck and head, but my mind had gone into a shutdown mode that scary thoughts couldn't penetrate.

At the opposite end of the spectrum, there were times that morning when I had been sentient and completely aware of my situation and surroundings. My ability to concentrate had been keen and my thoughts were sharply focused on analyzing my predicament. I tried to think logically and objectively, like my father would, about my now-dead friend and the part I had played in his tragedy. During these times, a vivid stream of "what if" scenarios had played out in excruciating detail in my mind. In each of these, like rewriting a story, if I altered my behavior in the past, a new chain of events would be set off and the ultimate outcome would be different in the present: Daniel would still be alive. That must mean that I was to blame for his demise, right? *Right?* Fearing the dispassionate, truthful answer to that question, the stress would become unbearable, and I gladly surrendered once more to the numbness.

During one of my alert cycles, I'd gotten angry. I cursed Daniel for what he was doing to me, how he was ruining my life. With my rage boiling over, I got up and went to my desk. Sitting there with my *Daily Missal*, the Roman Catholic liturgy and prayer book, I devised an elaborate ceremony to excommunicate him as my friend. I wrote it all in a notebook. I would perform the ritual as soon as possible, when no one was around at the bicycle racks at school, the place where I had last seen him alive. He was an inconsiderate coward, and I would petition the authorities on high that Daniel Carter should burn in Hell for all eternity. I was quite pleased with myself as I settled back onto the bed and waited for the dull, numb feeling to take over.

Thirty minutes later, when I was alert once more, I read my cryptic notes and gut-wrenching guilt set in. That I had sought to punish him for my stupidity and shortcomings was reprehensible. I ripped the pages out of the notebook and cursed myself for writing them. It wasn't his fault; it was mine. I had surely caused his death, and I begged my friend to forgive me.

Once, for at least 20 minutes, I kept playing "The Name Game" over and over in my mind. It was bizarre. I hated that silly, annoying jingle-jangle, but I was powerless to stop it. *Let's do Buddy! Buddy, Buddy bo Buddy, banana fanna* . . . And then, *What about Daniel? Daniel, Daniel bo Baniel, banana fanna* . . . *One more time! Buddy, Buddy bo Buddy* . . . *Can't stop now! Daniel, Daniel* . . . My father's knock on the door finally broke my trance and stopped the incessant gibberish.

Another time, on my bed with my eyes closed, numerous good-time memories of Daniel, Marty, and myself had paraded across my mind in vivid colors. They continued for several minutes like a "greatest hits" collection playing through a home movie projector, and they made me smile. But they were soon intertwined with dark scenes of Daniel rattling on about how he wanted to kill himself. The projector stopped as I wondered about his final thoughts. I tried to imagine what it feels like to have a bullet shatter your skull and rip through your brain. Did he hear the explosion? Was there an intense pain or did he just slip peacefully into oblivion?

I had also envisioned my own impending peril, to be played out at the hands of a host of curious adults: cops, shrinks, nuns, and my own parents. It was unlikely I could put them off forever. When their interrogation was complete, would they conclude that I was guilty of a crime? Would I be punished? Since I didn't yet have enough information about my nemeses to fully know their intentions and thereby devise a plan to thwart them, I had closed my eyes and invited the numbness to return. I needed to conserve my strength for the inevitable confrontation.

My mother sat dazed on the floor of our trailer. I was now the only thing between my father with his loaded pistol and the O.K. Corral, so I lunged for one of his legs and wrapped a python death grip around it with my entire body.

"I'm sorry! It's my fault! I'll get a job and pay you back for everything. I promise!"

"Let go!" the madman commanded, but I held fast. As he tried to jerk his leg free, Mom reached up and seized his free arm, the one without a loaded gun attached to the end of it.

"Mac!" she shouted.

"It's my fault, Dad!" I said. "I started it! Don't go!" I felt some of the tension go out of his leg.

"You said that colored boy hit you first. What's this 'bout you starting it?"

I was crying, screaming up at him between sobs. "I'll pay you back for the glasses and everything. I'm sorry! I didn't mean to do it. Please, Dad, please!"

"You didn't mean to do what?" His tone was gruff, but he had stopped struggling against Mom and me.

"To throw ink on her shirt—Norma Washington. Please, Dad, I didn't mean it. I'm sorry!"

Mom screamed at him, "Mackenzie Torrence, as the Lord God is my witness—"

"Quiet!" the madman roared.

He looked down and said in a more composed tone, "Buddy, Old Man Washington said something 'bout me bein' the one that owed money, not him. It had to do with his daughter. What did you do?"

I stuttered through a couple of confused sentences and then he stopped me. He told Mom and me firmly but politely to *please* let go of him. He promised not to leave until we had a conversation, and he wanted the three of us to sit at the table. Mom nodded at me and I released his leg.

After we sat down, I told him the whole story. As I spoke, I stared at the pistol and box of .38 caliber shells that he had set on the table, and I cried like a blubbering idiot. When I finished, the madman was gone and my father had returned. He inquired why I hadn't told him all this when he first came home. Mom defended me, shouting that he never gave me a chance. She said he just went crazy as soon as he heard it was a Negro boy who had assaulted me. She called him a bigot and stormed outside, slamming the trailer door behind her.

My father just sat there, his head bowed. I stared at the place on top where his hair was thinning and waited to see what he would do next. I was totally drained and felt the pain coming back into my face.

He finally got up and kissed me on the top of my head and said he was sorry. "I hope you learn something outta this mess I've made tonight. You know, for centuries whites have been struggling to dominate coloreds, and the coloreds have been struggling to throw off the whites. I guess I got caught up in all that crap without following my own rule—to get all the facts and think through 'em first." He gave a disheartened sigh. "I hope you do a better job when you grow up, Son."

"Aren't you going to go find her?" I asked.

He looked at his watch, just as he had when she first left the trailer. "In another minute," he said as he returned to his chair. The two of us sat there silently, each with his own thoughts as my father lit a cigarette. When it was finished, he picked up the gun and box of ammunition and returned them to the cabinet, locking it before he left to find Mom. Twenty minutes later, my parents returned. They clearly were not Ozzie and Harriet, but the overt hostility was gone.

The next day, my father paid another visit to Mr. Washington. This time, he was apologetic for his behavior the prior night and for my ruining Norma's clothing. He gave Mr. Washington an envelope containing $15 to replace the three blouses I had ruined.

Mom told him he was crazy. It was her view that the two wrongs—mine and Big Luther's—canceled each other.

Dad firmly disagreed. He said that I had started the whole affair and then failed to make an apology when I had the opportunity. Whatever happened thereafter was on me; it was my fault. He went on about how people must take responsibility for their actions and be accountable to themselves and to others. It didn't matter if the other guy didn't play by Dad's rules. He told us, "That's the way civilized people *must* act. Who knows? Maybe Mr. Washington and his family will learn something by seeing the honorable way we behave."

Yeah, good luck, I thought.

Dad said that the $15 was a loan from him to me, a debt that I had incurred through my foolish and inconsiderate actions. He expected it to be paid in full out of my first paycheck after I had completed college and begun my career. I was incredulous, wondering if he realized that I was only 11 years old, as he made me look him in the eyes and acknowledge that I understood these payment terms. Sometimes, I truly didn't know what to make of my father, but I was sure of one thing as we shook hands on it. After I graduated from college, when I was twice my age at that time, he would expect $15 from me, to be handed over in full and on time. He would never forget. But then, neither would I.

Alone in my room all morning, I never once shed a tear thinking about Daniel's death. I found this unsettling. During one of my alert periods, I had tried to force myself to cry, but the tears wouldn't come. What was wrong with me? Wasn't he my best friend?

In a curious way, I was relieved that finally, talking with my father after lunch, I felt a sincere sorrow for Daniel and his family, and I was suddenly overwhelmed by a sweeping sense of loss. I'm sure that Dad could sense it because he slid next to me on the bed and put his arm around me.

"For the life of me," he said, "I don't understand how a 12-year-old could take his own life. But you're right. According to Sister Mary Margaret, they're pretty much certain it was a suicide."

"Yes, sir."

"As the investigation continues and they get more facts, the reasons will probably become clear."

I tensed under his arm.

"You said that Daniel acted strange," he said. "Did he act, like in any way, suicidal—'round you? I mean, other than what you just talked 'bout, did he do anything specific?"

"Maybe," I said. The tears were welling up in my eyes.

"What do you mean, 'maybe'?"

"Well, he took some chances, you know, where he could have been hurt," I said.

"What?"

"But he joked about it later," I added.

"What else?"

"I don't know," I whined. "It's just that, over the last few weeks, he'd get all moody. And he'd never want to eat anything. And then—" My voice was shaking. I was losing control. "I guess he did act like . . . Oh, Dad, I can't—"

"But you didn't think much of it at the time, right? You thought he was kidding," my father said calmly. "In fact, he told you he was kidding, right?" The way he asked, it was apparent that this was the answer he was looking for, the response he wanted to hear.

"That's right. I never thought he'd really do it."

"I know, Son." He squeezed my shoulder and pulled me closer to him. He whispered in my ear, and there was no mistaking the sternness in his deep voice as he said, "But you should've told us these things 'bout Daniel. Why didn't you tell us?"

I couldn't answer. My best friend was dead, and I had no excuse for failing to report his recent dark, depressed behavior and obsession about his own death. Dad was clearly disappointed in me, and in that moment, all I could think about were those stupid forms that he filled out on the men at work. I had breached my duties and responsibilities as his son. I would have to suffer the consequences for my negligence, but this time I knew that a $15 IOU was not going to suffice. This time, someone had died. There was only one punishment I could think of to fit this offense. In my father's world, no exceptions could be allowed. I would have to be fired—as his son. My body trembled under his arm. I covered my face with both hands so he wouldn't see my shame.

To my relief, he let the question pass. He got up from the bed, went into my bathroom, and returned with several tissues. I used them to wipe my eyes and blow my nose. He took his seat across from me in the desk chair, where he could look straight at me. I got the impression that he was more comfortable with some space between us instead of right next to me. That was natural. You don't fire someone with your arm around them. When I was sufficiently calm, he began again.

"You know that the school administrators, your teachers, and the counselors they're using—these people are not the enemy. Right?"

When I didn't respond, he kept talking. "They're confused, just like you. They're trying to understand what went wrong with Daniel, and they need your help to do that."

"What if I don't want to help them?" I shot back. "What if I just want them to *leave me alone?*"

He sighed. "You've got to understand, Buddy. A terrible, inconceivable thing has just occurred. We need to figure out why on earth this happened. And maybe, once all the facts become clearer, some changes can be made to make certain the same thing doesn't happen to another kid." He paused before asking the question that I knew was troubling him. "You don't have any reason to be concerned 'bout talkin' to these folks, do you?"

I had expected it. He was continuing to gather data for my evaluation. To be believable, I needed to look into his eyes as I spoke. I blinked nervously as my gaze flitted back and forth between his two eyes, then down to his upper lip, and back to his eyes. "No, of course not. It's just hard, you know. I don't want to have to relive all this stuff and go through all their stupid questions about Daniel. They'll want to know, 'How did he act?' 'What did he say?' 'Why didn't you do this; why didn't you do that?' I don't need all that right now."

I was pleased to have been able to semi-lock eyes with him for so long. I wondered about my performance, what my father saw before I lowered my head with a sniffle and wiped at my cheek.

Dad took a deep breath and exhaled. "Listen carefully, okay?"

"Okay," I said.

"I want to cause you as little stress as possible under the circumstances, but you *will* have to speak with them. *Someone has died.*" He continued in a softer tone. "Buddy, this is not something that will just go away. Do you understand?"

When I didn't reply, he repeated the question. "Do you understand?"

I nodded without looking up.

"Good," he said. "Now, here's what Sister Mary Margaret and I have arranged. Sister, along with one of the outside counselors plus the Beaumont police officer assigned to this case, they'll all come over to our house after school today—at 4:30. They don't want to make this hard on you. They're just trying to understand Daniel's state of mind and hopefully find an answer to that question you were asking, 'bout why he did it. And besides that, Sister Mary Margaret and your teachers are worried 'bout you, Buddy. They're concerned how you're handling all this. It's the same thing your mother and I are concerned 'bout, first and foremost right now. So, Sister and I thought it'd be better to handle 'em all at once and get it over with as quick as possible. And I'm sure you'll be more comfortable taking care of this in the privacy of our home, with your mom and dad both there, rather than up at the school. Sorta like havin' the home-field advantage, huh?" He smiled reassuringly.

I nodded again, resigned to my fate.

So, he wasn't going to fire me, not yet. Dad had always said you should gather all the facts before reaching a conclusion. He would wait to see what additional information came to light in the afternoon, and then no doubt he would fire me as his son.

After the Washington incident, Mom and Dad started seriously considering taking me out of the public-school system and sending me to St. Christopher School. At night, I heard them through the trailer's thin walls debating the merits and, most of all, the cost—tuition, books, uniforms, et cetera. As my mother gathered more information, she discovered that it wouldn't be as expensive as they first thought. Members of St. Christopher Parish, like our family, received a discount on school tuition. Used books could be purchased at half price.

They also talked about the need to move. I overheard Dad say, "This trailer park is getting so bad—the potholes, nothing gets fixed anymore, the ignorant white trash moving in. And South Beaumont's bein' taken over by the coloreds. This is no

PART ONE: 12:40 p.m.

place for our family, Lon. I'm 'fraid it's gonna have a real bad influence on Buddy if we don't get outta this environment."

They finally concluded that they could afford to live in a better neighborhood and send me to a Catholic school if they cashed in their equity in the trailer and Mom kept her second job for the time being. Although our new neighborhood was only two miles north of the trailer park, it was a different world. It was a regular Norman Rockwell painting of lily-white, middle America, complete with rows of little houses, green grassy yards with colorful flower beds, picket fences, sidewalks, and Sunday barbecues.

I was no longer a trailer rat. I started seventh grade at St. Christopher, a fine parochial school, and I wore the same shirts and trousers as all the other guys. I met Marty Shannon and his good friend, Daniel Carter, and my life would never be the same.

*****

Dad stood and said, "I'll leave you alone now if that's what you want. Or I can stay if you wanta talk."

"I think I'd like to be alone for a while."

"Okay," he said. He picked up the tray of dirty dishes and started for the door.

"Dad?" I said, before he could get out of the room.

"Yes?"

"Marty, was he at school today?"

"Yes, he was, along with his mother. I specifically asked Sister Mary Margaret 'bout him."

"What did she say?"

"That she'd been with Marty and his mom for a while in her office, and she planned to get together with 'em again after the lunch break. She said they spent most of the morning with a psychiatrist fella—a Dr. Gibson. He had an assistant, a 'child psychologist' is what Sister called her."

"Did she say what Marty said?" I asked. But sensing he might find that question unusual, I quickly amended it. "I mean, did she say how Marty was holding up? I'm worried about him, Dad. He was such a good friend to Daniel and—well, for Marty, it'll be hard, you know."

"Sister said Marty looked dazed, kinda like he was lost in a fog."

"I know. Like me, just like me," I said weakly.

"I suppose so," he said. He glanced at his watch, a simple Timex with a leather band. "My guess is that Mrs. Shannon will want to bring Marty home early today. Maybe you should go see him when he gets back from school."

My heart leaped. "Great! Yeah, I'll do that. Good idea."

He gazed curiously at me but said nothing. He finally turned to leave the room.

"Dad?"

"Yes, Son?"

"Will you close the door, please?"

He balanced the tray on one hand and gently pulled the door shut with the other.

I took off my glasses and lay back on the bed. Talking with my father about Daniel had been stressful. It was so difficult to know what he was thinking, how he had interpreted my answers to his questions. But I was proud of the way I had maneuvered the conversation at the end, the way I had led him to the conclusion that Marty and I should get together to comfort one another. Didn't *I* lead *him* to that conclusion?

It didn't matter. I had to talk to Marty. I had to know what to expect when the Spanish Inquisition arrived at my house at 4:30. I needed to know how much Marty had told them. Hopefully, it wasn't much.

Chapter 9

2:40 p.m.

My bedroom was at the back of our house, across a narrow hall from the kitchen. It was quiet during the evenings, allowing me to focus on homework and my radio, which was always tuned to AM 1450—KAYC in Beaumont, where they played all the popular songs of the day. My parents' room was at the front of the house. Our two bedrooms were connected by that hallway running through the center of the house but separated by two bathrooms, theirs and mine, and a small laundry room between the bathrooms. Across from their bedroom, the hallway opened onto the family room.

That afternoon, the location of my room was fortuitous as it offered a good view out my window of Marty's home. The only partial obstructions were the short fence separating our back yards and a large pecan tree on our side of the fence that gave up hundreds of nuts in the fall, which Mom turned into scrumptious pecan pies.

After Dad left my room, I turned on the radio. I listened as they played "Downtown," "Mr. Lonely," and the other Top 40 songs as I sat on my bed staring out the window, waiting for Marty to return from school. I looked at my watch after each song. As the time slowly passed, I alternated between being concerned and annoyed. When "I Feel Fine" by The Beatles played for the second time in 60 minutes, I turned the radio off. I didn't feel fine. A thousand unsettling questions raced through my brain. *What was taking so long? What had Marty told them? Had I made a mistake by not going to school? Why did they keep playing the same songs over and over again on the radio?*

At 20 minutes until 3:00, Mrs. Shannon's old Chevy Bel Air pulled into the detached garage at the back of their property. Mrs. Shannon and Marty emerged from the garage and entered the house through the back door. I continued to stare trance-like out the window, breathing deeply and concentrating on what I needed to accomplish with Marty. After a minute had passed, I was ready.

I found my father sitting in the family room in his favorite chair, a large, well-worn recliner, reading a *Life* magazine. As I walked into the room, he looked up.

"Buddy, how are you? Oops, sorry, I'm not supposed to ask that. But you've finally—"

"Dad," I interrupted, "I'm going over to see Marty—like you suggested. He just got home."

"Would you like me to go with you?" he asked.

"No, sir. That's not necessary."

"You know, Marty can tell you what to expect from these people this afternoon. But you've already thought of that, right?"

"Maybe." Where was he going with this?

"That's okay. There's nothing wrong with that. Remember the Boy Scout motto. It's good to be as prepared as possible."

"I guess so," I replied. I glanced at the back door, then down at my watch.

"Would you like some iced tea before you go?" He held up his glass to show me the almond-colored liquid he was sipping on. In the evenings, he would sit in that recliner for hours and sip on his cocktail *du jour*—a vodka martini, gin and tonic, bourbon and Coke, or some other concoction—as he watched TV or read the newspaper.

"No, sir. I'm not thirsty. I'll be going now."

"Wear a jacket!" he shouted as I headed toward the door.

I detoured to my room, grabbed my navy blue windbreaker, and bounded out the door into the back yard. I wondered if it was really tea.

* * * * *

Mrs. Shannon opened her back door, and as I stepped

inside, she put her arms around me. I returned the embrace, surprised by how frail she felt. As Marty walked up, she slowly released me, but not before I felt her trembling. When I looked into her face, she seemed even older than usual.

Then it got a little weird with the three of us standing in a circle inside the door. No one spoke. We just stared alternately at each other and then into space and then back at each other. Mrs. Shannon's mouth opened a couple of times, but nothing came out. She seemed to be struggling with a lump as big as Texas in her throat. I felt immensely uncomfortable and disoriented, and I couldn't think of anything appropriate to say. After a short eternity, unable to stand there in silence any longer, I grabbed Marty and gave him a hug around the waist. I immediately regretted this move.

He stiffened in my awkward grasp as Mrs. Shannon raised her hands to cover her mouth. He allowed his arms to drape loosely over my shoulders, not wanting to disturb this "moment" for her. Marty was several inches taller than me, so the top of my head was positioned equal to his mouth. My hair must have tickled his face, and he tried to blow it away. Not certain whether he was spitting or blowing, I disengaged.

I made eye contact with Mrs. Shannon, but not before I caught a disapproving look from Marty. His lips moved, admonishing me, *You homo!*

"Do you mind if Marty and I go for a walk?" I asked. When she wiped her eyes before answering, I glanced quickly at Marty and mouthed, *Bite me!*

"No," she whispered.

As Marty and I turned toward the front door, she forced out the words, "Bundle up, boys. It's getting cold . . . out there."

As we walked down the driveway toward North Street, Marty and I tugged at our collars and pulled our jackets around us. It wasn't all that cold, about 55 degrees, but a strong north wind bit through my flimsy windbreaker, making me wonder what idiot came up with that name.

At the end of the driveway, we turned eastward to avoid having the afternoon sun in our eyes, and I wondered for the millionth time why North Street ran east/west. Why wasn't it a one-way thoroughfare running north? I also wondered why there was no South Street in this neighborhood. I assumed it was because North Street ran through the middle of our neighborhood. But if it ran east/west through the middle like that, what idiot named it North Street? Why wasn't it called Middle Street? And then I started worrying why I spent so much time thinking about stupid stuff like that—especially now. What was wrong with me?

We walked slowly for a block without speaking before Marty finally broke the silence. "I can't believe it. I just can't believe it," he said in a near whisper.

"I know, man. I can't believe it either."

We stopped at the busy Seventh Street intersection. Marty said, "I can't believe he's gone." He kept shaking his head as he spoke. "My God, Buddy, just like that—*gone*. And we'll never see him again."

I thought he was going to cry. "I know, man," I said.

"How could he do that, just check out and leave us like that? He was our friend, right?"

I couldn't answer. What could I possibly say? I wanted to reach out to comfort him, but I didn't want to get into a physical thing again.

There was a break in the traffic, so we walked silently through the intersection. When we got to the other side, Marty stopped and looked at his sneakers. "I guess we know why Daniel never called us over the weekend, huh?" he said. The soft voice was unnatural, out of character.

"And why nobody answered at his house when I called on Saturday," I added.

"Yeah," he whispered at his feet.

I needed him to snap out of this mournful, melancholy-man routine. I needed to get him focused. I didn't have all afternoon. "What was it like today?" I asked.

He looked up. "It was godawful, man. Girls were crying. Nuns were crying. I think that big shit-bird statue in the gym even started crying." His regular Marty-voice was back, even if he was besmirching St. Christopher's mascot, our beloved owl.

"You know what was really weird?" he asked.

I shook my head.

"None of them cared about him when he was alive. Some of them downright hated Daniel, never wanted him around. But now they're all sad and sayin' nice things—when he's gone, when it's too late. Why is that? Answer me that."

But before I could respond, Marty grabbed my windbreaker with both hands in a menacing fashion. He often played tough guy like this, but that afternoon I couldn't tell what was going through his mind. I stiffened.

"And you, ya little chickenshit!" he said. "Where were you?"

"Calm down," I said, pointing at the lady across the street. She had stopped sweeping her front porch and was staring at us. He let go.

"I couldn't, man. I just couldn't—"

"Yeah, you squirrel. I'm gittin' the third degree from cops, shrinks, and half the Catholic Church in this city, and you're safe at home hiding in Mommy's arms."

"It wasn't like that. I just needed some time alone."

"Right, like I didn't?" He looked puzzled and pulled my windbreaker open. "And what the hell are you doin' in that school uniform? You weren't at school today!" I still had on the button-up, powder-blue shirt and khaki pants that all boys wore at St. Christopher, the same uniform Marty was wearing under his denim jacket.

"Hey, I don't know, man! So what? What's the difference?" I said as I shrugged my shoulders. "I never thought about changing, you know, after my dad told me."

"Yeah, my mom told me this morning too. My God, I can't believe it." He poked me hard in the chest as he added, "But I went to school!" Marty started walking again and I followed.

"So?" I asked.

"So what?"

"C'mon, what happened at school, man?"

He spoke rapidly as we crossed Sixth Street. "Oh, God, it

was awful. They called an assembly first thing in the morning, but by then, I think most of them already knew. You know how everyone talks in the halls or around their lockers in the morning, how they—"

"So how did M Squared handle it? What did she say?"

"M Squared" was the nickname we used for Sister Mary Margaret. It was Daniel who came up with the name, and it caught on among our threesome.

"Not worth a shit," Marty said. "Not really like her, you know. Everybody was talkin' and she went a little ballistic when they wouldn't shut up, shouting into the microphone that she had something important to tell us, like we didn't already know."

"What did she say about Daniel?"

He stopped walking and glared at me. "Are you gonna let me tell this or keep interrupting?"

"Okay, sorry, but get to the point," I said.

He was irritated and looked like he was thinking that maybe he wouldn't tell me anything. That would serve me right.

"Please," I said as I nervously pulled my windbreaker tighter.

He stood pensively for a few seconds with his hands planted on his hips before he finally relaxed and gave in to my apology. "Okay, now let's see," he said as we started ambling down North Street again. "So, M Squared says Daniel is dead from a gunshot wound. She says they believe he may have shot himself on purpose. That they're still investigating, gathering facts. My God, Buddy! This is really bad."

"I know. What happened next?"

"She starts bawling and can't go on. Can you believe it?"

I shook my head.

"So, this psychiatrist guy comes out and—"

"A shrink?" I asked.

"Yeah, that's right. This fat little bald guy comes out. Says *Doctor* Gibson is his name, and he rattles off all the schools he's got degrees from, tryin' to impress everybody. Then he says, 'I'm here for you.' So, I'm thinkin'—what a joke, man! Like I'd want him *anywhere* for me." Marty laughed, as though he'd said something witty, and then continued. "Anyway, this shrink guy, he looks just like Elmer Fudd. I swear to God. You know, the 'Cwazy Wabbit' guy? Short, big cheeks, and he's got more hair growing out his ears than the top of his head. It was gross, man!" Marty shook his head and then gave me a blank look. He had completely forgotten what he was talking about.

"So, what did he say, the shrink?"

"Oh yeah. He starts talkin' about all the things we're feeling right now, like he knows, right? He says we have to get our feelings out. I wanted to walk up, puke on him, and then thank him for helping me get those feelings out."

I gave him a pained look but bit my tongue. I didn't want to antagonize him with another interruption. So, I tried telepathy to get him to see that I didn't care about the small stuff. I closed my eyes and beamed my thoughts to him. *Earth to Marty. Buddy to Marty. Come in, Marty. What did you tell them, asshole?*

It didn't work. He continued his rambling account. "But before anybody can get anything out about their feelings, he says he wants all the seventh graders to stay in the auditorium, and the eighth graders are supposed to go to the gym with his associate, who he introduces. Well, let me tell you, Buddy boy, you ain't gonna believe this associate! Out comes this gorgeous young thing that would have no problem passing the elbow test." Marty made an exaggerated wink at me, his entire face contorting with the movement.

The "elbow test" was something Marty said they gave to women before they could get certain jobs—like movie starlets, Playboy bunnies, receptionists for advertising firms, or secretaries for politicians. The woman in question had to stand facing a wall and put her two hands behind her head. With all ten fingers laced tightly behind her neck, her head up, back straight, and elbows facing straight ahead, she was then told to slowly approach the wall. If the elbows touched the wall first, she failed the test.

"You shoulda seen the knockers poking out under her tight red sweater," he said, pulling at the front of his jacket with both hands to create two jutting cones. He smiled at me, but my expressionless face provided no encouragement.

"And there we were, the seventh graders stuck with Elmer Fudd." Marty shook his head in disgust. "Anyway, after he drones on for another 15 minutes, talkin' about all these things we're likely to be feeling, he finally stops and asks if there's any questions. So, for the next hour, ten different girls figure out ten different ways to ask, 'How? How could this happen?' Or, 'Why? Why would he do it?' And it becomes pretty clear that the big expert, *Doctor* Elmer Fudd, he don't know shit! In fact, he doesn't have a clue about Daniel, who he was, and what was going on in his mind or in his life. He's like the last person you'd get any answers from. But girls, you know, they keep squealing and asking the same thing.

"Finally, he says that he or his associate will be available to meet with us during the day today—one on one, in private. Well, I'm thinkin' that he needs to know how much I'd like to meet with the associate—in private and definitely one on one—if you catch my meaning." He winked again.

Marty had this habit of winking his left eye with a wide grin and naughty-like look on his face when he said things that you weren't supposed to repeat or when he made innuendos, sexual or otherwise. Sometimes he'd do it a dozen times in a single day. It made him look ten years old and was annoying after a while. I made a mental note to tell him someday. I had a feeling that he would appreciate my honesty. Either that, or he'd pound me.

"Then," Marty continued, "Elmer Fudd says we're gonna skip first period—which was brilliant, 'cause it was already over by then—and that everybody needs to go straight to their homeroom. He says the teachers there would answer any further questions. Right! I think he was just ready to pass the buck.

"Oh, one more thing. Before telling us to leave the auditorium, he says if anyone feels like they need to go home, they could use the phone in the office to call their parents. They'd be excused for the day. So, that sissy, Tommy Wells, and his boyfriend, Mitchell Walker, they get up and leave, along with a few other girls. I didn't see the two of them the rest of the day. They probably had a hot date, you know, with each other!" He laughed and winked again. I let it pass.

PART ONE: 2:40 p.m.

When we reached the railroad tracks beyond First Street, we turned north, paralleling the tracks, walking into the wind. We walked for a short block, and Marty continued to tell me everything and nothing. When we reached Hazel Street, we turned left. The sun felt good, warm on my face. I had to get Marty to be more serious. I had to know what to expect this afternoon.

I said, "My dad talked to M Squared this morning and asked about you. She said that you and your mom spent a lot of time with the psychiatrist guy." It wasn't a question, but rather an invitation for him to go down a more personal path.

Marty squinted as he looked straight ahead, continuing to walk at a leisurely pace. There was more traffic on Hazel Street, so he stepped onto the narrow sidewalk that cut through the small front yards. I kept up at his side.

"On the way to homeroom, they asked my mother and me to go to the office," he said. "M Squared was waiting there. She was nice, kept askin' how I was feeling."

"What did you say?"

"I said I was okay, just shocked by what Daniel did."

That's good, I thought.

"But then the shrink and that cop came in," he said.

"A cop?"

"Yeah, but he didn't say much. He had this little notebook and scribbled down notes the whole time we were in there."

"He was Beaumont PD?" I asked.

"Yeah, a real Deputy Dawg. Oh, he did ask one thing, and he asked it about four different times, four different ways. But the same question." He paused. "He wanted to know if I knew any reason why Daniel might want to kill himself."

"What did you say?"

"What do you think?" he shot back. "I told him I didn't know."

But Marty had stopped walking and hesitated like there was more to tell. I tried to catch his eye, but he wouldn't look at me. He started walking again and I kept up—quiet, waiting for more. When the silence between us finally became too much for my friend to bear, he said, "I guess after havin' to spend the whole morning with that Elmer Fudd dipstick poking around in my head, asking all his questions, and with that Deputy Dawg writing everything down—" He stopped.

"What? Go on, man," I said.

"Well, I think they know that Daniel had a death wish," he said. Then he turned away and mumbled, "After they got done talkin' to me."

I suddenly felt the nervous fluttering of butterflies in the pit of my stomach. My knees were weak and I stopped walking.

"Buddy, why'd they need that cop there?" he whined. He looked back to see I wasn't keeping up and continued speaking as he rejoined me. "Do they think it's our fault? I mean, Daniel tells us all this crap about wanting to die, but we don't tell anyone else. At least, I didn't. Does that make me—or us—guilty under the law, you know, of some kinda crime?"

"You mean like accomplices or co-conspirators?" I asked.

Marty wrinkled his brow.

I was reasonably sure that I knew the meaning of these ominous-sounding legal terms. I'd spent countless hours watching *Perry Mason* on television and was fascinated with the legal process and its jargon. I loved the way Mr. Mason sorted through clever lies and schemes to ultimately bring truth and justice to light. Lawyers were the epitome of honesty and integrity in America, and I often imagined myself as a lawyer someday. Judging from Marty's confused look, he didn't watch *Perry Mason*.

Daniel and I had often joked about avoiding words with more than two syllables around Marty. We were always picking on him, but he took it well. Either that, or he didn't understand our clever put-downs. Or maybe he didn't care because he was too busy just being himself.

Because Daniel and I were so similar and Marty was so different, he stood out within our little triumvirate, a yang to our yin. He was the tough guy, not in an obnoxious way but more like big Hoss Cartwright protecting his brothers on *Bonanza*. Marty wasn't particularly troubled by his mediocre grades or not understanding what they were talking about on the nightly news, while Daniel and I competed for top scholastic honors and strived to be viewed as brilliant intellectuals. Marty acted worldly, dazzling us with detailed dissertations about female anatomy and sexual desires, what it takes to make it in the real world, FBI and CIA plots, and a myriad of other obscure topics. We struggled with our naiveté and subconsciously worried how Marty could know these things and we didn't.

Marty was always speaking without thinking while we were careful to think before speaking. He was trusting while we were skeptical and often cynical. He was optimistic. Marty was delighted to discover his glass half full, while we were discouraged to find ours half empty. Marty was happy-go-lucky while we wrestled with insecurity and worried about what other people thought. He was tough while we just acted tough. Daniel and I were ideal targets for the class bullies, but they didn't mess with us because of our friendship with Marty. He was the leader of our little band.

I thought that Marty's question about our potential complicity in Daniel's suicide was astute. It was the same thing I had fretted over in my room for much of the morning.

"My dad said that the cop is there to figure out if it was a suicide or an accident. He said that—"

Marty interrupted, "I think they're way past that, Buddy. It's like now they want all the gory details, so they know who to blame."

I stared into his eyes the way my father often did with me. What had he told them? Marty looked away, once again unwilling to lock eyes with me, and we began walking again.

After a block of awkward silence, I said, "Dad says it's routine for the police to investigate in this kind of case. Also, think about it. It doesn't make sense that we'd be held responsible, although—"

When I hesitated, he stopped. "Yeah?" he asked.

"Well, I don't know, but the cop, he might argue—that is, if he knew *everything*—that we screwed up big time by withholding critical information, you know, all that stuff Daniel kept saying about wanting to kill himself."

"And what would that mean?" he asked.

"I don't know, man, but I can't see how it's a criminal offense to be an idiot, especially if you're just a kid. It can't be a crime!" I was adamant, stomping my foot on the pavement for good measure. "I mean, what're they going to say, huh? That we knew something that was life-and-death important and therefore had some legal requirement to come forward? Will they say that just because we didn't tell anyone about Daniel, they weren't able to let his parents know or get him any help and stop him from dying? Okay, so is that a crime?"

I wasn't helping. Marty had been nodding in agreement as I spoke. He continued to nod as I asked that last question. His eyes were huge, wide open.

"Listen," I said, "I'm not too worried about whether we broke the law. I don't think we did, okay? But there were so many signs with Daniel that . . . Oh, you know, man."

"Yeah, I know."

"But I don't think they can put us in jail or send us to reform school, just for not snitching about Daniel acting all weird. I don't think so."

"But you're not sure?"

"Well, I don't think so."

He sighed. "I hope you're right, Answer Man."

"But I am a little worried that we could get expelled from school for not reporting all that stuff."

"Expelled! My old lady would die. I mean it! You have no idea what she had to do to get me into that school."

"Relax, man. Take a breath, for God's sake."

"Yeah, okay," he said. To ease the tension, we started walking again.

"Your mom, how'd she take it today?" I asked.

"She bawled."

"I know, but did she get all mad at you for not telling her about Daniel, not telling her how he got all depressed lately?"

"Nah. I kinda thought she would, but she didn't."

"She didn't say anything to you?"

"She acted weird but didn't say too much."

"What do you mean, 'weird'?" I asked.

PART ONE: 2:40 p.m.

"She cried a lot, like I said. She also kept looking up in the sky. It was like she was talkin' to someone or praying. She chanted a lot too."

"Chanted?"

"Yeah."

"Like what?"

"Like, she was sayin', 'I can't believe it; not again.' Something like that," he said.

"Again? What does that mean?"

"I don't know."

"Marty, I'm afraid my folks will be really pissed if they find out everything, if they find out about all the stuff Daniel said and did—around us, you know. That I didn't come forward like a Boy Scout and tell them."

"Yeah," he said, raising his eyebrows, "your dad, especially."

"I know. I'm afraid he's going to fire me or something."

"What?"

"You know, he won't want me around because—"

"Listen," he blurted out, "I can't get expelled, man. If it came down to it, I'd rather do jail time than get expelled."

Poor Marty. He was serious. I decided to move on or we were going to run out of time. "I don't know about getting expelled. That's up to M Squared and the school, not the cops. You met with her today. You met with the shrink and the cop. What exactly did you tell them, man? Were you able to resist that shrink's powers?"

"Yeah, for sure. At least, I think so." But then he was quiet, deep in his own thoughts. He kicked absently at some stones on the sidewalk as we passed the Lutheran church at the corner of Fourth Street.

"So, what happened? C'mon, man."

"Well, after a long time in M Squared's office with all of 'em there askin' questions, Elmer Fudd suddenly tells me and my mom that he wants to take us to the teachers' lounge. He says we'll be more comfortable there, have more privacy, and let Sister get back to work in her office. So, we go. Soon as we walk in, he points to the couch and tells me to sit down."

"Did you do it, sit on the couch?"

"Hell, no! No way I was gonna fall for that. I told him I preferred to stand, and we should let my old lady sit on that couch. I was a real gentleman." Marty extended his right arm over his waist in a sweeping motion and bowed low like some country squire. "Anyway, I stood in the opposite corner. I didn't let that mindfucker anywhere near me, you know, where he was close enough to lock onto me."

"That's good. So, what did you talk about?" I asked.

"He spent the first few minutes tryin' to loosen me up, askin' how I felt and all. He kept tryin' to get me to lower my defenses."

"How?"

"By gittin' me to describe a lot of personal stuff."

"Like what?"

"Like my feelings. He wanted me to talk about Daniel, how we'd gotten to be such good friends, and what it was gonna be like without him around anymore."

"And what did you say?" I asked anxiously.

"I answered his questions. I mean, what could I do? I talked about Daniel, what he was like, and how we had lots of great times together. How Daniel made me laugh. How I could talk to him about stuff, about anything. How I would, you know, miss him."

"And the shrink, what did he say?"

"He said it was all right to feel hurt. It was part of healing or something. He said it was all right to cry. It was part of—"

"Did you cry?"

"No!" he said, but his face softened. It gave him away. "Well, maybe I got some water in my eyes." Marty spoke more rapidly, making defensive gestures with his hands. "I mean, my old lady starts bawling her face off. It's so bad that she has to get up and leave. How am I supposed to feel, huh? I don't know, man. Okay, so, yeah, I guess I got a little emotional. It's only natural, right? Besides, they don't ask the yes-or-no kinda questions. You know what I mean? Instead, to answer their questions, you have to get into details, and they keep askin' for specific examples to back up what you're sayin'. You have to talk about things you don't want to talk about in order to answer the question. It's not fair! I don't know, maybe he did."

"Did what?" I asked.

"Maybe he did get me under his power, you know, for just a little while."

My friend hung his head. His tough-guy façade was gone. I patted him gently on the back and said it was okay. But inside, I was worried. My worst fears—that Marty had fallen under the psychiatrist's spell and told everything about Daniel—seemed to be coming true.

As we walked farther down Hazel Street, those fears were confirmed. With more prodding and encouragement, I gradually got him to confess. Marty had spilled *everything*. He had told them about numerous specific incidents, the times when Daniel had said things to us or done oddball things around us that had to do with his newfound fascination with death—his own death.

It sounded ghastly, listening to Marty. There had been so many signs over the past several weeks that Daniel Carter was unstable. The inevitable conclusion that people would reach after hearing this testimony was that Daniel's best friends must have been brain-dead idiots not to have taken him more seriously. And that was the best-case scenario. At worst, they'd judge us to be responsible for the whole mess through our shameful lack of concern toward a supposed friend.

The only silver lining I could find to this dark cloud was that Marty had not been immediately arrested or expelled for not reporting these events on a timely basis. In fact, he said that M Squared had hugged him as he was leaving school and told him not to blame himself. That part was encouraging.

Marty had told the truth. I just wished that he hadn't told so much of it. Now I was going to have to go through all the same details and tell a consistent story, or my examiners would wonder why I wasn't being truthful and cooperative. They would wonder what I had to hide. They would be suspicious. That might cause them to dig deeper into the circumstances surrounding Daniel's death. I couldn't risk that.

As we stood in front of my home and I wrestled with my burning conscience, my mood changed. I was suddenly overwhelmed with grief and guilt, a volatile combination.

Marty finally spoke. "We shoulda known, man. We shoulda known he was gonna do it," he said. "We shoulda told somebody. We shoulda sat down and talked to Daniel. Goddamnit! We shoulda done something, Buddy!"

"I know," I whispered. I didn't have the courage to look him in the eye. He might see that I knew something he didn't. I carried an added burden, much heavier than the ball and chain that we both wore for being uncaring idiots and failing to respond to our friend's pain. I had done something terrible and unforgivable, most likely illegal as well.

I wanted to cry, but I couldn't. I wanted to scream, but I couldn't. I wanted to inflict physical pain on my body, but I couldn't. I could only stand there, numb from the guilt and helplessness, the cold wind blowing in my face.

"What do you think they'll do to us?" he asked.

I shook my head. "I don't know. Whatever it is, I know I deserve it."

Chapter 10

3:40 p.m.

Mom had come home early from work, and both parents were sitting in the family room when I walked in.

"Was it cold outside?" Mom asked.

"Nah, not too bad," I said, removing the windbreaker.

"Come sit by me, sweetie," she said with a smile, and she reached out to take my hand as I moved toward her. I held her right hand in my left and sat next to her on the sofa. Dad was in his recliner to my right. They had me surrounded.

She squeezed my hand. "*Aloha nui loa.* You have all my love, my precious boy."

"I love you too, Mom."

"While you were out with Marty, we asked Mrs. Shannon to come over," Mom said. "She was at your school today, and she told us about their conferences with the psychiatrist and Sister Mary Margaret and with some of Marty's teachers. She told us about Daniel, what they know so far." She dabbed her nose with a tissue she had been holding in readiness in her left hand.

Dad leaned sideways across the big recliner to face us, and I shifted my focus to him. He said, "We just wanted to do a little preparation for this upcoming meeting, you know, like you were doin' with Marty."

I nodded, unsure why he phrased it like that.

"Thing is, you know we love you," he continued like he was reciting an unemotional fact. "And we know how close you boys were with Daniel," he added. With that out of the way, he came straight to the point. "It's only natural when an accident or a senseless tragedy happens that we try to assess responsibility.

That's human nature. It's also human nature for people who are closest to the situation to search their personal conscience to determine if they are in some way responsible. Do you follow what I'm saying?"

My face contorted. "Maybe," I said but quickly added, "I guess I'm not sure."

"Remember that Saturday morning when you were ten years old, when you fell outta that big oak tree at the trailer park playground?"

I nodded.

"You broke your arm and there was all that blood from your nose and your lip. You remember that?"

"Yes, sir." How could I forget?

"I was supposed to be watching you, but I was off talkin' to Mrs. Larkin. I remember seeing you outta the corner of my eye, up in that tree. I knew it was dangerous. I remember thinking I should walk over and tell you to get down. But I didn't. I was enjoying my conversation and didn't wanta interrupt it. Then you fell. For a long time, I thought your falling was my fault, that I should've been more attentive." He paused and then asked, "Well, what do you think?"

I knew he was taking a gamble here, hoping I would give the appropriate answer so that he could move on and complete the lesson. I didn't disappoint him. "To be honest," I said, "I remember thinking, just before I fell, that I had no business up that tree. But Jeremy Larkin, he'd dared me to go to that top limb. He said I was chicken if I didn't. I remember thinking later how stupid I was. So, I don't think it was your fault. It was mine."

"That's a good point," he said. "Do you remember how scared Jeremy was, looking down at you on the ground?"

"I don't remember much of anything after I hit the ground, except you carrying me home, me bleeding on your shirt, and Mom driving us to the hospital."

"Let me tell you, Jeremy was plenty scared. And a big part of the reason he was scared was 'cause he felt like your goin' up in that tree and then falling was his fault. I mean, would you have gone up that far if Jeremy hadn't dared you?"

"Probably not, but hey, I don't blame him either."

"That's not the point I'm trying to make here," he shot back, leaning closer to me. "He blamed *himself*. And I blamed *myself*." He paused to let the words sink in. "Blaming ourselves when bad things happen to people 'round us, especially people we care for, that's just human nature like I was saying."

To my left, Mom cleared her throat and squeezed my hand. I turned to face her. "Do you recall what I said to your father when he came running up with you in his arms, all dirty and bloody?"

"No, ma'am."

"I screamed at him. I said, 'What've you done? You were supposed to be watching him!' My first reaction was to blame him, and that wasn't right. It just made his pain worse."

I gave her a slow nod to let her know I understood, and the three of us sat in silence for a short while. Then, speaking slowly and deliberately, giving me his one-two-three logical summation, my father said, "We're a family, Buddy. We're on the same team. We're all we've got. We shouldn't try to place blame when misfortune happens, not on ourselves and not on others. That's the good Lord's job. Ours is to love and support each other as a family. And I'm damn sure not gonna let others try to place even a shred of blame—"

He stopped. Out of the corner of my eye, I saw Mom frowning at him. He took a deep breath and exhaled. "Let me clarify that, 'cause it didn't come out right. Mrs. Shannon confirmed it, like you suspected, that they now believe Daniel's death was a suicide. They know he said things to people—to Marty and you—like you were telling me earlier today. They know he talked 'bout killing himself, that he acted different, that he did some unusual things that were not reported by his friends—by you boys. Well, here's what your mom and I think 'bout that."

I swallowed hard as my heart rate increased.

"What Daniel did is a tragedy," he said. "It's terrible. I don't understand it, but I know this much for sure: *He* picked up that loaded gun, and *he* pulled that trigger. *He* did it. Do you see what I'm saying?"

My father was making assumptions and reaching a conclusion without knowing all the facts, which was uncharacteristic for him. I nodded in response to his question and grunted something between closed lips rather than trying to speak.

"His family didn't kill him. His school didn't kill him. His friends didn't kill him. *He killed himself.* Whatever Daniel Carter told you or did 'round you, don't you put a buncha blame on your shoulders on accounta his actions. You gotta be strong not to blame yourself, but don't you do it. And don't you worry 'bout those people comin' over in a few minutes. Mrs. Shannon told us they're just tryin' to understand as best they can what's happened here. And they wanta see if they can help you, Buddy. *They care 'bout you,* and they're not gonna insinuate or in any way imply that you did anything wrong. Your mom and I will make sure of that." He sat back in the recliner and then looked at me. "Do you understand?"

"I understand. Thanks, Dad. Thanks, Mom," I said, looking from one to the other as a great sense of relief flowed through me. After they had listened to Mrs. Shannon describe Daniel's death wish and the other things she had found out, it would have been easy for my mother to have gotten upset and cried out, "Why didn't you tell us?" It would have been easy for my father to have been stern with me, to have given me one of those icy stares that said I had screwed up big time, and then to have fired me as his son.

But that's not what they did. Instead, they made sure that I knew they loved me and would stand by me and protect me. I felt embarrassed for my doubts and trepidation over how they would react, but these were confusing times. It was reassuring to find an anchor in these swirling seas. I needed their love and protection. But most of all, I needed them not to blame me. I was doing enough of that for the whole family. I began feeling better.

My father reached over and took my free hand into his, so I was joined to both of them. He held it firmly as he looked at me, seeking the right words to conclude our conversation. "Son, we can't always understand the Lord's plans. I just hope that someday we can put all this in perspective. Until then, you have to keep your head held high, tell the truth, and do the best you can—one day at a time."

"I reckon so," I told him. I looked straight into his eyes as I said it. I wanted him to see my gratitude and strength.

He nodded as his eyes narrowed into a tight focus on mine. A confident little smile formed between his lips. It told me that he knew I could be strong and not give in to my own self-pity. It told me that he knew I could pull myself together and handle the shrinks, the cops, and the nuns. It told me that he expected me to show him how a man, not a 12-year-old kid, behaves under pressure.

Then it was my father who broke our eye contact. He looked over at Mom. It was like a telepathic signal. They both released me, got up, and walked slowly across the family room toward their bedroom to get ready for our guests. They held hands, and Mom turned and blew me a kiss before they disappeared into their bedroom.

I wondered if they would have felt the same if they had known the whole truth. "Oh, what the hell," I muttered to myself after they left. They loved me and I felt good about it. I wasn't going to disappoint them. I got up from the sofa and went to the window that faced Hazel Street—to think, to plan, and to wait for our guests.

Chapter 11

4:25 p.m.

They arrived at 4:25—a few minutes early—in four separate cars that pulled up in front of our house at the same time, led by the police car. My parents were still in their bedroom, and I was staring through the blinds from our living room window, about 50 feet from the street. My anxiety was high but under control. As they parked in a tight row facing the eastbound traffic, I was struck by the unnerving thought that it looked like a funeral procession.

The policeman was the first to emerge from his car. Next came Sister Mary Margaret, stepping daintily from the car at the rear. I noticed that the diminutive nun sat on a pillow in order to see over the steering wheel. Sister Katherine, my homeroom teacher, opened the door of the third car and stepped out. They all walked to the second car in the procession and waited. At last, its door swung open to reveal the most beautiful human being I have ever set eyes upon—*a goddess.*

Deputy Dawg extended his hand to assist her, but she either didn't see it or chose to ignore him. She pulled a clipboard and some papers into her lap. Clutching them with one hand, she grabbed the steering wheel with the other and swung her body sideways. She planted her feet on the curb, pushed against the steering wheel, and began scooching out of the car. As she did so, I got a clear view of her long legs protruding from a black skirt that had bunched around her waist and thighs. Where her legs met under the skirt, I saw a white blur of panties and short straps that held her stockings. I was mesmerized.

She closed the car door, and they stood chatting for a moment as she smoothed her skirt. I couldn't take my eyes off her hand as it ran slowly over her buttocks, hips, and thighs. Erotic thoughts filled my mind, and my entire body suddenly felt warm.

She looked like the young girls I'd seen on television in the annual Miss America pageant. But holding the clipboard and giving instructions to the policeman and the nuns, she was authoritative and in control, clearly not your typical airhead, 'I-only-want-world-peace' beauty contestant.

She was tall, a bit taller than the cop, and she towered over the two nuns. They turned and walked together toward our front door with her in the lead. There was a gracefulness in her stride, more like she was gliding than walking. She wore heels, but they weren't the slutty stiletto type. They were wider and more elegant.

She was slender. As she walked, I watched her breasts bouncing slightly under a closely fitted, strawberry-red, V-neck sweater. She stepped onto our porch, raised her chin, and inhaled deeply, causing her chest to rise, before knocking on the front door.

I tore myself from the window and ran awkwardly down the hallway toward my bathroom. Mom emerged from her bedroom to answer the door. She gave me a reassuring look as I scurried past her. I'm sure she thought I was having an attack of nervousness. I wondered what she would have thought if she knew the truth—that I wouldn't be able to face anyone until the raging boner in my pants subsided.

Marty talked about boners all the time. He even had a signal at school. When he was walking in the hallway or sitting in class and got a "pounding hard-on" or a "blue throbber," as he referred to them, he would put his notebook or textbook over his groin and walk or sit with the afflicted area shielded from view. If no such cover was available, he would pull out his shirttail and let it drape over his pants. If Daniel or I saw him in this fashion, Marty would give us that idiot wink, and we'd cover our mouths to keep from laughing.

Marty was perpetually covered or so it seemed. I suspected that most of the time he was faking, but that only heightened my curiosity. If Marty took delight in being in this naughty condition, didn't that mean it was cool, something that I too should strive for?

Like all young boys growing up, I had experienced boners when I had to pee badly, when I first awoke in the morning, or for no apparent reason. I had never given it much thought. But over the past year, they also seemed to *come up* when I thought about girls, which was an increasingly time-consuming pastime. Sitting in class or alone in my room, I would daydream about one of the popular girls in school, visualizing her strutting on the beach in a tiny bikini or stepping out of the shower, dripping wet. Sometimes I got the hard-on; more often, however, I didn't. Marty had made it clear that a stiff penis was an essential part of the sex act, and it was deeply disturbing that I had so little control over this important bodily function. What if opportunity came knocking someday, and I couldn't get prepared?

I tried experiments, but they only added to my confusion. Stacked on the top shelf of my parents' closet, under Dad's *Popular Mechanics* magazines, I had recently discovered three old *Playboy* magazines. When my parents left me alone in the house for a brief time on a weekend or if I beat Mom home by a few minutes on a school day, I would get a chair from the dining room and take it to their closet. Standing on the chair, I would gently remove the *Playboys* and then sit on their bed.

I'm sure my father had purchased the magazines for some special article he thought would be of interest. Guys are always telling their wives or girlfriends that *Playboy* has great articles, but I didn't have time for reading. I stared at the naked girls in the foldouts and pictorial displays. All the while, I kept a watchful eye out the window, my pulse roaring in my ears from the rush of doing something forbidden. If one of my parents suddenly drove up, I would have just enough time to jump onto the chair, return the magazines to their exact position in the stack on the closet shelf, rush out of their room, and replace the chair—seconds before they walked in.

My heart would pound from the sight of Amber, Dusty, Fawn, and the others with their naughty smiles and naked breasts and bottoms. However, much to my consternation, sitting on my parents' bed, trying to concentrate on all this naked flesh in erotic poses and keep an eye out the window at the same time, I never got the boner.

Alternatively, I periodically absconded to my room carrying the Sears catalog that my parents received with each new season. There, in the privacy of my room, I would admire the attractive young models pictured in various ladies' undergarments that could be ordered through the catalog. I didn't keep it in my room for long periods, but I wasn't overly concerned about having it in my possession. If Mom or Dad discovered the catalog was missing from its standard place in our kitchen pantry, I would say I was looking at the bicycles and other things for kids. No harm done.

Sitting in my room with the door securely shut, I invariably got a boner while staring at sterile poses of ladies and teenage girls displaying their brassieres, panties, and garters and stockings. It was unsettling. Why did gazing at the everyday women in the Sears catalog cause an immediate and predictable reaction, while sneaking peeks of nasty, naked women in *Playboy* did nothing for me? Did I have a perverted underwear fetish? It was all so confusing.

Chapter 12

4:30 p.m.

My father knocked on the bathroom door. "Son, are you all right?" he asked.

"I'm fine. Just give me a minute. Okay?"

"Okay, just remember what we talked 'bout." I heard his footsteps going up the hallway toward the family room where our guests no doubt awaited my presence.

After a couple of minutes, the stiffness that had overtaken my private parts finally subsided. Emerging from the bathroom, I ducked into my bedroom and changed into jeans and a long-sleeved, button-up shirt with green stripes. Tucking in the shirt, I took a deep breath and searched my mind for something inspiring. *Win one for the Gipper!* was all I could come up with on short notice. It was corny but had worked for some has-been actors in an old movie I'd seen on television. I opened the bedroom door, ready to get the show started.

As I walked through the kitchen and into the connecting dining room, Sister Mary Margaret was the first to see me. She threw her arms around me before I could get out of the dining room. My parents and the others rose from their seats in our family room, watching us.

She held me firmly and whispered into my ear, "Oh, Buddy, I was so worried. I lit a candle for you this morning. I prayed for you throughout the day and on the drive over." She pulled away slightly, so she could look into my eyes. "Your pain, your loss. I'm so sorry, my child." She raised her hands to gently cup my face. I was taller than her by several inches, but she cast a powerful presence that transfixed me.

"I won't ask if you're okay because I know you're not," Sister said in a low voice, so the others did not hear. "But you are strong, my child. I know that much about you, and I lift you up to God, that He'll wrap you in His love and give you strength and comfort to get through this tragedy." She dropped her hands from my cheeks.

Then she flashed the back of her left hand toward the family room as if flicking away a fly. "And don't worry about that policeman in there—Officer Powell. He's a caring Christian and he's just here to listen. You're not in any trouble. Your father and I got all that straight while we were waiting for you. He'll probably leave after a few minutes, anyway."

She smiled and I gave her a thank-you smile in return. I had liked her from the first day of school, and at that moment I felt a special kinship with her. She was on my side. I was feeling much better about what waited for me in the next room.

"Are you ready?" she whispered.

"Yes, Sister."

She took me by the hand, and we turned to face the others. They were standing in a circle. My father was in the far corner of our family room, his back to our front door. His right hand was on the TV set and his left rested on a dining room chair he must have brought in for this event. To his right, in the opening where our dining and family rooms merged, two additional chairs had been arranged facing into the family room. Sister Katherine stood in front of one and the other was obviously for M Squared, my new best friend. Across from the nuns, Mom stood by the family room sofa, facing the television. The place on the sofa to her right was open, no doubt reserved for me.

The goddess stood in front of my father's big recliner. It was closer to the sofa than I remembered and had been turned to face the sofa instead of the TV. She would be very close to me. To her right, stood the police officer. To his right, beside the TV, my dad completed our intimate little circle.

As M Squared led me toward the Inquisition, Sister Katherine was the first to greet us. She was my homeroom advisor and reputed to be easily confused by the eighth-grade math which was her specialty. She normally had zero interest in me during our homeroom time after lunch, and I was equally ambivalent toward her.

Sister Katherine stepped around the two chairs and stiffly embraced me like she was hugging a cactus. When she released me, she opened her mouth and struggled for something to say, but words failed to come to her. She could only shake her head and headdress slowly from side to side with a sad look. It made for a peculiar portrait—a huge bonnet encasing an empty head with an open mouth. M Squared, sensing this wasn't helping, gave a *That's enough* nod to Sister Katherine and steered me toward the goddess.

"Buddy Torrence, this is Allie Masterson," M Squared said. "Miss Masterson is a psychologist working with Dr. Gibson, and she's been a big help to us today. She's been accepted into medical school in Dallas, and she'll begin her studies in the fall. She's going to become a psychiatrist."

As I extended my right hand, M Squared whispered in my ear, "And she's every bit as intelligent as she is beautiful."

It caught me off guard. Was the nun reading my thoughts? Heat began radiating through my neck into my cheeks.

The goddess heard Sister's comment and shook her head as if to reproach the nun, but with a soft smile. I must have been crimson. Despite my embarrassment, I stared up into her face. This was partly to behold its remarkable beauty and partly because I was concerned about the consequences if I looked too closely at her body. She truly was the most beautiful thing I had ever seen—tall with radiant brown hair that hung straight and flipped up on her shoulders, perfect teeth and complexion, and rich hazel eyes speckled with an outside ring of green flecks.

She accepted my hand with hers and then stepped forward and placed her other hand on top of mine, surrounding and enveloping it like a cocoon, soft and warm. *She's touching me!* I couldn't breathe. I continued to focus on her face, but it wasn't easy. Because of her height and heels, her ample breasts were even with my uplifted chin and less than a foot away.

"It's good to meet you," she said. "I'm so sorry about Daniel."

The pleasing resonance of her voice matched everything else about her. I couldn't respond. I just stared into her face until she released my hand, and M Squared tugged on my arm to move along.

"And this is Officer Don Powell, Buddy."

The policeman was short and pudgy. His blue uniform was at least one size too small, particularly around his abdomen, and it made the spread of his middle-aged belly more conspicuous. He tipped his crew-cut head to acknowledge me but said only, "Son."

With his right hand extended to shake my hand, I saw the service revolver on his hip and the handcuffs on his belt. Regardless of what had previously been said—to not concern myself, that his presence was routine in these situations, that I was not in trouble—I wasn't convinced. Standing so close to me in his cop uniform, with his cop stare and cop weapons, he was frightening and intimidating as he grabbed my hand. My grip was weak. When he released me, I swallowed hard and quickly turned around.

Mom sat down and patted the sofa with her right hand. "Come sit here by me, Buddy."

"That's okay, Mom. I'll just stand over here," I said, and I moved to my father's side—the side away from the policeman—with the TV directly behind me.

"Don't be silly," Mom said. "Come sit by your mother, where you'll be comfortable."

I remembered what Marty had said about how he stood far away from his shrink. Even if the lovely Miss Masterson was still studying and not yet a full-fledged shrink, I didn't want to take any chances. She may have already learned enough to hypnotize me or otherwise gain control of my thoughts if I got too close, particularly if I was on a couch.

"Look, Mom, I'd rather be right here," I said. My words were harsh, too forceful, so I added, "Please?" I leaned back with my bottom resting slightly on the top of the television to reflect a more comfortable pose, and I frowned impatiently at her. She stared at Dad, and his indifferent shrug caused her to give up.

Everyone except the goddess took their seats. She looked at my father. "In that case, Mr. Torrence, could you help me turn this chair around?"

"Sure." He got up and walked to the recliner.

As they leaned over to each take an arm of the huge chair, the V-neck of her sweater fell open—not a lot, but enough. From my vantage, I had a clear view of her cleavage spilling into a white bra. It reminded me of one of my favorites from this winter's Sears catalog. The cups were thin and lacy with an intricate pattern, and the straps were set wide on her shoulders. The low-cut bra probably concealed little when she stood tall. But bending over, I was amazed the cups were able to contain their two prizes as she pulled sideways to move the heavy recliner.

I wanted to tear my eyes away but couldn't. It took three concerted pulls, each moving the big recliner two or three inches, for them to situate it facing the TV—toward me. She had turned slightly during the process, and by the third pull, Deputy Dawg also had a clear view. That was probably why he jumped up and moved toward them—to get a steeper angle—although he made it look like he was finally getting off his ass to volunteer some help with the big chair. The nuns and my mother missed the whole show since the goddess' backside had been turned to them.

But I had seen it all and my sex organ was growing again. *No, stop that!* I ordered myself, but the image of her breasts straining against that exquisitely dainty white bra was stuck in my mind, and I had no control over my own body. My jeans were constricting it, requiring me to lean forward at the waist with my hips back. At the current rate, in less than ten seconds, when everyone got situated and refocused on me, I would have a full-grown flagpole sticking out. I had to do something.

"You know what? Hey, I'm sorry but I think you're right," I blurted at my mother. I stepped awkwardly toward the sofa, hunched over slightly. At the same time, I tried to keep Mom's eyes focused on my face and upper body instead of looking down at my growing embarrassment by talking right at her and waving my arms like an airplane propeller.

"It'll be better by you, Mom, because . . . then, *Sister!*" I turned my head to the right, toward M Squared. "Then I can see you as well." She looked confused, but I didn't care as long as she was looking confused at my face and not my groin.

"And you too, Sister, thanks for coming," I said to Sister Katherine, waving my right arm high in a theatrical salute. She followed my arm motion with her eyes as I continued walking. Bending over even further with one step to go, I dove sideways at the right side of the sofa. The goddess, who was sitting forward in the recliner, had to draw in her knees and legs to avoid clipping me in my lunge.

I landed gracelessly on the sofa. The dive had caused my jeans to move roughly over the tip of my fully erect penis. It was intensely painful. I clenched my teeth and instinctively brought my knees up into my chest, forcing my body into a tight ball with my hands clasping those knees.

I pivoted on the sofa to face them. My chin was burrowed into my chest to help me silently endure the sharp burning in my jeans, and my line of sight was just over my knees. Through the pain, I smiled meekly at the nuns like we did this all the time in the Torrence household. To help put them at ease, I made a quick sign of the cross over my balled-up body. It had the opposite effect. M Squared's eyes were the size of saucers. Sister Katherine had her hands over her mouth and looked like she wanted to call one of the priests for an exorcism.

My gaze shifted to my father. He was shaking his head and didn't appear overly concerned by my bizarre behavior. Had he guessed my problem?

Deputy Dawg's searching stare told me he was thinking, *This kid is emotionally unbalanced.* He would no doubt be on his guard. Sitting in the big recliner, which now faced the TV, the goddess was straining to turn her head to see me.

She gave up and looked at Dad. "Well, Mr. Torrence," she said, "perhaps you can help me again." She stepped out of the chair and grabbed an arm.

Dad turned to the policeman as he rose. "C'mon Officer, give me a hand, will you?" They walked toward the goddess and my father said to her, "We'll get it this time." Then he looked at me and said sternly, "And you, no more playing 'round. You got it?"

"Yes, sir."

I had several seconds to compose myself as the two men picked up the big recliner and turned it to face me on the sofa. As they reseated themselves, I closed my eyes and tried not to think about how close the goddess-shrink was. I took a couple of deep breaths, placed my hands over my lap, and smiled through the pain like a twit.

"Buddy, if you're okay now, I'd like to tell you a story," M Squared said.

I nodded, relieved to have the attention diverted from me.

"It's an ancient tale that my mother told me when I was a small girl. It goes like this: There once was a small village in a country far away. A man lived there with his family. One day, his only horse ran away. The people in the village felt sorry for him and tried to comfort him. They all said, 'We are sorry you had such bad luck.'"

Her words were soft, and she leaned forward as she spoke, focusing all her attention on me. "But the next day, the horse returned. Not only that, but his horse was accompanied by a wild horse from the forest. Now, the man had two horses, and everyone came by to tell him, 'What good luck that your horse ran away and found another horse for you. You are blessed with this good fortune.'

"The next day, the man was riding the new horse and it threw him. His leg was severely broken. The people of the village cursed the new horse. 'What rotten luck,' they said. 'We are so sorry this happened to you. We wish that bad horse had never come.'

"Then, on the next day, an army marched by and forced all the young men in the village to join them. That is, all but the man whose leg was broken. The army had a battle that day with their enemies and all the men were killed. The widows came to the house of the man with the broken leg, crying, 'The horse that threw you was surely sent by God to keep you out of harm's way. Why are you so lucky?'"

Sister paused to give me a tender smile. "The point, Buddy, is that things aren't always as they first appear. It's so hard to understand God's will. Oh, I'm not trying to diminish this horrible tragedy, what happened with Daniel—to have him snatched from his family, from his friends, from all of us—at such a young age. But we who survive must learn from it. We must try to understand what happened, so we can be wiser and prevent it from ever happening again. And we must console each other. That's why we're here today. We want to try to understand why Daniel was so depressed. But more importantly, my child, we want to help you in any way we can, to deal with all the emotions you must be experiencing. Miss Masterson will tell you that grieving, feeling empty and sad—those are appropriate emotions right now. We must first go through grief and sorrow before the healing can begin, before we can become stronger and move on from this dark time."

The goddess spoke up. "That's right, Sister."

I turned to face her. The boner was gone, and I was determined not to let it come back, to exercise mind over member. I had to put away those "goddess" thoughts and see her as the dangerous shrink-in-training that she was. Sister's story had allowed me time to regain my composure. I needed to stay composed if I was going to pull this off.

"So, how are you doing?" she asked.

I looked at the floor. "Not great," I mumbled. "I don't get it. I don't see why, I mean, I don't know. But, to answer your question, I guess I'm getting by, ma'am."

I instantly regretted what I had said and how I'd said it with my head down like a little boy. *Concentrate, you idiot! Focus!* I implored myself.

"Please, do me a favor," she said.

"Sure."

"Don't call me 'ma'am,' okay? I appreciate your fine manners, but I'm not ready for that one yet. I'm just Allie, all right?"

"Sure, Allie." I loved her name. It rolled off my tongue so naturally. I wanted to shout it.

"And is it okay if I call you Buddy, instead of Lawrence?"

"Yeah, that's what everybody calls me."

"Excellent," she said, "You know, my middle name is Larice—Allie Larice Masterson. It's similar to your first name. I guess that gives us something in common right off the bat, huh?" She leaned back with a demure chuckle. I laughed too, just to be polite, but it wasn't funny to me. It was a sign.

Our laughter took the tension out of the room, and everyone seemed to relax until she asked her next question. "Buddy, do you think Daniel's death is in any way your fault?"

You can't get any more direct than that, I thought. Marty had said that the best kind of woman was one who came straight to the point and told you exactly what was on her mind—what she wanted and how and where she wanted you to give it to her.

I returned Allie's stare as she waited for my reply. I thought about our similar names and how easy it would be to live forever in those dazzling eyes. *Snap out of it!* I screamed in my mind. *Say something!*

"Well, my folks and I, we had a good talk about that," I said. "When something bad like this happens, I suspect it's natural for people to feel like they should've or could've done something different. It's like when your team loses a close game." I stopped. *That was a terrible example! How can you compare a lost life to a lost game, you idiot?*

"But I think Sister Mary Margaret is right. Maybe we can't understand God's will, but we've got to believe that there's a purpose for everything, like it says in the Bible and like in that story of hers."

"Tell me what you mean by that."

"Well, Allie—" I paused for a second to let her name reverberate in my head. I saw that she wore minimal makeup and no earrings. What little jewelry she wore was simple and it was all silver—a thin chain necklace with a cross, a ring with a small burnt orange stone, and a petite watch with a plain wristband. According to Marty, that also was a good sign in a woman. It meant that they didn't have expensive taste and wouldn't expect you to buy them costly jewelry all the time.

I said, "A lot of really good things happen in life. Whether it's by planning it out or just by luck, things can turn out great."

"That's right," she said. "And?"

"And sometimes things don't turn out so great, maybe even downright awful, for us or for a friend. Sure, they could've been different. But you can't change the past. I believe you have to be thankful for those good times and try your best to get by in the bad times."

"And what does all that mean?" She leaned closer to me, continuing to smile.

"It means you shouldn't go around making good-luck and bad-luck judgments all the time. You take things as they come. That's what my parents told me, and I think that's what Sister's saying."

"That's exactly what I meant with that parable," a very satisfied Sister Mary Margaret said.

"Oh, Buddy," Allie said, "that was lovely. It was so insightful. They told me at school how smart you are, how you always make the best grades. Now, I understand."

"Thanks, but you're wrong about that, Allie."

"Oh?"

"I didn't always make the best grades. Daniel, he was even smarter than me, and he made better grades, at least earlier in the year, back when he was really trying."

"Are you ready to talk about Daniel? Will that be okay?"

"Yeah, I guess so," I said.

The cop reached for his notebook.

After my walk with Marty and chat with my parents, while I was waiting at the window, I had laid out the script in my mind: what I should say, what I should avoid saying. I knew they would first want to know how I was doing. That's where they would start, just like with Marty. How was I coping? What was going on in my mind?

However, as long as I wasn't looking for a pistol to put to my own head, I knew we would eventually get around to Daniel Carter. There would be questions like, "Did he act strange, suicidal?" and "How did you react?" and "Did you ever tell any adults?" It was obvious where they would want to take our conversation. A ten-year-old could have figured it out.

I had their game plan thanks to Marty's detailed (albeit rambling) account of his sessions at school that morning. They knew *things* about Daniel, disturbing things Marty had revealed, that were true. They would be watching and listening to see if I would corroborate these things. Marty didn't seem to be in any trouble. So, I had decided to boldly cover the same ground in my own words, but be careful not to add anything, and hope for the best. In fact, I planned to readily volunteer all this information, all these *things*. A good offense, I had concluded, would be my best defense.

I was encouraged by the way the meeting had progressed so far, outside of my mad dash for the sofa. But I knew I could be forgiven for that momentary loss of sanity if the rest of the show went well. M Squared had been great, and I had the superb good fortune to have Allie in the room instead of Dr. Elmer Fudd. She was young and had a feminine sense of compassion which could be helpful when it came time to perform my critical scenes—the ones where I would pour out my naive childlike innocence. Allie was not yet a doctor-shrink with full powers. Although looking into her alluring eyes made me a little dizzy, I doubted that she knew how to hypnotize me or get control of my mind. I doubted that she could get me to reveal everything I knew.

Chapter 13

5:00 p.m.

"I've been expecting that question, Allie," I said in my most mature voice before launching into the opening remarks I'd rehearsed while waiting at the window. "My dad said that you—that all of you—" I leaned forward and slowly turned my head to look at each of them in the room. "You'd want to know what Daniel said to me about dying or wanting to die. I've been *contemplating* that," I said with extra emphasis on the four-syllable word like it was a regular part of my vocabulary, "as I thought about Daniel today and our, you know, our friendship. I guess there were four times—or situations or whatever you'd like to call them—that I can recall him specifically getting morbid and all, and I want to tell y'all about each of them. But first, if it's okay, I want to tell you about Daniel, what he was like."

"That's fine, Buddy," Allie said. She glanced at the others around the room and asked, "Okay?" All of them, including Deputy Dawg, nodded their approval.

"You have to understand," I said, "that Daniel, he's the smartest kid I've ever known. He was amazing! He loved to play mind games with people, and he was always two steps ahead."

"Define 'mind games' for us," Allie said.

"Well, that's where he gets you thinking one way, but it's a trick. Daniel was clever like that. He was easy to underestimate if you didn't know him. He liked to suck people into chicken-or-the-egg arguments, even with the teachers. He gets you convinced that 'chicken' is the correct answer, and then he says, 'What about the egg?' He liked to make people feel off balance around him."

"Do you think that was to make up for the fact that he was . . . you know, black?"

* * * * *

I didn't immediately respond to my father's question. I just stared at him, and the room became uncomfortably silent. I was surprised and disappointed that he had asked that question and had phrased it in that manner. I hated to see him display his prejudices so openly, but I knew he couldn't help it. He had these pre-conceived notions that included gross generalizations about people and social order that had been ingrained throughout his life, and he accepted them as fact.

I too had misconceptions about black people before I started going to school with them and getting to know them as one kid to another, before I met Daniel and we became close friends. Daniel and I often talked about our fathers, and one of my great hopes was that, through our friendship, Daniel's dad and my dad also could become friends. But it was a pipe dream. They were too much alike.

Daniel told me that his father had grown up in southern Louisiana, where their ancestors had suffered at the hands of the Cajun Ku Klux Klan. They were the meanest branch of the Klan. Daniel said they were so radical that they put white sheets on their dogs.

He said that his dad overcame all that prejudice and poverty to ultimately earn a medical degree from some big university up north. That's where Daniel's parents met and got married. He came along a few years later when they were living in New Orleans. To hear Daniel tell it, his father became some sort of Super Doctor there, working at a large hospital serving the inner-city Negro population. He was a regular Dr. Kildare and Ben Casey all rolled into one.

When Daniel was four, Dr. Carter moved the family and took up the more laid-back life of a country doctor catering to rural black families in Calcasieu Parish, near the Texas border. Times were tough in Louisiana, and they moved to Beaumont two years later, about the same time as our family. He said his father eventually got tired of country life and receiving chickens and vegetables in exchange for the medical services he provided. Dr. Kildare and Ben Casey never had that problem.

Dr. Carter's medical practice grew rapidly in Beaumont. The Carters lived in a modest two-story house in a black neighborhood near St. Christopher School. They were members of the Calvary Baptist Church, an all-black congregation where Daniel's mother sang in the choir and Dr. Carter taught Sunday school and spoke out on equal rights. Shortly after I met Daniel, he invited Marty and me to go with his family to church one Sunday. Marty got to go, but my father wouldn't even consider it. Dad said that we were Catholic and needed to go to a Catholic church. He said that I wouldn't understand what was going on because the Baptist service, particularly in a black church, would be so different from what I was used to, and I wouldn't get anything spiritual out of it. *Right*, I had thought, *because everything would be in English instead of Latin.*

Daniel and his eight-year-old sister, Jackie, went to a school that was nearly all-white, and their parents never made much of an effort to fit in with or get to know the other St. Christopher parents. Dr. Carter viewed school as a single-purpose institution—a place to learn, to get a good education. Period. He made a good income, and I'm sure he thought he was doing what was best for his children, getting them into a fine private school and out of the underfunded and second-rate Negro education system in Beaumont. But I think he underestimated the social challenges and pressures that decision put on his kids, especially Daniel.

The times I was around Dr. Carter at Daniel's house, he did his best to ignore Daniel and me—especially me. I tried to have a conversation with him once about the civil rights movement, but his response to most of my questions was, "You wouldn't understand." He seemed to have as little regard for white people as my father had for blacks. For the sake of their sons, Dr. Carter and Dad tolerated our friendship and were civil to one another at school functions. But that didn't mean they had to like each other or, heaven forbid, go out of their way to try to understand each other.

If it was confusing and frustrating for me, I can't imagine what it must have been like for Daniel. He had immense respect for his father, but Dr. Carter was consumed with his career and his causes. He didn't have much time for Daniel and couldn't relate to him when he took the time. Where Daniel was curious and open-minded, his father was dogmatic. Where Daniel was whimsical, his father was strictly business. Where Daniel was sensitive and fragile, his father was tough as nails. And Daniel's mom seemed content to take shelter in her husband's long shadow, where she doted on Jackie and left the raising of their son to his father. Daniel had heard her say, "Oh, you'll need to ask your father about that, dear" so many times that he had quit asking.

The black kids that Daniel tried to hang out with in his neighborhood made fun of him and treated him with disdain. They couldn't relate to someone who was intellectual, poor at athletics, and went to school with honkies. And most of the white kids at St. Christopher, other than Marty and me, stared at him like an amusement show freak and kept their distance, like they were afraid his skin color might rub off on them if they got too close.

I finally broke the silence. "No, Dad, Daniel played mind games because he could. He'd get bored, you know. School wasn't much of a challenge for him, and he liked to see if he could outsmart people. It didn't have anything to do with black or white. Okay?"

I gave my father a cold stare. Sitting next to him, Deputy Dawg raised his right hand, holding his pen in the air. He looked like he wanted someone to call on him. I thought that odd, that he needed to seek permission before speaking. He had a gun. Couldn't he do anything he wanted?

Allie turned her head to see what we were looking at. "Officer?" she said.

"Thank you, Miss Masterson," he said and nodded appreciatively as he lowered his hand. Unlike me, the policeman apparently was not on an intimate, first-name basis with the lovely Allie Masterson. I felt a smug superiority toward him. But then he bent forward in his chair and looked right at me with those cop eyes. I leaned back, trying to melt into the sofa.

"Young man," he said, "I'm still not sure what you mean by mind games. Can you give us a specific example, please?" Then he added, "And I'm sorry 'bout the loss of your friend. You have my deepest sympathy. This interview is a necessary part of our investigation under these circumstances, and I hope it isn't too, you know, hard on you."

How ironic that he had closed with the words "hard on you." It was probably a coincidence, but I couldn't help but wonder, *Is he signaling that I can't fool him?*

I forced myself to forget the play on words. I wrinkled my brow, deep in thought for a good example. Then it came to me. "Yes, sir, I can give you an example, a perfect example, but maybe I shouldn't."

"Why's that?" he asked.

"You see, it's about a delicate subject that we're not supposed to talk about in mixed company. I don't want anybody to get offended."

I cringed. But looking around the room at the ladies—the nuns, my mother, and then Allie—I got encouraging nods from all.

"Well, one day, Daniel, Marty, and me, we were together at Daniel's house when Marty starts accusing Daniel of cutting one—you know: pooting, passing gas. Do y'all know what I mean?"

They all nodded, but Sister Mary Margaret's look of anticipation had changed to one of concern. Mom shot an apprehensive glance across the room at my father, but his eyes remained glued on me.

"It's okay," Allie said. "Go on, Buddy."

"Are you sure?" I asked, all the while knowing I was hopelessly committed.

"I'm sure."

"Okay. Well, you see, I can't smell too good, particularly in the spring and fall with my allergies and all, so I say to Marty that I can't tell. I just know it wasn't me. Daniel looks at Marty like he's an idiot and says something like, 'Are you crazy, accusing me of that? Like, what is wrong with you, man?' Well, Marty says he knows that somebody let one loose, a real SBD. And Daniel, he just stares at Marty like he's completely out of his mind.

"Finally, Daniel says to Marty, 'Don't you know anything about black people? Don't you know we can't fart?'" I paused as curious looks came from all directions.

"Sorry, but that's what he said," I added.

Allie cleared her throat. "Go on," she said.

"We were just as surprised as y'all. Marty and me, we're both scratching our heads, but Daniel, he says it's the gospel truth. He says, 'Don't you know that's why we can eat all that spicy barbecue and beans and never have a problem?' With a totally straight face, he tells us that the Lord above made black folks different in that way. He says he's sure it's written somewhere in the Old Testament. He went on that God gave black people the curse of too much pigment in their skin, which makes them have powerful body odor when they get all sweaty. But, in His wisdom and fairness, God made up for it by designing their insides in a way that doesn't produce gases.

"Marty and me, we're listening, but not sure we believe him. Marty calls him out on it, and Daniel shakes his head and says he can't believe white people can be so ignorant. He says he can get his father, *Doctor* Carter, to explain it in medical terms, if Marty wanted him to—which of course Marty didn't.

"So, Daniel, he leaves and then comes back with one of his dad's medical textbooks, one with diagrams of the human body. He starts reading out loud about the digestive system, this part about the Negro race having a different system and all, using a lot of big words like 'fartulence.'"

Mom cringed. "You mean, 'flatulent'?" she said.

"What?" I asked.

"I think you mean, flatulent, Buddy. It's a word that—"

"It's okay, Lonnie," Dad said. "Just let it go."

All eyes returned to me. "Well, like I said, Daniel read right from this official-looking book." I raised my eyebrows and said, "Or he seemed to be reading. Then he points to the passage that he read, so we could see it, but he runs it by us real quick. Then he shows us the diagram, all the while explaining about the parts that are different in black people."

Mom interrupted again. "Is there a point to this, other than Daniel being able to take advantage of the fact that Marty is extremely gullible?"

"Oh, I believed him too, Mom. Daniel, he was very convincing."

"And?" she asked. My story was making her uncomfortable. I needed to get to the point.

"Yeah, there's just a little more to the story. You see, the next day in Sister Anne's social studies class, somebody keeps letting out these little toots." I paused as my eyes moved from one adult to another until Deputy Dawg finally gave a half-nod, indicating that elaboration wouldn't be necessary. "So, Sister Anne, she's really getting annoyed. Daniel, he keeps looking across a couple aisles at Marty and me, and all the while he's pointing at Tommy Wells in front of him with one hand and holding his nose with the other.

"Then comes this big one, much louder, while Sister has her back turned at the blackboard. She comes running over to Daniel, saying she knows he's the one doing it and he needs to stop it and also apologize to the class. Daniel, he's holding out his arms like, 'Who, me?' Then Marty jumps into it. He says, 'Sister, don't you know, black people can't fart?' I swear that's what he said. Then he says it wasn't Daniel. It was Tommy Wells.

"Well, Tommy, he freaks out. After what happened between Marty and him last year, I think he'd have a heart attack if Marty went up and said 'Boo!' to him. It got pretty strange after that. Marty explaining to Sister Anne about God trying to make up for the B.O. in black folks and all. Sister telling Marty to stay out of this because he doesn't know what he's talking about. The whole class laughing out loud. Tommy screaming that it wasn't him; it was Daniel. Marty screaming at Tommy that he's not only a twerp, but a liar. Marty describing for Sister the workings of the digestive system in black people. And all the while, Daniel has his head on his desk surrounded by his arms. But I could tell. I could tell he was laughing like crazy."

"I remember that," Sister Katherine said. "Marty was sent to the assistant principal's office."

"Yes, ma'am," I said. "He got Saturday detention for being disruptive in class. After school that day, when he caught up with Daniel out on the playground, Marty threw him down and got on top of him. He was screaming at Daniel and pulled back his fist to pound him. But Daniel, he made no effort to cover his face. He just laughed as hard as I've ever seen anyone laugh, right in Marty's big face. After a second or two, Marty unclenches his fist, calls Daniel a bad name, and then he rolls off him—onto the ground, looking straight up to the sky. Marty starts laughing—at himself—and he's shaking his head like he can't believe it all. Pretty soon, I fall down on the other side of Daniel, laughing just as loud as the two of them. We were like *The Three Musketeers*. That's what we used to say.

"That's about it, except for one other thing. While we were on the ground, Marty asks Daniel, 'How'd you know I'd do that and make a fool of myself?' Daniel stops laughing and rolls over to look at Marty. He says, 'I knew you'd come to my rescue. You're my protector, Marty.' That made us laugh even harder. I guess it's not so funny now."

I looked at the policeman. "That's what I mean, sir, by mind games," I said.

"Thanks. I see," he said as he gave me a nod and a little smile.

They had all laughed at the end of my story, even my mother. Now they were silent as I turned to Allie.

She smiled and said, "Thanks, Buddy, for that entertaining story. That must have been some scene in your classroom."

I smiled back. *My God, she was beautiful.*

"It's wonderful that you can tell that story," she said, "with enthusiasm and passion and humor all rolled together. You know, the willingness to reminisce and laugh with others is such a positive, healing sign. I'm so glad you shared that story with us, Buddy." But then she added, "You said there were four times that Daniel did strange or morbid things. Can you tell us about those?"

I was back on center stage. "Could I have a glass of water first?" I asked.

"I'll get it," Mom said as she rose from the sofa. After a couple of quick paces, she stopped and turned toward our guests. "I'm so sorry. We didn't offer refreshments when you arrived." She looked at Dad and said, "That wasn't very hospitable of us, was it? What terrible hosts we are. I can't believe that we—"

"I made some iced tea, Lon," Dad said as he stood, interrupting her apology. "We've also got soda pop—Cokes and 7-Up. Why don't you start with the Sisters, Lon, and see what everybody'd like? I'll get some glasses out."

Mom took their orders while Dad disappeared into the kitchen. The group made small talk for a couple of minutes until my parents returned with the drinks. I wasn't all that thirsty. I had asked for the water to stall them. I needed time to purge my mind and *stop all the goo-goo thoughts about HER!* I focused on the things I planned to reveal about Daniel, going over the script in my mind.

Mom and Dad distributed the drinks, and after a few sips, the Inquisition was ready, so I began. "First off, I thought y'all should know that Daniel, he talked quite a bit about dying, especially lately." I paused for a deep breath.

"It's okay. Go on, Buddy," Allie said.

"It began around the middle of November. He started off making sarcastic cracks like, 'Maybe I should just kill myself.' We thought it was a joke. It seemed like part of his thing."

"What do you mean?" Allie asked.

"We each had a thing. Marty's was to act tough. Daniel's was to make jokes about everything."

"And what was your thing?"

"I was the one always coming up with stuff to do so nobody got bored. My job was to figure things out and have the answers. They called me *Answer Man*," I said proudly.

"Tell me more about Daniel's thing."

"He made fun of stuff, but real clever-like. He never took anything serious. He cracked me up with that routine. Marty too."

"But it turned morbid, right?"

"Lately, he'd started talking about stuff going on at home and at school, mostly little things. Well, they seemed like little things to us. But Daniel, he'd say, 'I can't take it anymore!' He'd say, 'I just wanta die!'" I said his words in an exaggerated way. "I thought at first it was just Daniel being Daniel. But it got worse, more frequent."

"And he hadn't always talked like this—morbid?" Allie asked.

"That's right, but he was always sarcastic as all get-out from the first time I met him. You see, I only started at St. Christopher this year."

"I know," she said.

"Marty and me, we became friends during the summer when my family moved here, right behind his house." I pointed toward the Shannon house, across our back yard. "Marty and Daniel were friends from St. Christopher Elementary, where Daniel had gone since they integrated the school last year."

"And now you were all together at St. Christopher Junior High?"

"Right. I met Daniel over the summer, before school started. He'd come over to Marty's house and we'd all hang out. I liked him a lot, right from the get-go. I'd never met anyone like him. We were—" I looked at my father. "We were really good friends." Dad's face remained expressionless.

"Did Daniel have many friends?" Allie asked.

"Not really. Just Marty and me."

"You said he talked about some problems at school."

"Yeah, some of the kids, they called him names, you know, because he was colored. Daniel was smart and some of the real idiots called him 'Uppity.' He wasn't too good at sports either, not like most Negroes, so they made fun of him for that. They called him 'Spazmo.'"

"Who called him these names?" M Squared demanded.

"Oh, Sister, I don't know."

She glared at me, and I knew my denial wasn't going to suffice.

"It was just other guys. Daniel didn't take any heat when Marty and me were around. But we had different schedules, the three of us. I don't know all the details. I just know that some of them, they tried to, you know, to get to him with all that stuff."

"I would like some specific names, please," she insisted.

Dad looked at M Squared. "With all respect, Sister," he said, "I don't believe that would be productive right now. Can we set that aside?"

M Squared sat back in her chair. She realized he was right, but she fumed nonetheless.

Allie jumped in. "Buddy, what else can you tell us about this fixation Daniel had with death?"

I raised my right hand to my chin. Talking about my friend in front of all these people, with the cold realization that I'd never see him again, was more difficult than I had thought.

"He just talked about it a lot. If we told him he was screwing up a game we were playing, he'd say, 'Okay, I'll just go kill myself. Will that satisfy you?' If he did something good or won when we played cards, he'd say, 'That's great. Now I don't have to kill myself.' You know what I mean, Allie?"

"I'm beginning to, and I know this is hard, but when he talked like that, how did it make you feel?"

I closed my eyes and paused for three or four seconds to get the answer straight in my mind. Marty had told me that he was asked this question—a couple of times. He said he finally told them that he'd gotten "concerned," especially over the past month, but he never expressed that concern to anyone—except for me.

As I opened my eyes, I said, "I never, ever thought he was going to get a gun and shoot himself. I still can't believe it. But once or twice, I got a little . . . *concerned*. I talked about it with Marty. We were both concerned."

"Go on," Allie said.

"But I thought Daniel was just kidding around, like all this talk was maybe a new *thing* for him."

"Did you talk to Daniel about it?"

"Sure."

"What did you say to him?" she asked.

"Marty and me, we'd both tell him to knock it off; it wasn't funny. But every now and then, well, let's just say I got a little concerned."

"What specifically got you concerned?"

"I didn't like it when he'd go into details."

Allie's voice was soft and sweet. "What kind of details?"

Her eyes held mine, and I suddenly felt lightheaded and feared that she was beginning to hypnotize me. I pinched myself hard on the left arm. Marty had said that would bring you out of a trance. I bolted upright from the pain and grimaced. *Too much*, I thought, but it was a good sign—that I could feel pain.

"Are you okay?" Allie asked.

"Yeah. It, uh, it was just a chill. I'm okay."

"What kind of details did Daniel go into?"

"Just before the Christmas break, he began talking about the process he would use, you know, if he ever wanted to check out. He had begun calling it 'checking out.'" I looked down. I couldn't help it.

"And what were those?"

I swallowed hard and continued to stare at the floor. "He would go into these descriptions of all the pros and cons of where to shoot yourself—in the head, in the mouth, or in the heart." I looked up at my father. "Do I have to talk about this?" I implored.

"Not if you don't want to," Dad said. "But I'll bet that you've spent a big part of today pondering on those conversations with Daniel. You've probably fretted over it. Allie can tell you better than me, but I think it's good to get these things off your chest—to tell others, particularly someone like her, and to have them help you to understand it and deal with it."

"He's right, Buddy," Allie said. "Can you try to talk about this?"

"Okay. Daniel, he was a freak for neatness. His room was always picked up. He even made his bed." Then I repeated what Daniel had said. I said it numbly, detached, trying not to associate the description with my dead friend. "He told us that the side of the head was the best spot, but only if you put a big beach blanket down on the floor to lay on, and a pillow over that and a thick wash towel on top of the pillow. He said you should lay on your side so the wash towel and pillow would catch the bullet as it came out and would soak up the blood. You wouldn't make a mess that way. He said it was better than shooting yourself up through the mouth and . . . Well, you know."

Out of the corner of my eye, I saw my mother shiver. Allie was looking at Deputy Dawg, but he didn't look up from his notebook. He was writing furiously as I spoke.

"Allie?" I said in a bit of a whine.

"Yes?" she answered.

I cleared my throat. "Can we talk about something else?"

"Sure."

"Can I move on to the second thing?"

"Please do." She smiled.

"The second thing I thought you might want to know about was the poetry project that Daniel turned in for English class."

"We know all about that," M Squared said. Allie nodded in agreement.

"Well, I don't," Dad said. "What kinda project was it?"

I looked at my father. "You remember, Dad. We had to select a topic, any topic at all, and then find four poems about that topic and copy them into a notebook. And we had to find a picture in a magazine, or we could draw a picture ourselves, to illustrate each poem. We had to write an essay about why we chose the topic and why each poem was significant to us and to that topic. I picked 'Nature.' Mom got some old *National Geographic* magazines, and we sorted through them for pictures. Remember how I showed you my notebook, Dad?" I smiled and said proudly, "I got an A+."

"I remember now. Go on."

"Daniel chose 'Death.'" I paused for a second, chilled by the way I had cavalierly said the word. "Daniel's poems were all downers, things like 'Annabel Lee.' You know, the one by Edgar Allen Poe, where this guy plans to lay down in his dead wife's grave by the sea. And he picks 'Richard Cory,' where this rich guy that the whole town wants to be just like, he shoots a bullet into his head for no reason. He let me see his illustrations. They were all dark and gloomy. He didn't show me his essay, but he said he wrote about his own feelings—about death. I thought it was weird, offbeat, you know, but that was Daniel."

"This was back in November, right?" Dad asked.

"Yeah, the project was due right before the Thanksgiving holiday," I said.

"And he turned this report in, to a teacher?"

"Of course, but I don't know what grade he got. Miss Barton, our English teacher, she didn't give his notebook back. I think she kept it. Daniel didn't want to talk about it after that."

Dad turned his focus on the nuns. "You knew 'bout this?" he asked.

"Yes, and we were quite concerned by it," M Squared answered, more than a little defensively. "We summoned Daniel's mother to school to review the notebook with Miss Barton and me. She was concerned as well and said she would take it up with Dr. Carter. And with Daniel."

"Did they?" he asked.

"Did they what?"

"Did they take it up with the boy?"

"I'm not certain. I would hope they did, but I don't know for sure."

Dad exhaled loudly, blowing the air through his protruding lips so he looked like a fish. He rubbed his forehead as though his head hurt. "Did you suggest to Mrs. Carter that the boy might have a serious problem, that he might need help?" Dad asked.

"No, we left it to the parents to follow up."

"But you never checked back with them?"

Sister Mary Margaret lowered her head. "No, we didn't. I only wish now that we—"

Dad looked like he was going to interrupt, but my mother spoke first. "Mac! Stop, please. We said we weren't going to do this, remember?" Mom blew her nose into a tissue.

"You're right," Dad said. His face softened as he looked

toward the nuns, sitting rigid in their chairs. "I'm sorry, Sisters. I don't know what got into me, goin' off like that. Please accept my apology."

M Squared gave him a forgiving nod. Sister Katherine's head remained bowed with both her hands clasped together in her lap. She was gently fingering her rosary beads, silently praying. She had been in this position since I started talking about Daniel's deathbook.

"It's all right, Mr. Torrence," M Squared said. "We plan to cover this at the meeting tonight."

"What meeting?" my parents asked simultaneously.

"Oh, my goodness," M Squared said. She exchanged glances with Sister Katherine, who looked up momentarily before returning to her beads. "Buddy wasn't at school today. You don't know about the meeting. Oh, I'm so sorry. That was our oversight." She shook her head with her apology. "We sent a note home with each seventh-grade student to inform their parents that we've scheduled a meeting this evening for all the parents. It'll be in the school auditorium. The administration, our school counselors, and our psychological experts will all be there to brief the parents on this tragedy. We're encouraging parents not to bring their children, but if you need to, we'll understand. We want to openly discuss this matter on an adult level, focusing first and foremost on how we explain it to our children—at home and at school—in a consistent manner and in terms children can understand and ultimately come to grips with."

"Dr. Gibson won't be able to make it tonight due to a previous commitment," Allie added. "But I'll be there to cover some of the typical emotions that young people go through in these circumstances as well as grief counseling techniques—some dos and don'ts that might be helpful for parents in communicating with their children."

Dad must have had a skeptical look on his face because Allie looked at him and said matter-of-factly, "I have a master's degree from the University of Texas in psychology. My college studies were concentrated in *child* psychology, and I've been specializing in this area since I graduated last year. I think—"

"Whoa there, Miss Masterson," Dad interjected. "I didn't say that you—"

M Squared cut him off. "We don't start until 7:30. I do hope you can make it."

"I work tonight," Mom said. "There's no way I can get off on this short notice."

"I'm sorry we didn't let you know sooner. I feel so bad, but you must come, Mr. Torrence, please," M Squared said.

"I'm sure something can be arranged," Dad said. "We'll work it out after y'all leave. Now, what else?"

Allie started to respond, but M Squared waved her off as she leaned forward to look directly at me. She said, "It's been a long day and, as you can tell, Buddy, we're all a little on edge. But you, young man, you're holding up so well. I hope we won't need to keep you much longer." Sister then turned her head toward Allie.

But Allie looked at me and smiled again with those perfect teeth and gorgeous brown-green eyes. She lit up the room.

"Buddy?" she said.

"Yes, Allie?"

"You said there were four things we should talk about related to Daniel's mental condition. We've covered two. What are the others?"

The nuns and my mother sank back into their seats. Deputy Dawg picked up his pen and notebook. My father leaned forward in his chair, his eyes focused on me, intent on analyzing not only what I was saying, but also how I was saying it. He always said there was as much to be learned from studying a person's voice inflection and body language as from hearing the words they were speaking. He had told me that you had to keep your antenna up, constantly alert for the subtle signals people give off that can provide clues to the truth. It was apparent that Dad's antenna was up, way up.

Chapter 14

5:40 p.m.

"Looking back," I said, "another thing that seems strange is the way Daniel tried to give away his Christmas presents. That was the third thing I wanted to tell y'all about."

"Go ahead," Allie said.

"It was a couple of days after Christmas, about two weeks ago when we were still on break, out of school. Marty and me rode our bikes over to Daniel's house to see what he got. Marty took his new football so we could throw it around with Daniel and his two cousins who lived down the street. But Daniel, he kept trying to give us his things—for keeps. He tried to give me a sweater. We're the same size." I swallowed hard. "I guess I should have said that we *were* the same size."

"We know what you mean," Allie said.

"The sweater was fine. I told him I liked it, but I couldn't take something that was his. No way. I told him my folks had rules against stuff like that."

Dad gave an affirmative nod.

"So, Daniel's cousin said he'd take the sweater. He's younger than us, but big for his age. Daniel just gave it to him. I told him not to, but he ignored me."

Deputy Dawg had flipped back several pages in his notebook. As I spoke, he casually nodded his head as he looked down. I interpreted it as confirmation that I was recalling these events the same way that Marty had.

"Did Daniel try to give away other things?" Allie asked.

They already knew the answer. "Yeah," I said. "I couldn't stop him. It was nothing real valuable, but things you'd expect he'd want to keep. He gave Marty his Major League baseball, the one Turk Farrell had autographed. His other cousin, he gave him a Chinese checkers game and a model airplane that was still in the box, just waiting for someone to put it together. Then Daniel picks up the Bible in his room. It's got an old leather cover and had belonged to his great-grandfather, the one who was a preacher."

"It sounds very special," Allie said.

"Yeah, it was, except he hands it to me, that Bible. He says, 'Buddy, you've been a good friend. You have to take this.' He kept saying he wasn't going to need these things anymore, especially not the Bible. I told him to snap out of it. I couldn't take his Bible. It wasn't right. I also thought that maybe it was some new trick that he'd thought up—a trap—and I might step into it if I took the bait."

"Another mind game, right?"

"Yeah, that's right."

"Keep going," she said.

"So, he forces me to take the Bible. He shoves it in my arms and walks away. It made me mad, so I threw it at him. It bounced off his back and fell on the floor. Some papers that were inside went flying. Well, Daniel, he goes berserk. He comes at me and pushes me in the chest—really hard—and I fall backward and smash my knee on a big wooden bedpost. He jumps on top of me and starts swinging at me as hard as he can. But I've got my arms up covering my face, so he's mainly just pounding my arms."

"Did that surprise you? Had he ever done anything like that before?" Allie asked.

"No, never! But I didn't have much time to think about it, you know. Marty and Jason, one of Daniel's cousins, they're pulling him off when Daniel's father, who must've heard all the commotion, runs upstairs. He jerks Daniel off to one side and then yells at me to get up. He wants to know what's going on. Daniel says that I threw his Bible, and I say he made me do it. Everybody else, they can't believe what's happening. I can't either." I shook my head.

PART ONE: 5:40 p.m. 141

Allie leaned forward. "So, what did Dr. Carter do?"

"He asks the cousins if I threw the Bible. They both say, 'Yes.' But Marty, he steps up to tell Dr. Carter to hold on a minute. He says something about me being provoked by Daniel and how it's part Daniel's fault too. Well, Dr. Carter, he cuts Marty off real fast. He makes it clear that he doesn't like the idea of the Good Book being thrown, not for any reason. He orders me to leave the house, and then he orders Marty to leave, even though Marty wasn't the one in the fight."

"It's probably 'cause he thought you two white boys were ganging up against Daniel," Dad said.

Here we go again, I thought. I wanted to call him out for putting things—complicated things—in such black-and-white terms. But I let it pass. "How would I know what his father was thinking?" I said. "And, do you know what, Dad? It doesn't matter. All I know is that Marty and me, we were ordered to leave, and Daniel, he looked strange the whole time. He looked like he was glad to see us go. I didn't get it. Anyway, Marty stuffed the Turk Farrell ball in his pocket and we left." I paused for a second, wondering if I was getting Marty in trouble. *Too late now,* I thought as I continued, "My knee hurt so bad I could barely pedal my bike. Mom put ice on it when I got home."

"And you told your parents what happened at Daniel's house?" Allie asked.

"Of course," I said. "I told them *everything*: How Daniel and I had a fight and I fell in his room and hit my knee. How Daniel was giving away stuff, acting all weird, and how upset I got about it." I looked to my mother and then my father for confirmation. The others watched as both parents nodded in agreement, confirming that I was a regular George Washington.

"That's right," Dad added, "but you said you had a fight over a book that he wanted you to take. That he got all mad when you told him you wouldn't do it."

"Well, the Bible's a book, ain't it? And that's what we had the fight over." I was annoyed. George Washington didn't have this much trouble confessing about the cherry tree.

Dad wouldn't drop it. "All I'm saying is: I'm clarifying that you didn't tell us 'bout Daniel trying to give away *so many* of his possessions and him saying he wouldn't be needing a Bible. This is the first time your mom and I have heard that. I didn't want anyone here to get the wrong idea."

"Wrong idea about what? You think I'm trying to give people the wrong idea?"

I was leaning forward on the sofa, and Mom reached out to put her arm around my shoulders. "It's okay," Mom said. "Your father wasn't implying that you didn't tell the truth."

"That's right," Dad said, looking around the room. "He just didn't tell us all these details back when he told us 'bout the fight."

"And you keep twisting everything!" I shouted at him. "It's all my fault now for not getting into a lot of detail and not saying it was a Bible?" I knew then that I was going to cry, that I wouldn't be able to hold back the tears.

Mom came to my rescue again, placing a tissue in my hand. "Don't get upset, Buddy," she said.

"That's right," Dad said. "There's no need to get upset. I'm not trying to be critical of the way you handled this situation. I'm just trying to avoid a misunderstanding for these folks over how much information your parents had."

Why couldn't he drop it? Why did he have this burning need to keep explaining things, to get all the details stated so precisely? Now he had succeeded in making it look like I had withheld important information. With Mom leaning into me, trying to comfort and protect me, I lashed out at him. "Do you think I lied? Did I do something wrong? Tell me!"

Allie said calmly, "I'll tell you, Buddy. You didn't—"

"I don't want you to tell me! I want *him* to tell me."

Allie recoiled into the recliner as I pointed an accusing finger at my father. I said, "I'm 12 years old, okay? I'm sorry, but my knee hurt, and I tried to tell y'all what happened as best I could." My voice broke as I continued, "Don't you think I'd have told somebody if I knew what it all meant?"

My father didn't speak. Instead, he rose from his chair. With great calm and no expression on his face, he stepped toward me. He wedged into the space between the coffee table and Allie as he said to her, "Excuse me, young lady."

Then, oblivious to the others in the room, he got on his knees in front of me. I turned away to nuzzle against my mother, but I felt Dad's hands gently covering my knees. "Look at me," he whispered. I didn't respond, and he said it again in a voice that was still soft but deeper, more insistent, "Look at me."

Forget the power of shrinks. My father had a power over me that was stronger than anything they might concoct. I couldn't resist him. As I turned my head and body from the protection of my mother's arms, I put on my fiercest scowl for him to see how angry I was.

On his knees, his head was slightly lower than mine, and his voice was slow and deliberate. "I'm sorry," he whispered. "You told the truth, and you haven't done anything wrong. My clarifying comments—and that's all they were meant to be, Buddy—they weren't worth upsetting you. You're doin' a great job here today, telling us things that can't be easy for you. I am so proud of you, Son. You're showing a ton of courage and maturity. Now, please forgive me for being so picky and let's move on."

All my stress and anxiety vanished. I reached forward to rest my hands on his shoulders and whispered, "Don't worry, it's okay." Then I slid my hands around his neck and hugged him.

You could feel the tension leaving the room and folks breathing again. Dad acknowledged me in a voice that was barely audible, so the others couldn't hear. "Don't squeeze so tight. I have to pee," he said.

I was confused at first. I pulled away from him, and he gave me a wink. We smiled briefly at each other, and then Dad stood and said to our guests, "Let's take a short break and then see if we can wrap this up, okay?"

Everyone nodded in agreement. Dad headed for the hallway that led to their bathroom. M Squared followed Mom to the kitchen to refill her drink. Deputy Dawg stood to stretch and then signaled to Allie that he wanted to speak with her. I remained on the sofa and tried to compose myself for the final act.

* * * * *

Near the end of that break in the action, Allie and I had a private chat in the family room. She asked why I hadn't been in school that day. I told her that I needed time by myself and didn't want to be around a lot of people after I heard the bad news. I told her that I was a thinker. As the others regrouped, she leaned close to me and said that she was the same way. She liked to have time to think through issues or problems and generally trusted her own intuition on important matters.

"However," she said, "in times of high emotional stress, we all need someone to talk openly and honestly to, someone to confide in and seek advice from. I hope you know I'm available, that I'm here for you, Buddy, if you need someone to talk to."

I was dumbstruck. When she talked right at me—so sweetly, so intimately—it was like we were the only two people in the world. As she turned to pick up her glass of 7-Up, I pinched myself again, even harder this time.

Dad and the policeman were the last to return. They had been standing in the front yard smoking cigarettes. When we moved into this house in June, Mom had declared that she was going to have a rule: Dad would have to do all his smoking outside the house. She told him that she would do the same, although my mother wasn't a heavy smoker like my father. At first, Dad told her she was crazy. He said that people had a right to smoke anywhere they wanted. It was in the Bill of Rights or something, and he accused her of being un-American. He argued that they wouldn't be able to invoke a rule like this with guests. It would be embarrassing, not to mention impolite, to ask someone to go outside to smoke their cigarette. But Mom refused to relent, claiming she didn't ask for much and this was important to her. Finally, my father caved.

I was glad. I hated breathing the cigarette smoke when they lit up around me. I knew it wasn't like I was the one smoking and doing damage to my lungs. But I hated that smell and the queasiness I felt because of the reeking, pungent odor that had permeated our trailer and our cars and everything in them. I was glad that Mom had instituted this policy for the house on Hazel Street, and I knew, once Dad had accepted it as a rule, he would obey it, even if he was all alone in the house. It was, after all, a rule.

Mom rarely lit up in public. However, I would occasionally see her puffing on a cigarette in our back yard, where she would just stare at the big pecan tree. She sometimes lingered to have a second one. I often wondered what she was thinking about. What were her dreams?

Over the recent holiday break, my curiosity got the better of me. It was the day after New Year's, a Saturday. Mom had just come home from working at the hospital, and I was watching her backyard ritual from my bedroom. She was so deep in thought that she didn't hear the kitchen door shut nor my footsteps as I approached her.

"Whatcha thinkin' 'bout, Mom?" I asked in a little-boy voice.

She jumped. "Oh, Buddy, you frightened me."

"Sorry."

"It's okay." She gave me a reassuring smile and draped an arm loosely over my shoulder. She held the half-smoked cigarette in her other hand. "What are you up to today?" she asked.

"Not much. I'm waiting for Marty to get home. He's off with his mom. I think they're shopping for school uniforms. He's already outgrown the ones he got in September."

"That's nice," she said absently.

"Mom, do you think I'll get a big growth spurt like Marty?"

"Oh, I don't know. What about your other friends?"

"Yeah, some have had a recent growth spurt and some—"

"No, I meant, what about other friends that you could play with today?"

"Well, Daniel and I aren't on good terms just now. You know, we're not really speaking."

"That's too bad," she said.

"In fact, I don't get it, Mom, why Daniel has been so—"

"Don't you have any other friends, Buddy?"

"Not really. You see, Daniel, he's been—"

But she didn't let me finish. "Now I can't believe there is absolutely no one else." She let the words hang in the air.

"Well, no one I'd want to call up on a Saturday and hang out with."

She looked puzzled as she took another drag on the cigarette.

"Mom?"

"Yeah?"

"What do you think about when you come back here?"

"Oh, my goodness." She stepped backward and placed her hand over her heart like it was some deeply personal question. "Why do you ask that?"

"No particular reason, just curious. I bet it's your New Year's resolution."

"What?"

"I'll bet you're thinking about your New Year's resolution, right?"

"No, not really," she said.

"That's okay. New Year's resolutions are for quitters." I gave her a big smile, but she just stared at me. "It's a joke I heard."

"Oh, I see," she said with a forced smile.

"Then I bet it's your second job. I bet you're thinking about that—about giving it up like Dad thinks you should, right?"

"No, not really."

"About how Sister Bethany at the hospital doesn't realize what a great job you're doing and what a sacrifice you're making, you know, like you were saying the other night at supper, right?"

"No, not really," she said again.

C'mon! I thought. Her evasiveness was annoying. It was like listening at the end of a record when the needle gets stuck on the same three words.

"Well, what then? You come out here in the back yard to think about something, Mom. What is it?" I had tried to ask it in a semi-polite tone, but maybe I'd said it wrong.

"What I think about in my private time is my business, young man."

"I know. I know that, but do you think about the same things when you come out here, or is it something different each time?"

"I don't want to talk about it. Okay?" She stared at me with a sullen glare. She continued until I had to look away.

I swallowed hard and said, "Okay," with a shrug like it was no big deal. I turned and walked back into the house.

In my room with the door safely shut, lying face down across my bed, tears came into my eyes. I wiped them on my pillow. I didn't understand. They said we were a family and that families were supposed to be close. We were supposed to be able to talk to each other. Why wouldn't she talk to me? Why was it so hard to communicate with your parents?

I knew so little about my mother, deep down—about her hopes, her dreams. I wanted to know what she was thinking about that day, but I also had another agenda. I had hoped we would strike up a casual conversation, and during its course, I could ask about something that was bothering me, bothering me a lot—something about Daniel and how strange he'd been acting.

I looked out my window. She had lit another cigarette and was once again focused on the pecan tree. I could have been a million miles away for all she knew.

Chapter 15

6:00 p.m.

I was talking about what Daniel's friendship had meant to me, what it was like to have a really good friend. Allie continued to provide an encouraging smile. Dad continued to listen and observe everything. Mom continued to sniffle. Deputy Dawg continued to scribble notes. Sister Katherine continued to pray over her rosary beads. M Squared continued to stare out the window. She had already heard Marty's version of these events, which I had every reason to believe was highly consistent with mine. M Squared was no doubt thinking about the meeting with all the concerned parents that was scheduled to start in just 90 minutes. It was getting late. I was tired, but I felt reasonably good about my performance as we headed into the home stretch.

"Did you and Daniel resolve your differences last week?" Allie asked.

"After our fight, I didn't see Daniel again until the holidays were over. But we had a good talk at school on Monday morning, a week ago." *Daniel's final week on Earth.* The thought was suddenly unsettling, stirring my emotions. I blinked twice, trying to concentrate. *Get a grip, man! You're almost done.*

"And you got everything cleared up between you?" Allie asked.

"Yeah. Daniel apologized in front of Marty for coming after me in his room. He was in good spirits. He said we should get together and play some football after school."

"Did you play?" Allie asked.

"Yeah. We had a great time. Then Daniel and I talked on

PART ONE: 6:00 p.m.   149

the phone that night—and a couple other nights last week—about math homework problems. He seemed happy, you know, *normal*."

"Anything else unusual from last week?" she asked.

"No, not really," I lied.

"Daniel seemed fine to you?"

"Yeah, pretty much." I slumped back on the sofa, fatigue setting in.

"That's interesting because Marty said he saw Daniel give you a big hug on Friday afternoon, like a goodbye hug, just before Daniel went home from school that day," Allie said. She stared at me, measuring my reaction as she spoke. "Marty said it was at the big bike rack, just before Daniel pulled out his bike. Marty said you pulled away, but then walked back and Daniel hugged you a second time. He said it looked 'odd.' That's how he described it to Dr. Gibson."

She stopped speaking but continued to stare at me. So did everyone else. I wasn't aware that Marty had seen us at the bike rack. Even worse, during our little walk, my Peeping Tom friend neglected to tell me that he had said something to the Inquisition about it. I wanted to throttle Marty's fat neck. This wasn't in my script. There wasn't a question on the table, so I tried to remain calm and concentrate without volunteering a response until Allie finally broke the silence.

"What was that about?" she asked.

"Oh, Daniel just wanted to thank me. Remember, like I said, he had talked to me on the phone about homework. I had been helping him. His grades were coming back up."

"In one week?" she asked, her tone clearly skeptical.

Dad leaned forward in his chair. Like a reflex action, I pushed backward, harder into the sofa.

"What I mean is: He had pledged to get his grades up. It was like a New Year's resolution. He was glad I was helping him, and I was glad that we had, you know, made up . . . or something like that."

I was uncomfortable with the reference to "made up." That was an expression we used at school for couples—a boy and a girl. I didn't want to use it for two guys who were seen hugging, especially if one was me, but I couldn't think of the right words with all of them staring at me.

"And it wasn't a big hug or anything like that," I added, when no one else would speak. I looked at Allie and shook my head in disbelief. "I can't believe Marty called it a hug. It was more like a handshake between two friends."

Her look said she wasn't buying it.

"Marty probably had a bad angle, you know, when Daniel and I were just standing there next to each other. He had gone around the corner to watch for his mom. She was picking us up. No big deal, okay?"

My eyes darted from one person to the next. They all stared back at me. Why wouldn't someone speak? I nodded at Allie to indicate that I was ready for the next question, but she only narrowed her eyes and continued to stare at me. When the quiet in the room and her expressionless face became unbearable, I opened my mouth wide and snapped my fingers. "Oh, I remember now. Silly me." I put my index finger to my temple like I was having trouble with my memory. "Daniel, he also wanted to apologize about my knee. That was the second hug, or handshake, that is. He was still feeling bad about my knee. He noticed I was still limping a little on Friday as we were leaving school. I didn't stop limping until the weekend. Isn't that right, Mom?"

She thought for a second. "Yes, I think that's right, honey, but to tell the truth, I'm not sure. So much has happened since then."

Thanks a lot, Mom.

"How did you play football on Monday if your knee was hurt so badly?" Allie asked.

"Oh, I didn't play much. I mean, I tried. I just couldn't get around too good, so I quit. I mean, after a couple of hours. You can ask Marty. He'll back me up on that."

"That won't be necessary, Buddy. We believe you," she said.

But I wondered if she did. If my father leaned any further forward in his chair, he'd be in my lap. That damn Deputy Dawg hadn't looked up in forever; he was too busy recording everything I'd said in his little notebook, no doubt so he could trip me up on it later. He suddenly looked intimidating again. And why was our house so hot? I felt beads of perspiration forming on my forehead.

Even Allie's look was different. The smiles and sympathy were gone. It felt like her eyes were burning through me, like my father's, as she said, "You don't have to be nervous—"

"I'm not nervous!"

"Or defensive—"

"I'm not defensive!"

"Or afraid of anything—"

Oh, God help me, I must be under her spell, I thought. The room was spinning as I interrupted her again. "I'm not afraid or anything else, okay?" I blurted. "I'm just tired. Look, can I please tell y'all about the fourth time where Daniel acted strange, so we can get through all this—*please*?"

"If that's what you want, Buddy," Allie said. "If you don't want to talk about that last time you saw Daniel, then—"

"I did talk about it! I just told you all about it."

I was talking to Allie but looking desperately at my mother. She turned her eyes away from me and gave Allie a sad look that said, *Enough, please.*

"Okay, then. Let's move on," Allie said.

"Good," I said. I tried to lean forward, but the perspiration along the middle of my back had soaked through my shirt and it was sticking to the sofa. I leaned back and tried not to think about it.

"Well, this one is really strange, I have to admit," I said. I was relieved to be back to my script, to once again be in control of *my* meeting. "It was a Sunday afternoon and the three of us, we're all at Marty's house listening to records while his mom was taking a nap."

I smiled to myself thinking about what brought us together that afternoon. Marty had bought the 45 RPM recording of "Louie Louie" by The Kingsmen. After Mrs. Shannon had gone to her room, we listened to the song, trying to make out the lyrics.

Marty said they were singing about getting "*way down low*" on a girl, and there were lots of other nasty words in the song. He said the FBI had been called in to investigate whether the song should be classified as obscene, and it had been banned by at least a thousand radio stations. It sounded like "*we gotta go*" to me, and Daniel said it was "*away I go*," but Marty said we were both deaf. Frankly, I wasn't sure. The singer slurred the words throughout the song. In the end, I was willing to give Marty the benefit of the doubt since it was cool to think they could slip dirty words and hidden meanings into a song that was so popular and got played all the time on the radio in Beaumont. After about the hundredth time we'd listened to the song, Daniel had completely lost interest.

Looking around the room, I decided to skip the part about "Louie Louie" and our lyrical quest. I went straight into the bizarre events that took place later that afternoon. "While Marty and I were inside the house," I said, "Daniel walked outside, out to the curb on North Street. We thought he was just getting some fresh air."

"When exactly did this take place? Do you remember?" Allie asked.

I suspected that she already knew the answer. Marty had said he told them that he thought this incident had occurred during the second weekend in December. I was positive that was correct.

"I can't be sure," I said, "but it was a Sunday and it was December, probably early that month when we were still in school."

She nodded as the cop checked his notes. Yeah, they knew.

"What happened next?" Allie asked.

"Marty and I went outside to see what Daniel was doing. He was all glassy-eyed, and he says, 'I think I'll get me some death.' Weird, huh? We laughed at him like it was a joke, but Daniel, he closes his eyes and lifts his arms out like a cross. Before we can figure out what's going on, he starts walking—right into the street!

"A car was coming, not too fast, thank goodness. Daniel, I

PART ONE: 6:00 p.m.

swear, he walks right in front of that car. It's a little car, like the Shannons' Chevy, with a lady driving. I see the car and I see Daniel, but he's already halfway across the street and we can't do anything to stop it. It all happened so quick, you know. She slams on the brakes and swerves to the right. The car, it bounces off the curb and comes to a stop down the street. It came this close to hitting Daniel," I said with my hands extended, a foot apart. "And I don't think he ever opened his eyes. He just kept walking real slow until he reached the other side of the street."

I broke eye contact with Allie, who I was sure had heard the story secondhand from Dr. Elmer Fudd, and I looked across the sofa at my mother. Her eyes were open wide.

"What did you boys do?" Mom asked.

"Well, there was a break in the traffic, so Marty and me, we ran across the street. We were both pretty scared. I screamed at Daniel, but he just laughs and says, 'I told ya I'd show ya.' It was a sing-song rhyme he kept repeating—'I told ya I'd show ya; I told ya I'd show ya'—until he looks around and throws his arms back again. He was crazy. He says, 'Wanta see it again?'

"Well, Marty's really mad now. He throws Daniel down, and he bangs his head on the curb. It starts bleeding over the top of his ear. About that time, the lady gets out of her car and starts walking back to us. She's screaming, 'Are you insane? I could've hit you! What's the matter with you?'

"Daniel jumps up off the curb before we can stop him. He walks straight toward her all stiff-legged with his arms out just like the zombies in the movies. He's shouting at her in this weird, spaced-out voice, 'Yes, masta, I must have some death. Please give your poor slave some death, masta.' Something like that. And the blood's coming down pretty good now. It's over Daniel's ear and on part of his face. The poor lady. When Daniel starts coming at her, she turns around, jumps in her car, and lays rubber getting out of there."

"What happened then?" Mom said.

"Nothing. At least, nothing freaky after that."

"What did Daniel have to say for himself?"

"That's probably the strangest part of the whole thing. After the lady drives off, bang!" I snapped two fingers together. "All of a sudden, he's back to normal. It's like he had, you know, temporary insanity."

I had seen a TV show over the Christmas holiday where a nice enough guy had these fits of what his lawyer kept calling "temporary insanity." It was all because his medicine kept getting screwed up. It caused him to act like a madman and do all sorts of horrific things that he had trouble remembering. By the end of the show, they had figured out the problem, and everybody said the man wasn't responsible for his actions. The cops arrested a guy who was spiking his pills. They got him some new medicine, and everyone lived happily ever after, except for the people he had killed when he was a temporarily insane madman.

"Daniel went into Marty's house with us," I said. "Marty, he's boiling mad, but he has to stay quiet because his mom is taking a nap. Daniel goes in the bathroom to wash his head, but we don't leave him alone in there on the chance he'll flip out again, right there in Marty's house. But Daniel keeps saying he's fine, and he washes his head real good. Marty finds a Band-Aid. He puts it on the cut and it stops the bleeding.

"Then Daniel made us promise not to tell our parents what happened. He begged us, so we said, 'Okay.' After that, we watched a football game on TV. Daniel was like normal, except he didn't say much. Then, before the game is over, he jumps up and says he needs to leave. He gets on his bike and, as he's pulling out, waves goodbye and smiles at us, like nothing ever happened. It was like *The Twilight Zone*." I shook my head and continued.

"I saw him the next day at school and tried to get him to explain what happened. He said he couldn't remember too much about it, you know, just like temporary insanity. He told me he was on some medication that had gotten all fouled up, but now they had it fixed. So, it wasn't likely that it could happen again." I paused for a second. "That's what Daniel told me. Marty wasn't around when he said that to me. But that's about it."

PART ONE: 6:00 p.m.

They were all spellbound. I had always fancied myself a good storyteller, and I was confident that my version of these events, although factually consistent with Marty's, must have been more entertaining. Also, I was sure that the ones who heard Marty's story didn't know about the last two items—Daniel swearing us to secrecy and then telling me the next day that his medication was to blame.

That's because they weren't true. I had made them up. I lied about those two points because the added facts were needed, in my opinion, to somehow, in some way, justify our failure to notify our parents. According to my version, we couldn't tell anyone without breaking a pledge to our friend. Kids are taught to be faithful, right? We're supposed to keep secrets when promised to a friend. Plus, the part about the medication explained why Daniel behaved like a whacko on a death mission and why, later, I wasn't particularly worried that he'd do it again. It was a clear case of temporary insanity, just like in that TV show.

I wasn't overly concerned about being caught in these lies. I had thought it through. On the off chance that Marty was questioned again and failed to corroborate the promise that I said we made to Daniel, I could claim that Marty just didn't remember. No big deal. I would remind them that it got totally crazy that afternoon. Daniel was a madman, and Poor Marty was almost a madman. Poor Marty must not have been paying attention when we made that promise. That was typical for Marty, whose attention span was measured in nanoseconds. Everyone knew he didn't have as good a memory as me. He couldn't be expected to remember *everything* we said or did. Yes, I convinced myself that I would be safe with this little white lie.

The part about the medication seemed even safer. That conversation, according to my account, was just between Daniel and me. If anyone investigated or asked Daniel's parents about any medication for their son, the Carters would no doubt say it didn't exist. Then we would all conclude that Daniel was lying to me. He had acted so outrageously during that time. It would be easy to believe that he lied about this. No problem, right?

Not quite. Assuming I got away with the lies, which I thought was a safe bet, I was still going to be living with the truth—that I couldn't explain why we didn't tell anyone about this freaked-out, death-wish experience of Daniel's. It scared the hell out of me and was such a clear harbinger of the dark forces that were taking over Daniel's mind. Marty was right, what he had said during our walk. We should have told someone. We should have let them all know how close he came to killing (or seriously hurting) himself that day. I still can't understand how we could have been so naive.

Worse than simple naiveté, there's another possibility that still haunts me. What if Daniel acted out this scary death scene for our benefit? Was he screaming out to alert us, his best friends, to his inner pain and how desperate it made him feel? Sometimes, you just can't communicate with your parents about personal stuff, especially when they want so badly for you to be somebody that you aren't or can't be. Daniel obviously didn't confide in his parents about his death wish. However, contrary to what I had told the Inquisition, he never said that we shouldn't tell ours. He never said we shouldn't tell the teachers, Sister Mary Margaret, or *somebody*, for Chrissake! Maybe Daniel went crazy that day because he wanted to scare us into telling someone—to get him some help. Maybe he was crying out in anguish to his so-called friends, but we were too stupid to hear. Or maybe we closed our ears because we were too caught up in ourselves—at the center of our own universe—and didn't care enough about him to listen. That one really hurts.

After that story about the zombie of North Street, my interrogation mercifully came to an end. M Squared summed up with an apology on behalf of the group for the intrusion and was commenting on my fine performance under such difficult circumstances when my mother interrupted.

"I have a question for Officer Powell, if I may."

"Please, ma'am, call me Don."

"Thank you, Don. What I want to know is how in the world does a 12-year-old child get his hands on a loaded gun?"

PART ONE: 6:00 p.m.

He put down his notebook and pen as the question hung in the air. "That's a mystery, ma'am. Dr. Carter keeps two hunting rifles and a .38 caliber pistol in his house. The rifles are locked in a cabinet—a real fine gun case—whereas the pistol, the one the boy used, he keeps it in a drawer at the bottom of that cabinet. There's no lock for that drawer, but—"

"That is totally irresponsible!" Mom blurted out. "You're saying an unsecured gun was in their house while children, including our son—"

"Now, hold on a minute. You have to understand, the doctor says that none of the guns in the house, including that pistol, are ever loaded. 'Never!' is what he claims. He keeps all the ammunition locked in a safe in their bedroom closet. They also keep important papers in there. The doctor, his brother, and Mrs. Carter are the only ones who know the combination."

"So how did Daniel shoot himself with an unloaded gun?" Mom asked.

"Obviously, it wasn't unloaded," he said. "Somehow, there was one live round in the pistol—just one—when the boy fired it. As best I can figure, there's only three ways the bullet got there. First, maybe the doctor's mistaken 'bout the gun being unloaded. He said he took one of the rifles and the pistol out to a firing range over the holidays. Who knows? Maybe he missed one of the chambers before he put the revolver away."

"What does he say—Dr. Carter?" Mom asked.

"He says there's no way. He claims to have fired every single round at the range, and then he thoroughly checked the guns again before returning 'em to the cabinet."

"But you don't believe that?" Mom said.

"Whoa, hold on! I didn't say that. I'm just telling y'all what the possibilities are. We don't know for sure how the bullet got there. Chances are good we never will."

"So that's one possibility. You said there were two others," Dad said.

"That's right. It's possible the boy knew the combination to the safe and got a bullet that way. He coulda seen his father opening the safe one day and memorized the sequence.

Or maybe his parents mentioned the combination in a casual conversation; they didn't think nothin' by it, but the boy heard. Not likely, you know, but a possibility. Also, the doctor's brother kept the combination on a piece of paper in his desk at home. It's possible that the boy found it there in his uncle's desk."

The policeman raised his eyebrows and looked around the room. When no one offered a comment on this hypothesis, he continued. "The final possibility is that, through trial and error, the boy cracked the code. The three numbers corresponded to family members' birthdays. So, you know, the boy's just flipping to the right and to the left whenever he's home alone, trying various numbers, and then one day—Bingo! The safe pops open and there's the bullets. But that's the most unlikely scenario."

"You think the first scenario, that a lone shell got left in the gun, that's the most likely?" Dad asked.

"Well, I'm not one to dispute the good doctor's word, but I know this much: The bullet got there somehow. None of us are perfect, and Dr. Carter coulda made a mistake. I know that's a huge burden, so we're not pressing the question. Besides, it doesn't really matter how it got there. Only thing that matters in the end is what the boy did with it."

I had listened carefully, and I liked the way that he had logically determined all the possibilities. It was the same way that my father would have approached this dilemma and, presumably, reached the same conclusion.

Mom gave a sympathetic nod to the officer. "And Dr. Carter and his wife and their family—how are they doing?" she asked.

It was M Squared who answered. "Not well at all, as you can expect."

"Oh, Sister," she said, turning to face the nun, "that didn't come out right. Of course, they're devastated beyond description. He was only 12 years old. I'm so sorry. I didn't mean it to sound like that." Mom hung her head.

M Squared rose and motioned for Mom to move toward the center of the sofa, even closer to me. She complied and the little nun took a seat next to her. She embraced my mother, then spoke slowly and calmly to her, just as she had done with me before beginning this meeting. "There, my child. Please, you must be strong too. Father Bernard and I spent time with the family and poor Daniel in the hospital on Saturday, when we didn't know for sure that it was a suicide. And then I paid a visit at their home yesterday. Family members and friends from Calvary Baptist Church have all gathered to provide support for the Carters."

Sister Mary Margaret continued talking to Mom in a soft whisper. I couldn't make out the rest of what she said because Mom had wrapped her arms around me, engulfing me in a protective manner. Mom kept repeating in my ear, as she listened to Sister, "He was only 12. He was only 12."

I was able to peek through her arms and saw my father lean to his left and ask the policeman, "Are you sure it was a suicide? I mean, isn't it possible the boy was playing with the gun? Maybe he didn't know there was a live round in there. It coulda been an accident, right?"

"My report will conclude that it was a suicide," he said matter-of-factly.

"But how can you be so sure?"

The policeman seemed uncomfortable. He looked at Allie, who had been listening to their conversation. They both glanced in my direction, and I pretended that I wasn't paying attention to them. I buried my head in Mom's rib cage, but my ears were tuned in, awaiting an answer.

Allie must have given him an affirmative nod because he leaned toward my father and said, "You see, Dr. Carter found the boy lying in the entryway, right behind the front door. It was like he wanted his body to be the first thing his father saw when he came home. The gunshot wound was angled down into the temple and through the back of the boy's jaw. It's remarkable that he didn't die instantly."

"And?" my father asked when the policeman hesitated.

"And the boy was on his side, laid out on a large beach blanket. Under his head was his pillow from upstairs and a couple of thick hand towels he'd placed there to soak up the blood."

Chapter 16

6:30 p.m.

After our guests finally left, Mom phoned St. Elizabeth Hospital to report that she would be a little late that evening. I heard her explain to Sister Bethany, who was in charge of the hospital's medical records department, that a family problem had arisen. She hinted that it might be better for her to stay home that evening, but Sister Bethany clearly had a different opinion. Mom managed a feeble, "Yes, but—" and an "Oh, I see, but—" before the conversation ended, and she set the phone back on its cradle.

"Sister Battle Axe says they're way behind," she said to my father. "Lots of surgery since the holidays, and one of the nine-to-five girls was out sick today. She asked me to think about coming in an extra night this week. Drat! I'm sorry, dear."

"It's okay, Lon."

She turned and headed for the kitchen. Dad and I followed. Mom opened the refrigerator door and stared inside. "There's some leftover chicken and potato salad," she said. "I didn't have time to cook anything for supper. I'm sorry, but everything's happening so fast."

Dad put his arm around her as she stared into the refrigerator. "It's gonna be all right," he said. "I've got a plan."

He kissed her cheek and closed the refrigerator, telling her, "Don't worry 'bout supper." He motioned for me to come closer. "We'll rustle something up, right, Buddy? You just go freshen up and get over to the hospital. Buddy and I will go to the meeting at school. We'll be—"

"But they said not to bring children tonight."

"Sister said they *recommended* that we not bring our children. In this case, on such short notice, I believe it's better for Buddy to come with me than to stay here alone. I'm sure no one will mind."

I had a thought. "Dad, I could stay with Marty, and you and Mrs. Shannon could go to the school."

"No, that's not a good idea, Son," he said. "I'd prefer we stick together tonight." Mom nodded her agreement.

I looked down. "Okay, it was just a suggestion. I'm just trying to help."

"I know you are," Mom said. She put her hand on my shoulder. "My sweet little boy's growing up. You've grown up so much today," she added with a sigh.

"Yeah, it's been a lot," my father said. "We just want you with us for the remainder of the evening."

That settled, he looked at Mom. She was biting on her quivering lower lip. *Oh no, here it comes*, I thought.

But Dad put his hands on his hips and commanded in his deepest voice, "And you—you're late, madam, and we don't tolerate tardiness in this army. Now get into the bedroom and get ready for duty. Now! That's an order, soldier."

He gave her a big smile, and she managed a weak one in return. But then she suddenly stood erect and made a mock salute. She spun around and marched out of the kitchen in an exaggerated high step, like a soldier on parade, but not before Dad gently patted her on the bottom as she filed past us.

I smiled. I couldn't help it. *How does he always know what to say?* I thought as I watched her disappear around the corner.

"It's not that hard, you know," he whispered to me, "if you just pay attention."

Chapter 17

7:30 p.m.

It was unusual for my father to be driving so fast. We traveled briskly down Seventh Street until encountering a red light at the busy intersection with Calder Avenue. Dad's fingers tapped nervously on the steering wheel as he leaned forward, fixing his sights on the dangling traffic light. When it finally changed to green, he turned our little Ford Falcon left onto Calder, one of Beaumont's major east/west thoroughfares.

The drive from our house to St. Christopher School took 10-15 minutes, depending on how fortunate one was with the numerous traffic lights en route. Our luck was bad that night as we caught another red light at Fourth Street. Dad was fond of saying that it always takes longer to get somewhere when you're in a hurry. "That's why," he'd say, "it pays to have patience." That night, he had no patience, and he pushed hard on the accelerator the instant the light turned green.

We continued down Calder, the car bouncing roughly over the railroad tracks past First Street. But then Dad had to brake sharply as we slowed to a complete stop behind a city bus unloading passengers. He cursed to himself and focused his attention over his left shoulder for an opportunity to switch lanes. After four or five cars had passed, he whipped the Falcon into the other lane.

It made me recall how Dad was also fond of telling me that it was easy to predict which lane of traffic was going to move the slowest.

"Whichever lane I'm in," he would say in a disgusted voice, but then look over at me with a big grin. I'd heard it a hundred times, but it still made me smile. That night, however, he was quiet as he drove, deep in his own thoughts. I didn't like it. Was he analyzing something I had said during the Inquisition, a slip-up on my part?

He glanced at his watch as we stopped for yet another red light. It was already 7:35. If the big powwow at school was on time, we were going to be late. Dad hated to be late for events. When the light changed to green, he made a quick right turn onto Mariposa Street. We continued in silence. After another traffic light, I saw the familiar dome of St. Christopher Cathedral, lit up in the night sky. In another minute, we arrived at my school, a rambling two-story brick structure situated across the street from the cathedral.

* * * * *

We hurried into the school auditorium to find people wandering around or chatting in the aisles. Only half of the parents were seated. The meeting was clearly late getting going.

Allie was the first to greet us. She was still wearing the red sweater and black skirt with the sheer stockings and black heels. My pulse quickened as she joined us at the back of the auditorium.

"Hi, Mr. Torrence. Hey, Buddy. We're about to get started," she said. "I'm glad you were able to make it. Mrs. Torrence couldn't come?"

"No. She tried, but no. And one other thing: Please call me Mac, okay?" They smiled at each other in a way that I immediately resented.

Allie took Dad's arm and gently tugged at it. "Can we talk for a minute, Mac? Please excuse us, Buddy." They walked a few steps, just out of earshot, and she began speaking softly to him. I stared at the two of them, feeling indignant about their sudden chumminess.

My attention eventually turned to the other people in the auditorium. There were 60 students in seventh grade at St. Christopher, and my quick headcount tallied about 70 parents in attendance. The women outnumbered the men, and they all looked somber.

Up front, Sister Mary Margaret was motioning to the parents to take their seats. She was flanked by Sister Rose Anne and Mrs. Johnson, St. Christopher Junior High's assistant principal and student counselor, respectively. I was surprised that none of our teachers were present. I also noticed that none of the priests from the cathedral were there. And there were no other kids in the auditorium, which I found especially disconcerting.

I wanted desperately to know what would be said about Daniel in this meeting and what might be said about his best friends. However, as Dad and Allie walked back to me, I also had a strong sensation that I didn't want to be there.

"Son," Dad said, "Allie has suggested that it might be better if you didn't stay here for the meeting."

Yes! I thought.

"She says there's six or seven other kids that came tonight, and they're all in the science lab with Sister Bridgette. You should join them there."

Heaven help me, please! Sister Bridgette taught health class and an occasional P.E. class for junior high girls. None of the girls could stand her. She was old and wrinkled like a dried prune. When she finally dies, they'll have to use carbon dating to determine her actual age. And I never saw her when she wasn't hunched over with a plastic ruler in her hand. Marty said she used the ruler to wrap the knuckles of girls who committed minor offenses in her class and on their naked bottoms after they showered from P.E., but he never finished the story. He had to rush off to find his notebook.

Another glance around the auditorium told me that I had no choice in the matter. Dad must have sensed my uneasiness, and he draped an arm around me. "You'll be just fine. In fact, I can't imagine you'd wanta sit here with us old fogies." He smiled and added, "I'll leave early if this thing starts dragging out, I promise. Now, you run on."

"Okay, but Dad?"

"Yes?"

"Is Marty there? Did he come tonight?"

Dad looked at Allie. "No, Buddy," she said. "Mrs. Shannon

PART ONE: 7:30 p.m.

told Sister Mary Margaret that they wanted to be alone tonight, just the two of them. She said they needed some quiet time."

"Yeah, I can understand," I said.

Allie gave me a sympathetic look and touched my shoulder. The contact was exhilarating, but before I could get all wound up, Dad motioned for me to go.

I turned and walked up the center aisle and through the huge double doors at the rear of the auditorium. Alone in the spacious lobby, my pace slowed as I began thinking about how gorgeous Allie had looked. I walked slowly through a side door into a long corridor. It wound through the administration offices and then past the nurse's station and band practice room. It felt creepy, being there alone so late at night. Although I tried to walk quietly, the sound of my loafers on the tile floor bounced off the walls and echoed ominously down the corridor. The heat was off for the night in this part of the school, and I blew warm air into my hands as I tried to stop thinking about *her* and focus on my predicament.

My anxiety increased with each step. There was no way I was going to be able to handle the next hour with old Sister Bridgette, especially not in the science lab. Thinking about the science lab resurrected a specific memory of Daniel that I couldn't face right then.

I stopped walking. *Why do I need to go to the science lab?* I thought. Sister Bridgette couldn't possibly know that I was there at school. She no doubt thought the parents' meeting had already started, and she'd commenced her torture of the unfortunate kids in her charge. I logically sized up the situation and convinced myself that I didn't have to be one of them.

I was contemplating going to the library or the gym when I had a second inspiration. If I could risk going to those deserted places, I could just as easily go backstage in the auditorium. I had noticed earlier that the stage curtains, long heavy drapes that reached to the floor, were closed. No one would be backstage, and I could hide in the wings behind those curtains and possibly hear what was being said in the meeting.

I walked rapidly, with purpose. Just past the ground floor

restrooms, I found the unmarked hallway door that led into a room where performers applied their makeup and stored their costumes and props. This makeup room was connected by a door at the other end to the back of the auditorium stage. I took a deep breath as I reached for the doorknob. It was unlocked. After a quick look up and down the deserted hallway, I opened the door and stepped inside.

Light from the hallway bathed the room while I took a quick mental survey. The rectangular room was about 50 feet in length. There were several racks of costumes against one wall and storage cabinets against the other. A narrow aisle ran down the center of the makeup room, separating two neat rows of desks. I focused intently on the door on the opposite side before I closed the hallway door behind me and stood in darkness.

* * * * *

Standing there waiting for my eyes to adjust, I was thankful that I was so familiar with the auditorium and backstage area. The previous month I had been asked to narrate St. Christopher Elementary School's annual Christmas pageant for first through fourth grade. The music director always enlisted a junior high student for this task, and it was a big honor since I was a newcomer to St. Christopher School. I spent hours rehearsing my lines in front of the mirror in my room until I had them down pat.

The little kids dressed up in costumes and each class got to sing one or two Christmas hymns after the narrator—me—set up the songs by reciting a passage of Scripture. I was constantly popping out from behind the curtain and walking to the microphone at center stage. I recited my lines and then walked off until the next song or scene. It was kind of cute with all the kids shuffling on and off stage and the high-pitched chirping of their little voices.

Some of the third and fourth graders got to portray Mary, Joseph, shepherds, angels, wise men, and other important characters in the Christmas story. A few of them had a line or two, but nothing too taxing. Some of the kids were animals in the stable. Daniel's little sister, Jackie, was a sheep.

PART ONE: 7:30 p.m.

Daniel and his parents had come to the pageant. He delivered Jackie and her sheep costume to the makeup room before the show. She was distraught because Daniel was putting her on about being the black sheep in the performance and how no one liked a black sheep. I'd never heard him mess with her like this. She was young and vulnerable, and she adored her brother. I gave him a disapproving glare, and Daniel quickly came to his senses.

"I didn't mean that, baby. I'm the only black sheep 'round here," he said. Then he knelt at her side. "I'm leavin' now, Jackie, but you gonna be just fine." He pointed at me. "Buddy there, he'll take care of you."

"Affirmative!" I said with a nod.

"Break a leg, bro!" Daniel shouted as he got up and walked out the door.

Jackie locked eyes with me. She was adorable. She gave me a gorgeous smile that seemed to say, *I'm glad you're here. I feel safe with you.* She blew me a kiss before scurrying backstage to join the other sheep.

The only hitch in my otherwise flawless performance that evening came about a third of the way into the pageant. It was dark in the auditorium to highlight the performers onstage. My mother had crept up and was kneeling at the foot of the elevated stage as I began reciting a long passage of Scripture, the one where the angels appear to the shepherds and tell them not to fear. I was really getting into it, speaking the lines with passion and conviction.

In my mother's hands were her camera and its five-thousand-megawatt flash attachment. She whispered, "Buddy," and I looked down in the middle of a line. At that instant, she clicked the camera and popped me with the powerful flash. I saw stars and went completely blank. I couldn't remember where I was, what came next.

Offstage, Sister Agnes, the pageant director, was desperately trying to feed me the lines, but I was in a total fog, furiously rubbing my eyes under my glasses and unable to concentrate. I heard the audience in front of me stirring uncomfortably and felt their eyes on me. So, I did what all the great thespians do when they can't recall their lines: I improvised.

I pray that St. Luke has a sense of humor because I absolutely murdered his beautiful verses, telling the little shepherds assembled on the stage in my most serious voice, "Don't you guys be afraid. I want you to go find this baby—swaddled in a stable and lying in a manger. When you see him, fall on your knees and shout, 'Good God, almighty!'" I had said the last three words with my best Billy Graham voice and thought it was a good place to stop.

Still squinting, I turned and took a wobbly step to commence my walk offstage, but then I remembered the last part. I reached backward, feeling with my right hand until it made loud contact with the microphone on its stand. I drew it toward me, leaned over, and added, "And on Earth, peace to men of good will." I nodded in the general direction of the pianist and began walking slowly with arms extended, feeling my way toward the blur of light from the left wing.

Sister Agnes was waiting there. She had pulled back the curtain slightly and reached out to me as the children launched into "Hark! The Herald Angels Sing." She guided me behind the curtain, holding me steady as she whispered, "That was most interesting, Buddy."

Then we both cracked up. Sister hugged me while trying to stifle her laughter, and I continued to rub my eyes while laughing with her. It had all happened so fast that I didn't have a chance to get embarrassed. The song was a long one, and I had plenty of time to regain my composure and eyesight for the rest of the pageant.

Unfortunately, my mother didn't witness that remarkable recovery. She had fled from the auditorium as soon as she realized what she'd done. She spent the next 30 minutes in the cold back seat of the station wagon, too embarrassed and distraught to return. Dad eventually joined her, so he missed the last half of the show as well.

On the drive home, I sat in front with Dad. Mom said that she preferred to stay alone in the back. Between sniffles, she apologized profusely to me. I kept telling her it was okay, but she kept chanting how she should have known; she should have known. How she ruined the show; she ruined the show.

Finally, I couldn't stand it anymore. I turned to look at her and said, "Mom, stop it! It's not that big a deal. I did fine, so quit going on about it." After a second, I added, "Please, ma'am."

She was silent with her head bowed, avoiding my eyes. I turned my head and looked at my father. We were stopped at a red light. I thought he would chastise me for speaking that way to Mom, but he just stared at me like he couldn't figure out what to do next.

And then, simultaneously, Dad and I smiled at each other, and we both began a gulping kind of laughter, the kind where you're trying not to laugh, but it just sneaks out in little gulps. It was infectious like when you see someone yawn and it makes you yawn. Looking at my father and hearing his little gulps made it impossible for me to stop and vice versa. I covered my mouth, but it was hopeless. At first, Mom got upset and told us to stop. But we couldn't. Pretty soon, she started gulp-laughing too. When Dad shouted in his deep voice, "*Good God, almighty!*" all three of us died laughing.

When we got home, Mom fixed hot chocolate with tons of little marshmallows. We sipped our drinks while sitting around the Christmas tree, and we all laughed as my father entertained us with confessions about embarrassing things that had happened to him at various times in his life. When I finally had to go to bed, Mom apologized again but this time with a big smile. I don't think she ever got that picture developed.

✳ ✳ ✳ ✳ ✳

In the days immediately following Daniel's death, I was haunted by his words to his little sister the night of the pageant: "I'm leavin' now, Jackie . . . but Buddy, he'll take care of you." I wanted to comply with his request—to seek her out, to try to comfort her like a big brother. But I was a coward. I couldn't bear to face her, knowing how she loved her brother and how I'd failed him.

I stared numbly at the back of her head throughout Daniel's funeral service. She sat motionless between her parents. They held her tightly like they were afraid that she too would slip away forever if they lost physical contact with her. It was the last time I ever saw her.

* * * * *

I walked through the makeup room without bumping into any obstacles and moved quietly through the unlocked door on the opposite side. I was backstage. I continued up the left wing—the side "stage left" for the performers, but to the right for the onlooking audience. I stopped when I reached the spot where Sister Agnes and I had embraced and laughed at my *faux pas*. There where the heavy stage curtain ended was a long, narrow gap between it and the wall. I pulled back the curtain just slightly and peered out. I had a clear view cutting across the backs of the two nuns, Mrs. Johnson, and Allie as they faced the parents. They were seated on fold-out chairs on the auditorium floor, the same place my mother had squatted when she looked up to take my picture, about three feet below the elevated stage.

M Squared rose, microphone in hand, to begin the meeting. She stepped forward and stopped in front of the wide center aisle that separated the auditorium's navy blue chairs into two sections. I could see her back as long as she didn't wander too far to her left as she spoke.

I also could see the parents who were sitting in the first dozen or so rows on the opposite half of the auditorium. They were focused on M Squared. From my experience with the Christmas pageant, I was confident that they couldn't see me in the backstage darkness, even if their gaze shifted to my direction. I slowly settled onto the wooden floor.

Scanning the faces, I found my father. He was in the fourth row by the outside aisle, sitting next to a man and woman I didn't know. I would be able to watch all the action and still have plenty of advance warning if he got up early to leave. I congratulated myself on my cleverness.

PART ONE: 7:30 p.m.

M Squared made some introductory remarks. Her tone was somber. She then introduced Sister Rose Anne and Mrs. Johnson as well as Allie Masterson, doting on Allie's credentials as a child psychologist. I could hear it all thanks to the microphone and the auditorium's fine sound system.

"We want you parents to know everything that we know," she said. "I will explain as candidly as I can all the facts that we have at this time. Then I will turn the discussion over to Miss Masterson. She will cover the topic that I know is your most immediate concern—what to say to your children and how to help them deal with their confusion and grief over this tragedy."

She paused and bowed her head. When she began again, her voice quivered. The words were difficult for her, and they came in halting phrases. "Our seventh-grade student, Daniel Carter, is dead. It is my understanding that, ah, the police report will conclude that his, ah, his death was a suicide." With that last word, she lost it.

"Oh, I'm so sorry," she managed through a full-fledged sob. "I thought I could do this and not get emotional." Sister Rose Anne jumped from her seat and embraced M Squared, followed by Mrs. Johnson, one on each side. After a few seconds, M Squared nudged them away. As they returned to their chairs, she raised the microphone back to her mouth.

"I'm sorry, but all my ministry has been in education, and I've never had to deal with anything like this. Please excuse me. If you don't mind, I think I'll do better if I can just read from the notes that I made in preparation for this meeting."

As she picked up several note cards from her chair and began arranging them, I studied the parents in the audience. My father was leaning forward in his chair, his fingers laced under his chin. His antenna was up.

Sister looked at the cards in her left hand while her right held the microphone to her mouth. "Daniel's parents discovered him at home after school last Friday. It was shortly after the incident. They rushed him to a hospital, where he died on Saturday. As I mentioned, the investigating police officer has concluded that this was not an accident. It was a suicide." She looked up and then turned to the next card.

"I was first notified by a relative of the family on Saturday morning. Father Bernard and I rushed to the hospital and got there just prior to Daniel's passing." She looked up at her audience and said, "We prayed together with the family. As you can imagine, the shock and pain they are experiencing, I can't put it into words."

She took a deep breath and exhaled slowly into the microphone as she returned to her notes. "There was no suicide note, and it's unclear to any of us—his parents, your school faculty and administration, his friends, and the mental health experts we've called in to help us—what specifically drove him to commit this tragic act. However, I can provide some details about Daniel to hopefully help you to better understand him.

"Daniel Carter began attending St. Christopher School in the fall of 1963, in our sixth-grade program. Daniel and his sister, along with five other Negro children, joined our school family at that time as part of our commitment to make St. Christopher School available to all of God's children, regardless of color or religion. Daniel proved to be a brilliant student here. He achieved highest honors in each of his four quarters in sixth grade. On the National Education Development Tests we administer annually, he scored in the 99th percentile in almost every subject. His raw intelligence, his IQ, it was nothing short of extraordinary.

"I wasn't here at the time, but I am told, on the social side, Daniel struggled to make friends and faced prejudice from certain classmates. Most of you are aware of the unfortunate incident last year where three boys ganged up on Daniel and harassed and beat him. He didn't sustain serious injuries, thankfully, as another student intervened on his behalf."

* * * * *

I had heard this story about a thousand times from Marty and Daniel. Three guys in sixth grade with them—real punks—cornered Daniel when he hung around too long after school and forced him into the bathroom. They called him names and pushed him onto the floor. One of them held him down while the other two punched at him and kicked his ribs. Marty, who happened to be passing by on his way to an after-school detention, heard the commotion and cries for help coming from inside the bathroom.

Marty said he didn't know Daniel very well back then, but he sure disliked those other boys and their prissy little clique, especially Tommy Wells. Marty would always add in his typical braggadocio that he had been looking for a good reason to kick their butts. When he walked in, his loathing for them plus his instinct to help the underdog took over and he went wild.

Marty loved to tell this part. He would describe in infinite detail how he was carrying his science book and his three-ring binder when he entered the bathroom. He caught Tommy by surprise, slamming the big book and binder into his face with all his might. The force broke Tommy's nose, and blood started flying everywhere. At the sight of so much blood, Mitchell Walker made a run for it, but Marty tripped him and he went down hard on the tile floor. As Mitchell crawled on his hands and knees toward the door, Marty repeatedly kicked him in the ass as hard as he could, right out the door. That left Bobby Mosley, who was cowering in a corner. Marty said that he got in a few good licks with his fists before Bobby was able to hightail it by him and make it out of the bathroom.

The three-on-one gang, as they came to be known—Tommy, Mitchell, and Bobby—were each suspended for three days. Mitchell was absent for five days. Marty claimed it was because his tailbone was bruised so badly from the ass-kicking that he couldn't sit for a whole week. Sister Martha, the elementary-school principal, told Marty that he should not have fought with those boys, that he should have run to find one of the nuns or another adult to break up the beating that Daniel was receiving. For his part in the fight, she gave Marty a one-day suspension.

But Mrs. Shannon called big-time bullshit on that. She showed up at school the next morning with fire in her eyes and the Carters at her side. Daniel said his father threatened to sue the school for not providing a safe environment for children and for allowing Daniel's civil rights to be violated. He told Sister Martha that Daniel might have been beaten to death if Marty hadn't intervened. They both said that Marty deserved a medal, not a suspension. By the time they were finished, the school was ready to give him one to avoid their wrath. Marty's suspension was revoked.

Daniel missed one day of school nursing his wounds, and Marty said he looked pathetic when he returned. His face was puffy, one eye would only open partway, and he had to wear thick bandages under his shirt to protect his bruised ribs. If you asked Daniel, however, he'd say that the beating was worth it. He became a martyr in the eyes of his classmates, an innocent victim of egregious foul play and bigotry, and they started going out of their way to be nice to him. Marty and Daniel started hanging out together and soon became best friends. The three-on-one gang, who were ostracized from the rest of the student body after their gutless actions, never bothered Daniel again.

Marty no doubt basked in his heroic glory for months. He said the incident made him even more popular with the girls. I wasn't there, but I had my doubts about that part as well as some of the other details that always got embellished a bit more each time Marty and Daniel retold the story. But that didn't matter. It was an exciting, real-life story of good triumphing over evil that made me feel secure and righteous about my friends.

Chapter 18

8:00 p.m.

M Squared continued to read from her notes. "Daniel's grades for the first quarter of seventh grade were excellent—straight A's—and he earned highest honors, as we all expected. However, beginning in late November, his grades became notably lower. They were still good by our high standards—above 80 percent. But they were not the grades of 95 to 100 percent that we had come to expect from Daniel Carter.

"In early December, I asked Mrs. Carter to my office, so we could review an English report of Daniel's. Several of you called me today when you heard about this project and Daniel's particular report from your children, so I want to comment on it, just briefly. It had to do with selecting a topic—any topic—and finding poems and illustrations on the topic as well as writing an essay relating the student's personal feelings or experiences to the poems. Daniel chose 'Death' as his topic."

I heard the murmur of parents in the audience whispering to one another. M Squared looked up momentarily but then went back to her note cards.

"His essay was disturbing to us and to his mother, who read it for the first time in my office. For confidentiality purposes and out of respect for the Carter family, I won't go any further into the specifics of what Daniel wrote or the follow-up actions taken by the Carters. Suffice it to say that the school dealt with this matter swiftly—and confidentially—with a parent."

I shifted my position on the hard stage floor to relieve the pressure and soreness that was creeping into my legs and backside as M Squared continued.

"The quality of Daniel's schoolwork did not improve during December. In addition, he wasn't eating much at lunch and seemed to be losing weight. His attention in class and participation in classroom discussions decreased. As you know at St. Christopher Junior High, we require students to get a parent to review and sign all major tests after they are graded and returned to the student. This is an excellent policy, and it keeps you parents up to date on how your children are performing academically. We now know that Daniel forged his mother's signature on the four major tests that were sent home during December. His teachers didn't recognize the forgeries, as they were good likenesses. We therefore thought that his parents were aware of his declining grades."

Another collective buzz went through the parents in the auditorium. Like them, I thought about how things might have turned out differently if just one of his teachers, concerned by these disturbing changes in Daniel, had reached out to his parents. Were our teachers sitting at home right now with the same guilt-ridden thoughts as me?

M Squared lowered the hand holding her notes, apparently finished with her prepared remarks, and added, "I don't know why Daniel's parents didn't notice an absence of tests to be reviewed and signed by them. But it doesn't matter because our objective tonight is not to second-guess, try to find blame, or make excuses for anything. Daniel Carter is dead, and all of us are in a state of shock, including your children."

I shifted my weight again as she exhaled softly before continuing. "I don't know what else to say. I feel so devastated, so infinitely sad. I know it's not productive to try to find fault with ourselves, but I have to tell you, one minute I feel like asking for God's forgiveness for my lack of attention and the next I want him to punish me for being so blind."

She stood silently in front of them for an uncomfortably long time until Allie got up from her chair and wrapped an arm around her shoulders. Allie took the microphone from M Squared's hand and spoke softly into it. "Sister, your response just now is completely normal. You are experiencing sorrow and remorse because you are in mourning." Allie released M Squared, and the little nun took her seat as Allie stepped forward to address her audience.

"Your children are also in mourning. And they're confused. Feelings of grief, anger, and confusion are all normal reactions to a tragic event like this, whether you are 12 years old or a full-grown adult. We wouldn't be human without them. It's also okay and even productive to express our feelings and our confusion, to lay bare our sorrow and regrets like Sister Mary Margaret did just now.

"When you return home tonight, talk to your children. Find a quiet place with no TV or radio. Look at your son or daughter, and ask with as much sincerity as you can possibly put into it, 'How are you feeling?' Try to get them to open up, and I can't stress this enough—be a good listener for them. Don't interrupt and don't try to speak for them. Don't offer, 'I bet you're feeling this or thinking that.' Let them say it in their words and just listen to them. Listen closely. The more they talk, the better. Don't let them say, 'Fine' or 'I'm okay' and just stop there. Get them to talk about how they *really* feel.

"I'm going to tell you something that you already know." She paused to let their anticipation build. "You have some remarkable children. My colleague, Dr. Gibson, and I spent all day today with them, and I can't begin to express how impressed we are. Your children are amazing—so intelligent and articulate. And because they're smart, caring, and naturally curious, your children want answers—some that we have and some that we may not have. Be honest with them. Explain how life is filled with disappointments and tragedies. Give them some personal examples you may have had with the death of a loved one or with people you know who've taken their own lives. You know, suicide is, unfortunately, more common than you may suspect, particularly among our young people."

Allie turned and walked to her chair. It was good to see her face again. She removed some papers from the clipboard she'd left in the chair, careful not to clang the microphone in the process, then turned to face her audience again.

"Every year in this country, about 2,000 teenagers take their own lives." She looked up from her notes and added, "Let me repeat that another way, so you can appreciate the enormity of this statistic: Every five hours, an American teenager takes his or her own life."

Allie paused for a few seconds so they could comprehend that Daniel's action was not an isolated incident. According to my quick calculation, another 15 kids had died by their own hand since Daniel Carter put that gun to his head on Friday.

"That's an amazing and tragic statistic," Allie said, "and it ignores many *hidden* suicides that are not reported as such due to shame or fear. I believe that the alarming number of teenage suicides is a by-product of the turbulent and fast-paced 1960s that we live in and the enormous pressures that we place on our young people today in the United States.

"Here's another statistic for you: For every adolescent who kills himself, there are around 200 others who attempt suicide in some form or another, from superficial to very serious attempts. Most of the unsuccessful attempts are by females. That's because most male suicides occur with guns, whereas most females use pills or other drugs.

"I can tell you that suicide is rare for someone as young as Daniel Carter, but certainly not unprecedented. Many of you came here tonight looking for answers, for information on what specifically drove him to take his own life, for reassurance that it couldn't happen again. You want some form of closure. Well, you're going to leave here disappointed in that regard. Daniel was a complex young man who kept most of his feelings to himself. As Sister Mary Margaret told you, we have not been able to determine exactly what pushed him to this desperate act."

Looks of concern had crept into the faces of the parents I could see. What was going through their minds was obvious: If this could happen without warning to Daniel Carter, an intelligent kid with a loving family, could it conceivably happen—sometime, somewhere down the road—to their 12- or

13-year-old son or daughter? I suspected that they'd never contemplated a question like that, and it rocked them to their core.

Allie continued, "I don't believe it would be productive for us to spend time in this meeting or with your children speculating on the things that may have made Daniel so unhappy, so despondent. However, I would like to spend a couple of minutes discussing, in a very broad sense, the principal reasons why adolescents attempt suicide. I'll begin with a sobering statistic in that regard: About 90 percent of suicidal adolescents feel misunderstood by their parents and believe that they cannot effectively communicate with their parents." She paused and then repeated the point to let its impact sink in.

"Adolescence is filled with conflict between feeling a need for continued parental security and guidance and a natural desire to begin pulling away. The most important thing that you can do as parents is to remain actively involved in your children's lives and always maintain open lines of communication. That way, you'll know when something serious is bothering them, and they won't be afraid or embarrassed to talk with you about it."

Judging from the faces in the crowd, communication with their kids sucked and they knew it. One couple was holding hands and staring at each other like they wanted to get up and run home to check on Junior. One mother had covered her mouth with one hand as she wiped tears from her eyes with the other. I imagined that she was reflecting on a recent confrontation where her seventh grader had said, "You won't listen," or "I can't talk to you."

Back in September, for Miss Barton's seventh-grade English class, we had to interview someone in our family and write a paper about them. Or we could write about one of our ancestors that a parent or other family member told us about. The assignment was supposed to teach basic interviewing skills, along with writing concisely to weed out the long-winded bullshit that you were sure to get when you asked people to talk about themselves or someone in their family. It taught me that I didn't want to be around my father when he was drinking.

Dad generally had one or two drinks each night, which he sipped leisurely while we passed the evening hours watching television. About once a month, however, he'd go out with the men from work or he'd get with Uncle Johnny or sometimes just sit at home in front of the TV, and he'd drink more than one or two, lots more. I couldn't understand what compelled him to do that, not any more than I understood why Mom smoked cigarettes and daydreamed in the back yard. Maybe it was just his way of breaking up the boredom and monotony that consumed our everyday lives. But it wasn't pretty, not from my perspective.

Uncle Johnny was over on the evening I had to write this biographical paper. He had supper with us and then, after Mom left for her second job, he and Dad settled into the family room to drink cocktails and watch television. I had gone to my room to do homework. After finishing my other assignments, I decided to write about Grandpa Torrence. Feeling like a regular Ernie Pyle with my notebook and ballpoint pen in hand, I walked into the family room.

"Dad," I said, "I've got a favor to ask."

"Your command is my wish," he said. Uncle Johnny made a barking sound that I assumed was supposed to be a laugh.

"I'd like to call Grandpa."

"Call 'im what?" my father slurred. Uncle Johnny barked again.

"No, call him on the telephone."

"Well, just don't call him on the carpet. He hates that." Now they both broke into barking laughter.

"Dad, this is serious. I have an English project. I need to call Grandpa for this project."

He wrinkled his forehead and eyeballed me. I hated this. I couldn't tell if he was finally getting serious or still screwing with me. Dad wasn't mean or abusive when he drank, just weird and uncomfortable to be around. Sometimes he'd get silly and make stupid jokes. Sometimes he'd try to wrestle and horse around with me or get all lovey-dovey with Mom. Sometimes he'd get on a soapbox and wouldn't shut up about some meaningless issue, even if Mom and I complained that we didn't care and couldn't hear the television.

"Calling Dallas, that's long distance. It costs money. Why do you need to talk to Grandpa?" he asked.

"Don't you think he'd like to hear the sound of my voice?" I shot back at him.

"Don't get smart with me, young man!"

Great, I thought, *talk about double standards.* I was tempted to scrap the whole interview and make up some stuff about Mom's brother battling kamikazes and being eaten by sharks when Dad said sternly, "I asked you a question."

"I need to talk to him for a paper I have to do. We're supposed to interview someone in our family and then write about them. Miss Barton wants a two-page essay. I thought Grandpa would be a good subject, you know, growing up in Scotland, coming to America, traveling all over. It's perfect. But I need to ask him some questions and get some details."

Dad's eyes lit up. "Have I got a terrific idea for you!" He rose from the recliner as he spoke. "There's no need to waste precious funds on a long-distance phone call when you have in this very room one of the most fascinating personalities in the entire galaxy." He took a sidestep so he stood over Uncle Johnny, who looked up with glazed eyes from his seat on the sofa. "Drum roll, please," Dad said.

Uncle Johnny leaned over on queue to tap rapidly on the coffee table with his two index fingers.

"John Gallagher, 'This Is Your Life!'" They both applauded enthusiastically like some idiot studio audience.

Dad whispered something to Uncle Johnny. The only part I heard was *Queen for a Day*, an obvious reference to another TV show, which caused them both to double over with gut-splitting laughter.

I tried to protest, but Dad wouldn't listen. I wished that Mom was there, but she wasn't due home for an hour. I couldn't wait that long, so I tried another tactic. I said something about Uncle Johnny not being my real family, but that pissed Dad off. Not wanting to provoke him any further, I decided to play along. What the hell? Maybe this would work.

Dad turned off the TV and went into the dining room for a chair. He placed it across from Uncle Johnny, where he would have an excellent view of the entertainment from his recliner, and I sat down.

When they were both situated, I began. "Okay, we'll start at the beginning. Tell me something about your birth."

"Ah, yes," he said. He took a swig from his drink and then continued. "Well, Buddy, I'll speak slowly so you can get all this down."

"Thanks," I said, positioned like an ace reporter with my pen poised over a blank page in the notebook.

"If you must know, I was born at a very early age."

I wrote it down and then looked up for more.

"And I've never been older than I am now," he said. "Right now!"

I lowered my head to write it down but not before I saw Uncle Johnny glance sheepishly at my father. When I looked up, Dad was covering his mouth with his hand, the one that wasn't holding a drink, trying to stifle his laughter. I gave him a *This isn't funny!* stare.

"Okay, now get this, Buddy—seriously," Uncle Johnny said. "Buddy, look at me."

So, I turned my scowl toward him.

He just smiled and said, "C'mon!"

I lifted my pen and assumed the position.

"I was born in Mississippi," he said.

"What town in Mississippi?"

"Shagnasty," he replied. "Shagnasty, Mississippi. That's S-h-a-g-n-a-s-t-y." As I wrote, I heard a giggle escape from behind my father's hand. Uncle Johnny ignored him and continued speaking. "I was very naughty as a kid, drove my parents crazy."

"Really?" I asked.

"Oh yeah," he said, "and when I was five, my parents moved to Biloxi."

"How do you spell that?"

"B-i-l-o-x-i," he spelled out. "Then, when I was six, I found them."

I stopped writing. "Found who?" I asked.

"My parents. Get it?" The two of them howled. They gulped at their drinks and then laughed some more when they saw the frustration in my face.

"Okay," Uncle Johnny said, "now write this down, Buddy. C'mon, I'm serious now."

I assumed the position again.

"Like I said, I was a bad kid. I had a tough childhood, always getting in trouble with the law."

"Really? I didn't know that," I said.

"Oh, yeah. When I was 12—your age—I ran away with the circus."

Now we're getting somewhere, I thought. *This part might be interesting.*

"Yeah," he said, "but they made me give it back—the circus. Get it?"

That made them both convulse with laughter and reach for support to keep from falling over. My father spilled his drink and cursed. "See what you made me do," he said to Uncle Johnny as he jumped up. "You ready for another?"

"Sure."

As Dad headed for the kitchen, I got up from my dunce chair and stormed back to my bedroom. I threw the notebook against the wall and bit my lower lip. I could hear their laughter through my closed door and the taunts they shouted from the family room.

"Oh, c'mon, Buddy!"

"We didn't mean nothin' by it!"

"We was just clownin' 'round!"

"Come talk to us! C'mon back!"

The next morning, my father apologized for tooling me around with Uncle Johnny. He was very contrite for about ten seconds, and that apology was his way of settling the ledgers, like it righted the wrong he had done and put his relationship back in balance and harmony with me.

I told him it was okay. But it wasn't. I wanted to say, "I hate you for doing that to me," or "You don't know anything about me," or "I can't talk to you." But I couldn't. That would have been disrespectful. It would have broken one of his rules.

At school, I asked Daniel which family member he had chosen for his essay.

"My sister," he said.

"What?"

"Yeah, she's the gravy, man."

"I know," I said, "but she's only eight years old. Why didn't you get your dad to tell you about his grandfather, the one who became a famous preacher and stood up to the Klan? That would've been cool."

Daniel shrugged his shoulders. "I thought about it, but I just couldn't talk to him—my old man. Not about personal stuff like that. Besides, he probably woulda used it as a *teaching opportunity*, ya know what I mean?" Daniel shifted to a low-pitched, lecturing voice mimicking his father saying, "You must get stronger in mind and body, boy, like Grandpappy was. Stop daydreaming and start reading the Bible. Exercise and build up those puny muscles. Now get down and gimme 20." He laughed.

"Yeah, I get it," I said. "But how could you write about an eight-year-old?"

"Read it and see."

I know it sounds corny, but as I read his essay, I thought I might cry. It was that beautiful: Daniel recalling going to the hospital to meet his baby sister for the first time and how tiny, how helpless, and how lovely she looked; her explaining how they walked hand in hand to school on her first day and how confident she felt with him at her side; describing games they played and how, no matter how angry or unhappy she got, Daniel could always make her laugh. It wasn't just from one perspective but from both of their views, cleverly intertwined. Daniel got an A+. My report on Patrick O'Conner growing up in Hawaii, going down with his ship, and being eaten by sharks got a B–, and Miss Barton scribbled a big red question mark at the end. I didn't have to ask what it meant.

PART ONE: 8:00 p.m.

* * * * *

"The reasons for adolescent suicide generally fall into three broad categories," Allie said, "but they each have to do with a lack of communication. First, threatening or attempting suicide is seen as a means of gaining love, affection, or sympathy from someone who is denying it or as a way to punish that person by inflicting pain and guilt on them. The target is often a parent or an ex-boyfriend or ex-girlfriend. As parents, don't be afraid to openly show affection and say, 'I love you' to your child. Be especially attentive when your son or daughter is going steady—as they call it in junior high and high school—and be sympathetic if they break up with their steady. Or if the steady breaks up with them. As parents, you may be uncomfortable with these relationships, but these are emotionally vulnerable times for your children. Please don't demean them or brush them off as puppy love.

"Second, a suicide attempt is often a desperate cry for help. Children are generally inexperienced and poorly prepared to deal with a multitude of problems all at once. They get confusing messages from rebellious rock-and-roll music and the alarming number of bedroom scenes that are creeping into popular motion pictures. Being a preteen or early teen in the mid-1960s is very different from past eras. It's much more pressure packed. When the weight of the world gets to be too much, these kids are no different from you or me. They need a helpful ear to listen to their problems and perhaps even a shoulder to cry on. But too often, adults, including parents, are too busy or not available, too judgmental, or just poor listeners. Sometimes, kids feel that it will take a desperate act to get our attention, to get us to see how heavy their burdens seem—*to them*. Most suicide attempts in this category are halfhearted, but sometimes they unfortunately succeed.

"Finally, and this is the one that is the most dangerous, suicide becomes the adolescent's only way—in their mind—to relieve the pain and pressure of an otherwise unbearable situation. Someone, I believe it was a military officer, once said that there is a tremendous sense of freedom that comes when one realizes that he is in a totally hopeless situation. Just like adults, children can get into what they perceive to be a hopeless situation with no one to help them and no way out—except one.

"It's also important to understand that suicide is rarely an impulsive act," Allie continued, "irrespective of what we may see portrayed in the movies for dramatic effect. Suicide victims generally contemplate their death over an extended period, often with a great deal of forethought and preparation.

"There's usually a defining event that occurs, a *That's it, I'm done* moment in time when the conclusion is reached to go through with the planned act. This deciding moment generally occurs after less drastic options for solving one's problems consistently fail. With Daniel Carter, however, we don't know what event specifically committed him last week to this fatal decision. As I said, we probably never will."

I lowered my head and thought, *Yeah, unless I tell you.*

"I want to discuss one more topic: the warning signs that we psychologists look for that may indicate that adolescents are potentially suicidal. Then I want to open the meeting for your questions."

I scanned the audience as Allie paused. Like me, they had been listening attentively, often appearing surprised and disturbed by her revelations and statistics. Suicide was ugly, uncharted ground. I anticipated that there would be lots of questions.

Allie looked at the paper she was holding and read the list. "These warning signs include: changes in eating and sleeping habits; recurring headaches, stomachaches, or fatigue; neglected personal hygiene; mood swings; isolation and withdrawal; inability to concentrate for extended periods; decline in the quality of schoolwork; loss of interest in previous activities, sports, or hobbies; recurring death fixation in written or verbal communications; reckless behavior; giving away possessions or setting affairs in order; and saying goodbyes to friends and family."

She looked up. Everyone was thinking the same thing, so

Allie said it. "Daniel Carter displayed an inordinate number of these signs over the last several weeks of his life."

No shit, I thought.

"With hindsight, it's now apparent that Daniel was a very unhappy young man and may have been suffering from a form of mental illness broadly referred to as 'depression.' I can't tell you exactly why he may have been depressed. I do know that depression is difficult to recognize and diagnose in adolescents, even for professionals. That's because developing young teens and preteens tend to be moodier than adults. We come to expect them to go through a new and different personal crisis each month. Radical mood swings in young people, like those exhibited by Daniel Carter, may actually be manic-depressive incidents. One week they're happy and the next they're extremely sad. We tend to remember the happy and shrug off the sad as merely having a bad day or going through a stage. Or we blame it on hormones.

"Also, let's not forget that Daniel was extraordinarily intelligent and manipulative for his age. If he wanted his parents, teachers, or classmates to see him in a certain light, I'm sure that he could have put up the appropriate façade for a short period of time.

"And so, in conclusion, please try not to be critical of your faculty and administrative staff at this fine school for not recognizing the warning signs and not taking steps beyond what has been described to you tonight. When a tragedy occurs, we need to pull together as a community. We need to support and encourage one another and show all the love we have for our children. I hope that's what's going through your minds right now."

Allie nodded at her audience. "Thank you for your attention, and I apologize for rambling on for so long. My daddy would say that's the price you pay for giving the microphone to a woman. But I hope this has been helpful." She motioned at the three ladies seated behind her. "Sister Mary Margaret and the others here, we'll all be pleased to respond to your questions and concerns now, as best we can."

Allie turned and placed the papers back on the clipboard on her chair. There was brief, polite applause from the parents. I stared at her, completely spellbound. Not only was she a physical goddess, but she also was caring, compassionate, and had to be the most intelligent and articulate woman on the planet. She was perfect in every way, and I knew at that moment that I was hopelessly in love with her, that I would be in love with her for the rest of my life.

Chapter 19

8:20 p.m.

Sister Mary Margaret and Allie fielded a barrage of questions for the next 40 minutes. Many were more like rambling speculations and opinions instead of real questions. These soliloquies made me want to puke. They were self-serving blather.

Hardly any of the parents there actually knew Daniel or anything about him. Those who acknowledged that fact acted like it gave them a license to talk about him in a dispassionate, clinical manner like he was a piece of meat. That royally pissed me off.

On the opposite end of the spectrum, others talked like they knew what his most intimate thoughts must have been. They said they knew these things because their particular child was *sooo* close to Daniel. They talked about how upset their precious little children were and tried to explain the emotions that "Daniel's little friends" were feeling. That really got me mad. How in Hell, a place that I was becoming intimately familiar with, could they possibly know what his *real* friends were feeling? They were idiots, hypocrites, and liars. They didn't know shit! I wanted to tell them all to shut up, to let him lie in peace, and to quit torturing me.

Allie's warning signs had me concerned. I wasn't feeling good. I hadn't eaten much at supper and had no appetite. My mouth was as dry as the Sahara Desert, yet my body felt clammy. My head and stomach had started hurting. Maybe I was suffering from depression. I felt isolated. I couldn't concentrate. Yes, I was certain that it was deep, dark depression. I recalled lying in my room that morning when I had daydreamed about killing myself, particularly if all the facts concerning Daniel's death came to light. Maybe I was suicidal. I wished that I had a copy of Allie's list in order to check.

I wanted to get up, walk around, clear my mind. But I was concerned about tripping over something if I started wandering about in the darkness, and I dared not let Dad out of my sight. He had said we might leave early. I had to be ready to move quickly—straight back to the makeup room door—when he got up to leave the auditorium. So, I remained squatted on the floor.

The questions were getting worse. People started bringing up race as a possible factor. There were no black parents in the audience, as Daniel was the only Negro in seventh grade, and several in the all-white crowd felt emboldened to ask questions that might, under different circumstances, seem offensive. A woman asked if blacks were more prone to suicide than whites, implying by the way she phrased it that they had less to live for, so suicide must be a common answer, right? She seemed disappointed when Allie shot down her hypothesis. Allie told her in a curt, but professional manner, that she couldn't quote from any specific research in that regard, but she was highly confident that was not the case.

Another lady asked if the school would now scrap its poorly conceived integration plan.

"I wouldn't think so," M Squared said. "None of the other black students at St. Christopher have exhibited behavioral problems or instability. In fact, they have as a group adapted very well here. Daniel himself was a model student until recently. Our school board has been completely committed to a racially integrated school, and I would be surprised if they considered reversing that decision when there's nothing to suggest that Daniel's suicide was driven by racial issues."

That opened Pandora's box. A man shouted, "But you said ya don't know why he did it! How can y'all be sure that ya aren't puttin' other children at risk by unnaturally mixin' blacks and whites like this?"

M Squared defended the school's policy as best she could

and continued to classify Daniel's tragedy as an isolated event. But there were more questions and comments along this line. The more vocal parents clearly had not been happy that a parochial school had voluntarily integrated while most public-school systems in Texas were resisting integration or were making only token efforts.

A few eyebrows were raised when Allie grew frustrated by their ignorance and prejudice. "Look," she said, "being a black student in a predominately white school no doubt added to the pressure on Daniel Carter, but racial differences alone aren't going to push the children at St. Christopher, a fine private school, toward suicide. Especially your *white* children. There are too many other options."

Thankfully, a lady changed the subject before the discussion turned uglier. She asked, "If Daniel was so depressed like you say, then why didn't he tell someone—his parents, a favorite teacher, or better yet, his best friends? Why was this such a surprise?"

I looked at my feet and pondered the question.

* * * * *

On a Sunday afternoon in mid-November, four weeks before the zombie of North Street incident, Daniel came over to my house. It was the first time I could recall him acting differently.

We were sitting on the floor in my bedroom waiting for Marty to arrive so we could play three-handed Hearts. I had the cards in my hands, shuffling them to pass the time.

"Who do you say I am?" Daniel asked in a deep tone that cut the silence in the room.

I let out a snicker. "Who do you want to be?"

"No, that's not the question. Who do *you* say I am?" he asked.

"Why do you ask?"

"You can't answer a question with a question, Answer Man. It's irritating."

"I can if I need more info," I said.

"Okay, well, the lesson this morning in Sunday School was 'bout Jesus askin' that question to his disciples and—"

"So, you're Jesus?" I interjected.

"No, dummy. Just listen, okay?"

"Okay."

"Jesus wanted to know if his followers—his friends—knew who he was, if they *really* knew him."

"And what did they say?" I asked.

"Peter answered for 'em. He said he thought Jesus was the Messiah, sent from God."

I cocked my head to one side. "And?" I said, drawing out the word.

"And I wanta know, Buddy Torrence, who do you say I am—me?"

"Well, you ain't Jesus!" I laughed and gave him a big grin, but his silence and expressionless face told me he was waiting for a serious response. This was getting uncomfortable.

"Okay," I said, "you're Daniel Carter. There!"

"C'mon, you can do better than that. Ain't you supposed to be smart? *Think about it*, okay? Who do you say I am?" He folded his arms over his chest, waiting for my reply.

I put down the cards, took off my glasses, and rubbed my eyes, stalling for a little time. This was a different Daniel. I put away smart-ass Buddy and tried to think.

"Okay," I said, returning my glasses on my nose, "you're intelligent, you're funny, you're—"

"Them's things, just traits. Who do you say I am?" he asked for the hundredth time.

"Okay, let me think. Well, you're a human being. You're a guy, you know, like me."

"If I'm like you, then tell me who I am."

Daniel was generally three steps ahead, and he was clearly looking for a specific answer that I was failing to deliver. So, I took a chance. At the risk of sounding girlie, I decided to tell him the truth, straight out.

"Okay," I said, then cleared my throat and found my most serious and sincere voice. "You're Daniel Carter, my best friend, the best friend I've ever had. Well, you and Marty are, but it's not the same with Marty. You're unique. You're not like anyone

I've ever known, but in some ways I think you're a lot like me. You're—"

"How am I like you?" he interrupted.

"Well, we're both 12 years old and—"

"And you be thinkin' small—like a 12-year-old. Am I white like you?" he asked.

Where is this going? I thought. His face gave away nothing. His dark eyes stared at me with an intensity that I'd never seen before.

"No," I said, "but that's not—"

"Do the teachers like me, the way they all like you? Do those jerks at school like me? If you didn't sit with me at lunch, would anyone wanta sit with me?"

"Now, I don't know if—"

"I'm not white. I'm black. But do I have any black friends? Do any of the kids in my neighborhood like me? Or do they just make fun of me? Like, *all the time*—for how I act, how I talk." He leaned in. "And do my parents like me? I mean, yeah, they gimme food and clothes and pat me on the back like a good doggie if I bring home A-pluses. But do they really like me?"

"Your sister likes you and she's the gravy, right?" I smiled but he didn't return it.

"Yeah, and she's eight. She'll probably grow out of it."

"What do you want me to say, man?"

"You have no answers, Answer Man?"

I couldn't think of a response, so he kept talking. "I ain't like you. I damn sure ain't white. But I don't think I'm black either. I don't know what I am, but whatever it is, no one seems to like it."

"Look," I said, "I don't know about all that. I'm sorry if you're not the most popular guy in town, all right? I just know that *I like you.* I like being around you and hanging out, going to school with you. You're my friend, my best friend. Okay? There!"

He leaned back and it took some of the tension out of the room. "Do ya know what Jesus told the disciples after Peter answered the question?"

"No," I said.

He unfolded his arms and his voice was softer. "Jesus told 'em that He had to suffer many things, that He was gonna be rejected by His people, and that He was gonna have to die in order to be reborn." He paused, then raised his voice like a preacher would, like a regular Martin Luther King. "Uh-huh, that's right! Jesus *could see* His fate. He knew what was comin' and He told 'em."

My forehead wrinkled as I kept asking myself, *Why is he telling me this?* The muscles in my body felt like rubber bands being pulled ever tighter as I stared at him. He returned the stare, unflinching.

Daniel, I don't understand! I wanted to scream it at him, but I waited—uncomfortable in my own skin, wanting him to speak first.

Marty opened the door. He was out of breath. "Hey, sorry I'm late."

Neither of us looked up.

"Did I miss anything?" Marty asked.

Daniel closed his eyes and gave me a slow nod and soft smile that I interpreted as *It's okay, man*, before turning his head toward Marty. "Nah, ya big donkey," he said. "Sit down and prepare to have yo'r ass kicked."

"Oh yeah? Deal!" Marty said, so I picked up the cards.

Over the ensuing weeks after that aborted conversation with Daniel, I couldn't stop thinking about how he had opened up and exposed his feelings to me. I wanted to follow up with him and, lord knows, I had opportunities. But I never did. I wanted to understand what he was going through and the prejudices and conflict that he felt. But how could I? We came from different worlds and getting into those details was a hundred miles outside of my comfort zone. I wanted to be that best friend I professed to be, a confidant who could offer encouragement and sage advice. But I never was. I failed him. In fact, I betrayed him later, when I should have known better.

* * * * *

I swallowed hard as Allie repeated the question for the crowd, "If Daniel Carter was so depressed, why didn't he tell someone—his parents, a favorite teacher, his best friends?" She paused and gave a sad sigh before answering. "Our society puts so much pressure on young boys to hold their emotions inside. How many times do boys hear, 'Don't be a sissy, big boys don't cry, be a man,' and things like that? The message we send is that boys shouldn't let on if they're feeling depressed. They should just deal with the pain like John Wayne would do. Unfortunately, young boys are not John Wayne. As they struggle with the pressures and confusion of puberty and adolescence, they're torn between the need to confess their feelings to a nonjudgmental ear, assuming they can find one, versus the fear that their confession will compound the problem by making them appear unmanly. It's a real dilemma. The only hope for the boy who won't confide is that someone will notice the clues and signs that he'll inadvertently give and will say in a caring way, 'What's wrong? You can tell me.'"

"But Daniel Carter gave signs," a woman shouted, "and 'parently no one noticed 'em."

I hung my head and looked away.

"That's right," I heard Sister Mary Margaret whisper into the microphone.

"What I mean," the woman said, "is will y'all be able to learn somethin' from this horrible mess—to be more observant, to change some procedures here at school to try to make certain it can't ever happen again?"

"Yes, absolutely," Sister said. "We must learn from this tragedy and make changes. One of the sad things we've discovered is how little our faculty and staff, me at the top of this list, understand about depression and suicidal tendencies in children. Dr. Gibson and Miss Masterson have agreed to spend a Saturday with us, educating our staff on this subject. We hope to offer this same seminar at a later date to our parents. Once we are better acquainted with the warning signs, we must look at improving our counseling services for students and establishing even stronger communications with parents. I'm sure I'll have more specifics in the near future, but rest assured that changes will be made."

The evening was dragging on when a lady asked the *Why did he do it?* question again, this time in a more roundabout manner. That question had already been asked and answered at least three other times with a resounding, "We don't know." That answer, however, was difficult to accept.

"But what can we tell our children tonight?" the lady implored in a shrill voice. "You've given us a lot of generic comments and statistics. Please, be more specific. What can we say about Daniel Carter—about *him*, to make them understand why someone they know, someone in their class at school, their friend—why Daniel resorted to such a desperate act?"

"Be honest. Tell them that we don't know for sure," Allie said. "And then tell your son or daughter how much you love them. Tell them that all of us need love and understanding in our lives. Then ask if they feel like they can come to you when they have a problem, no matter what that problem may be. Ask if they trust Mommy and Daddy. Then listen carefully to their answer."

Dad was listening carefully to Allie. He rarely showed emotion, but I saw concern in his face and tightness in his body language. He looked down and shifted positions, uncomfortable in his chair.

"If I can be of help to any of you in understanding or interpreting their response, please contact me," Allie said. "Dr. Gibson is out of town until Thursday, but I'll be here at school for the remainder of this week—and longer if needed. The faculty will send any student who is showing emotional strain directly to me for counseling, and I'll advise the parents immediately. I'll let you know if I think there's anything specific that you should be doing or watching for."

Allie glanced at her watch. "It's getting late, but please allow me to make a final point. Many people—no, let me change

PART ONE: 8:20 p.m. 197

that to *most people*—think there is a stigma associated with seeking help from a psychologist like me or a psychiatrist like Dr. Gibson. It's like the stigma that used to be associated with having to wear eyeglasses. Remember those days? Well, it's now the 1960s and we are fortunate to be living in a more enlightened time. Today, if our vision isn't in focus, it doesn't mean we are lesser human beings. It means we need help from an optometrist, and we need an aid—eyeglasses in this case—to see correctly, to get our vision back into focus.

"The same is true for our mental health. The way we interact with others and view our lives can get confusing, out of focus. This can be due to a chemical imbalance or a neurological disorder. It can also be due to extreme stress that comes upon us when we aren't prepared to deal with it. Whatever the reason, there are doctors and other professionals who specialize in understanding and diagnosing these kinds of everyday human problems. Please don't be afraid to use us."

M Squared took the microphone from Allie. "Thank you so much, Miss Masterson. As you said, it's getting late. I'd like to suggest that we adjourn this meeting. Miss Masterson and I, as well as Sister Rose Anne and Mrs. Johnson, will be here for as long as necessary this evening if you'd like to talk to us or ask additional questions." She paused and, seeing no objections, said, "Thank you for your attention and your—"

But then someone spoke from the audience, a deep baritone voice. "Wait a minute, please, Sister. I have something that I'd like to add, something that I think needs to be said."

I thought I would faint. It was my father. In all my 12 and one-half years, I had never seen my father speak up in a large gathering. Another nine and a half years have passed since that night, and I've never seen him do it again.

Dad was great in a small group. Although he never dominated the conversation, when a few people were around in a casual setting he could be charming and interesting, sometimes even downright funny if he'd had a few drinks and loosened up a bit. But he was always reserved in a larger setting such as a Scout meeting or a father-son catechism class at church.

Yet here he was, standing to address this emotional crowd on this somber occasion. My anxiety level skyrocketed as I pushed on the hard floor of the stage and tucked my legs under me. *My God, what could possibly be going through his mind?* I feared that my father would embarrass himself and thereby shame our family, in front of Allie no less. I should have had more faith in him.

Chapter 20

9:00 p.m.

As all eyes turned toward him, my father cleared his throat and flexed his hands to crack his knuckles. With a tightness in his voice, he said to Sister Mary Margaret, "I feel awkward saying this, you bein' a Sister and all, but I have to confess that I'm disappointed with one aspect of this meeting here tonight and the answers that you fine folks have been givin' us."

"What is that, Mr. Torrence?" M Squared asked.

"Well, ma'am, it's the lack of any spiritual emphasis here tonight." He rotated his head to look at the other parents as he said in a stronger voice, "We should never underestimate the power that prayer and a strong spiritual belief can play in the healing process. And no one has yet said anything 'bout that."

"Oh, you are so right, Mr. Torrence," M Squared said, "and we should—"

"If I could just continue with my train of thought here, please," Dad said to her.

"By all means. Sorry I interrupted."

"You see, I'm not a highly educated man, certainly not in these matters, Sister. Also, I'm not much of a public speaker, and I feel more than a little uneasy standing here. I know what I want to say, but if I don't get it all out, I'll probably lose it."

"Just say what's on your mind."

"Okay, you see, I know that the Catholic Church has an official policy that people who take their own lives ain't supposed to make it to Heaven. I'm Catholic, like many of you here tonight, and I'm sorry but I just can't agree with the Church on this point." He looked around for a reaction to his blasphemy.

When there was no response, he continued. "Anyway, the thing is, I assume that this suicide matter, involving a boy attending a Catholic-sponsored school, is especially sensitive. That may be why we haven't seen any of the priests tonight and why they weren't over at the school today."

M Squared interrupted again. "What are you saying, Mr. Torrence?"

"I'm getting to that, Sister. We've spent a lot of time talkin' 'bout what we should say to our kids tonight. I appreciate your advice, and I plan to use some of the good tips we've been given." My father wiped his forehead. "But I also plan to pray with my boy," he said.

"You know, someone asked tonight what we could do to be helpful to the Carter family. I heard y'all mention a few things, but what I think you should've included is this: *We should pray for them.* Even better, *we should get our kids to pray for them.* You see, praying for someone in need takes our attention off our own problems. It focuses us on helping others like the Bible says we're supposed to do.

"I'm not sure how many of you folks know the Carters. Well, I do. Oh, not real well, but well enough to know they're a Christian, God-fearing family, and if you'd ask Dr. Carter that question, 'What can I do for you?' I think he'd ask for your prayers for his family."

He paused before adding, "I think he would also ask you to pray for the soul of their poor, confused son. And that's what I intend to do tonight. I don't think my boy is gonna get all hung up on church theology when it comes to one of his best pals. He'll want to ask Jesus to take Daniel into His lovin' arms to give him comfort and peace from those demons that've been torturing him. And despite what the Catholic Church teaches, that's what I'm gonna encourage him to do.

"You folks keep askin', 'What should we say to our kids?'" Dad scanned the faces in the auditorium before continuing. "Well, I sure don't have all the answers, and that's why I plan to ask for God's help. I pray that He'll be able to help me explain to my son how the wiring inside someone's head can get as messed up as Daniel Carter's did." Dad pointed briefly with his right index finger to his temple before he continued speaking.

"I'm a mechanic by training, and I tend to view things in mechanical terms. I think our human mind is like one of those huge NASA computers. Each of those computers is wired different 'cause they're built for different purposes. I believe that's the way God made people, each of us wired with different personalities and different likes and dislikes. It's what makes life such a beautiful mystery."

He had their complete attention. "Now and then, I guess the wiring can get all screwed up, and it makes the computer go haywire. But a wiring problem, it's not like a physical defect—you know, a baby that's born with a crooked spine or an accident that cripples someone later in life. A wiring defect is on the inside. It's like Miss Masterson said—it's a lot harder to figure out when there's a problem.

"I don't know the specific reason why Daniel Carter's wiring became defective. I just know that it was. That's obvious now. It's tragic that we didn't catch it before it blew, *but we didn't*. We can't change that. Our job now is to help our children get through all this and come to peace with it in their minds. And I believe the best way to do that is to tell them that Daniel is in Jesus' hands. Jesus was the greatest mechanic that ever lived. I believe that He's accepted Daniel Carter and He's fixed his wiring. He's taken away all that pain that wasn't Daniel's fault any more than a baby born with a crooked spine could be at fault for his defect. That's what I think."

Dad paused like he was finished. One hand reached down to his chair and his knees bent as though he was going to sit. But he stopped suddenly. He looked around at the other parents and said, "Just one more thing. Please, if I may, let me impose on y'all to please bow your heads with me for a brief moment of silence. I hope during that silence that you'll ask God for strength to help you get your family through this. I hope you'll think 'bout the Carter family and 'bout how precious our children are—white, black, red, yellow, or any color. I hope you'll ask for His strength for them and for His mercy on Daniel

Carter. If we could please have that moment of silence—now, please."

He bowed his head and everyone I could see did likewise. The quiet was deafening. I bowed my head and closed my eyes. I imagined Jesus placing His healing hand on my friend's head, gazing lovingly into Daniel's eyes, and then giving him a big welcoming hug. I liked that image.

Dad was right. It was helpful. I felt peace and serenity in the silence. I knew that my feelings of guilt, anxiety, and sorrow would each return soon. I knew that I would have to deal with my own demons, but it was good to have something to think about that was as tranquil as this mental image, even if it was just for a moment.

"Amen!" Dad said. "Please excuse me, but I have to get home now." He stepped into the outside aisle and walked up toward the exit, out of my range of vision.

At best, I had 45 seconds. That's how long I estimated it would take for him to walk out of the auditorium, through the lobby, and then wind his way down the hallway to the door to the makeup room. He expected me to be farther down that hall and around the corner in the science lab. I planned to intercept him at the bathrooms beside the makeup room door before he discovered me AWOL.

In a rush, I pushed up from the floor only to fall backward, hard on my bottom and elbows. For a second, I couldn't imagine what had happened. Had I tripped on something? Then it hit me. Sitting on the hard backstage floor with my legs tightly crossed, so intensely focusing on what my father had been saying, I didn't notice the blood being cut off from my legs. They were both fast asleep and entirely useless.

I pounded my right thigh with my fist to confirm my diagnosis. Nothing, no feeling at all. *Stay calm*, I thought. I tried to lift my legs with my arms and rise to my feet. It was hopeless. I couldn't walk.

If I was to have any hope of beating Dad into the hallway, I had to crawl. Using my elbows, forearms, and hands, I slithered over the stage floor for the 40 feet it took to reach the makeup room door. When I got there, I was panting and my legs were beginning to tingle. It was an awful feeling, but it was a good sign—that the blood flow was slowly returning.

Supporting my body with my left hand, I stretched my right hand upward to pull on the door handle. It opened toward the stage, and I had to curve my body and numb legs around the door like a contortionist to get into the little room. It was dark inside, but I identified my objective across the room by the sliver of light spilling in from under the hallway door. Using the first desk I could crawl to, I pulled myself into the chair and then up onto my feet. The pins and needles in my legs were excruciating. Stiffly pulling my pants legs with one hand and balancing myself on the desks with the other, I dragged my legs like a Frankenstein monster, trudging from one desk to the next until I reached the door.

I cracked the door open and peered around it to see into the hallway. Miraculously, it was clear from both directions, but I heard footsteps and voices around the corner coming from the administration area.

Supporting my weight with the inside and outside door handles, I employed a series of quick little jerks to pull myself into the hallway. Breathing rapidly, I pushed the door shut with my back to it. My feet and legs were tingling madly, and a low groan escaped my lips. I checked to see if I could lift my right foot off the floor. Balancing precariously on my left foot and straining hard, I raised the right heel upward about an inch, but my toes remained stuck to the floor. There wasn't enough feeling to walk, so I decided to make a stand there in the hallway. I reached down to lock my knees and then leaned back against the door to maintain my balance.

I'm sure I looked wobbly, like the proverbial drunken sailor, as my father and two other parents rounded the corner. My heart was racing. *Stay calm*, I kept repeating in my mind.

They were deep in conversation, but Dad slowed when he noticed me leaning against the door.

I gave him a big smile. "Hey, Dad. Meeting over?" I asked in my most nonchalant voice, like there was no problem here, like I went around all the time leaning against walls like a dork.

They walked up to me. The man and woman accompanying Dad looked unusual together, his barrel chest and high Cro-Magnon forehead in extreme contrast to her petite frame and bony cheeks.

"What are you doing out here?" Dad asked. "I thought you were in the science lab."

"I am," I said, trying not to grimace too much from the painful tingling.

"You are what?" he asked.

"In the science lab," I said, but their confused looks demanded further explanation. "I mean, I *was* there, but now I'm in the hallway." I smiled through clenched teeth. I couldn't think clearly.

"And why are you in the hallway? And what happened to your pants? They're filthy."

"Oh, I had to use the bathroom. You didn't expect me to stay in the science lab when I had to use the bathroom, did you?"

He shook his head. "Are you goin' or comin', Son?"

"Where?"

"To the bathroom! Are you on your way to the bathroom or on your way back from the bathroom?" He was losing patience.

The impulses continued to torture my legs like electric currents, but the worst was over. I figured that I only needed another 30 seconds, max.

"Oh, I'm finished," I answered. "And was it ever dirty in there. Yuck! See what happened to my clothes? Well, we should be leaving, Dad. I mean, we can leave soon, in half a minute or so."

The man standing next to Dad stuck out his hand. "Buddy, we've never met. I'm Joe's dad, Bart Stoddard, and this is Joe's mother, Janet Stoddard. Joe says you're jest 'bout the smartest kid he's ever known."

"I'm sorry," Dad said. "I got distracted and forgot my manners. I should've introduced you."

"Glad to meet you," I said. My right hand had been gripping the door handle behind me for support, and I extended it to shake his hand. As he grasped my hand and then pulled firmly on it, I slowly toppled forward like a tall tree being felled. I couldn't stop my forward progress without unlocking my knees. But I was afraid that would cause my legs to buckle, leaving me on the floor again.

So, I put my left hand forward onto Mr. Stoddard's big chest to catch myself. I pushed against him, causing me to reverse direction and tilt back upright against the door. Mr. Stoddard released my right hand as he took a step backward from my thrust.

"Buddy, what in the world is wrong with you?" Dad said.

"Wait a minute there, Mac," Mr. Stoddard said to Dad in a twangy east-Texas drawl as he moved forward to regain his position. "I think I know what's wrong." He broke into a huge smile as he stared at me.

"Lemme guess, Buddy. Ya came outta the bathroom yonder," he said as he pointed to the restroom door. A snorting sound that I took for laughter exploded from his nose before he could continue. "You was in there, ya know—*sittin' on the throne.*" Now, he was having difficulty speaking, gulping for air between guffaws. "And ya sat on there fer so long, har har, yer butt and yer legs, har har, they fell asleep on ya, har har. Am I right, har har? Am I right?"

I looked at him like he was crazy. What kind of idiot would let that happen? It was ludicrous. I was about to vehemently deny his accusation when I realized the golden opportunity that he was handing me—a way out of my predicament. They were all staring at me, waiting for an answer.

"Yes, sir. How'd you know?" I asked as sincerely as possible.

"Oh, heck, it happens to me all the time, har har."

"It does?" Dad and I said in unison.

"Sure!" he said as his wife nodded her head.

He gave me a wide grin that exposed his tobacco-stained teeth. "Now, don't you go gittin' embarrassed, boy. It's no big deal." Stoddard patted my shoulder.

He looked at Dad and said, "It's that darn cons'terpation, makes you sit there *sooo* long. Ya probably need to give him a dose of lax'tive when he gets home, Mac."

My father looked perplexed and didn't respond.

Without thinking, I said to the idiot, "Yes, sir."

"See, Mac, the boy is practically beggin' fer some relief," Stoddard said. "Ya probably need to give 'im a big dose."

"I meant, 'No, sir,'" I said, realizing my mistake.

"What?"

"I mean, I think I was able to get it all."

"All what?" Stoddard asked.

This was ridiculous. I said, "I mean, with all respect, I won't be needing that laxative. I was able to . . . well, you know." I looked at Mrs. Stoddard. Her hand covered her mouth, but I could tell she was laughing at me. The feeling was back in my legs and feet, and I wanted to kick this cretin in his numb ass.

"Nonsense," Stoddard said. "A good—"

My father walked between us and cut him off. "Bart, I think we can take it from here." He looked at me. "Are you ready to go?"

"Yes, sir, I'm ready," I said. "The feeling's all pretty much come back."

"Good night, Bart and Janet," Dad said to the Stoddards. "It was a pleasure meeting you. When you get Joe, please tell Sister Bridgette that I have Buddy, okay?"

"Sure thang," Stoddard said. His wife nodded at us.

I got a sudden rush of adrenaline. What specifically would the idiot Stoddard say to the old hag about me? Would her reaction give me away? Would my parents get a call from confused Sister Bridgette saying that I hadn't been in the science lab?

It was just one more thing that I couldn't control. *Que sera, sera.* If the call came, maybe I could say that I'd been in the bathroom so long, Old Sister Bridgette must have forgotten about me. Stoddard would probably fall for that one but not Dad. If I got caught, maybe I'd confess about being backstage. But I couldn't think that far ahead or play out hypotheticals, so I decided not to worry about it. I just wanted to get out of there.

Dad extended his arm to help me, but I shook my head. So, he started walking down the hallway.

I turned to follow him, but Stoddard reached out and held my arm until I looked him in the eye. "I jest got one word fer ya, Buddy," he said softly, leaning closer like it was some big secret he was prepared to divulge. "Jest one word."

"Yes, sir," I said.

"Are ya listening?"

"Yes, I am."

"Lax'tive," he said. He paused to let the word sink in before adding, "Think 'bout it. Will ya think 'bout it?"

"Yes, I will," I said.

He brought his finger to his lips and quickly added, "Shh. Nuff said." He released me and walked away.

I hurried to catch up with my father.

Chapter 21

9:30 p.m.

"Dad?"

"Yes?"

"Dad, do you pray?"

He kept both hands on the steering wheel as he looked over with a puzzled expression.

"I mean, I know you say the prayers at Mass on Sundays," I said. "We say a blessing before every meal, and you help me to pray at night. We do all that together, but do *you* pray? Do *you* talk to God on a regular basis?"

"No, not on a regular basis. I reckon it's more when the mood or the need strikes me."

"How do you do it?" I asked.

"Come again?"

"How do you pray? Do you say a Rosary?"

"No, I'm not much on the Rosary. That's more your mother's style."

"Then what's your style?"

"I'd say it was more personal than a Rosary."

"Like how?" I hoped he didn't mind me pressing him. He was watching the road, but I saw a reluctant smile come over him like when you finally decide to share a secret with someone.

"You know how we make the sign of the cross?" he asked.

"You mean like this?" I crossed myself.

"Right. You touched your head and abdomen and then across your chest. Well, I like to think that making the sign of the cross is like pulling on an imaginary zipper that first opens our minds, then our hearts, then unzips our whole body. We're opening ourselves for God, totally and completely, for Him to enter us and communicate spiritually with us. Once I open myself to Him like that, a whole different mood comes over me, a peaceful mood as I try to get in touch with the Holy Spirit deep down inside. Do you follow?"

I nodded. "I think so."

"After I open myself with the sign of the cross and feel that spirit, that's when I start to concentrate really hard on the people and the things that are important to me at that particular moment. You see, when I pray, I don't generally say a lotta words and sentences like I'm talkin' to somebody. I think that's the way most people pray, but I've never been too good at expressing my emotions with words. Besides, I believe that God is so powerful, so overwhelming, that we humans don't need to communicate with Him in our slow and crude language. The Holy Spirit of the Almighty, it's right there inside us, and believe me, He knows everything we're thinking and feeling. I don't need to say, 'Today is January 11th, blah, blah, and I would like for You, God, to please watch over blah, blah.' *God already knows all that.* It's right there in the Book of Matthew, just before Jesus teaches the Lord's Prayer. He says that the Father knows what you need before you ever ask, before you ever say the words."

"So, you don't speak to God?"

"Not like you and me are talkin' just now," he said. "That's partly 'cause I've found that there's a big advantage to not doin' a lot of talkin' in your prayers."

"What's that?"

"Well, if you're the one doin' all the talkin', how can you ever hear what God might have to say?"

"Does God talk to you, Dad?" I asked in an excited voice.

"I can't be sure, but I think He does." He glanced across at me as oncoming headlights lit up our car. "Sometimes, when I'm real still and deep in prayer," he said, his voice barely above a whisper, "thoughts just start swirlin' 'round in my head. It can be a specific idea, a new plan, or maybe a whole different way of looking at things that I probably would've never come up with if

I hadn't taken that quiet time. Oh, I know it's comin' from inside my own mind, but I like to think that the Holy Spirit of God has a hand in planting those thoughts."

"So, how do you ask for stuff if you don't speak any words?"

"Like I said, I mostly just concentrate on things."

"Like what?"

We slowed to a stop for a red light that cast a warm glow on his face. "When I pray," he said, "I like to start off with a mental picture of your mother. There's a smile on her face, and she's all happy in the picture in my mind. I don't generally say any sentences or anything. I just think wonderful thoughts 'bout her. You see, God is inside me and He knows all my feelings for her.

"Then I repeat the process for you. In my mental picture, you can be playing baseball or taking a test at school. Or you're doin' whatever's goin' on in your life at that time. My eyes are closed, but I'm staring at that picture of you. And the good Lord, He knows exactly how I feel. He knows all the things I want for you without me ever having to say 'em, you know, with words that could never express all the right feelings."

"And what is it you want for me, Dad?"

"Right now, I want you to be happy and be safe. Beyond that, I want you to learn good values, to be able to know right from wrong, and to make good decisions when it's your time to be a man."

"How do you pray for special things, like somebody that's in trouble?" I asked.

"Same way, I reckon. I just think 'bout 'em. Remember when your Grandpa Torrence had that gallbladder surgery last year?"

"Yeah, he came through it okay."

"Yes, he did. I remember up there in Dallas in that hospital waiting room while he was in surgery. Every few minutes, as the need struck me, I opened myself up to God and then concentrated on a mental picture of your grandpa, all healthy and strong. One time, he was out hunting. Another time, he was fixin' something 'round his house. It varied. But you see, God knew exactly what I wanted for my father without me havin' to put it all into words. Whenever I was finished, I'd make the sign of the cross again, this time using that imaginary zipper to close myself up.

"Now, this is important: By closing myself up, that doesn't mean I'm closing God out. Making the sign of the cross at the end of a prayer just means I'm finished for now with my inner time with God. But He's always inside us and watching over us, and I know He'll be there when I need to open up again."

"How do you know for sure that He'll be there?" I asked.

He grinned at me. "That's why they call it *faith*, boy."

We rode in silence for several seconds before I summoned the courage to ask the question that was weighing heaviest on my mind. "Dad?"

"Yes?"

"How do you pray for forgiveness?"

"Same way. With my eyes closed, I think real hard 'bout something I've done wrong, a sin—like, maybe I was rude to your mother. She may've forgiven me, but I still feel so bad that I need to seek forgiveness from an even higher authority—that is, if there could possibly be such a thing." He looked over at me with a smile.

To be polite, I gave him a superficial grunt-laugh. But I wanted him to be serious, and I nodded to encourage him to continue.

The traffic was light as he turned the Falcon onto Calder Avenue and then said, "Inside my mind after I've opened up to the Holy Spirit, I replay whatever act it is that needs forgiveness. Painful as it may be, I try to analyze what I did and why it was wrong. Remember, this is just God and you. He's inside you and you can't lie or sugarcoat the facts, 'cause He and you are one. I ask myself if I'm truly sorry with all my heart and if I'll try to make certain that it never happens again. If that's the case, then God forgives me, and I forgive myself."

"What happens if the sin is so great that it can't ever be forgiven?"

"Oh, I don't believe that's possible. If we sincerely repent, God *will* forgive us."

It irritated me, the way he demeaned my question with such

a simple answer. He was thinking small, like minor infractions, and dishing out platitudes. I was thinking big, like Major League sins. "But how can you be sure? How do you know you'll be forgiven?" I asked.

"Jesus asked the Father to forgive the men that tortured and crucified Him. Think 'bout that, Buddy." He glanced at me with a reassuring smile before his eyes returned to the road. "If He can do that, He can forgive anything," he said.

"Anything? You're sure?"

"Anything, even suicide. I know the Catholic Church may disagree, but I don't care. He can forgive, and He does."

"But what about things worse than suicide?" I asked.

"Like what?" he shot back.

"Oh, ah, I don't know," I stuttered, sorry that I had pursued this point so far.

"He can forgive anything," my father declared emphatically.

"That's good," I mumbled.

As we approached Fourth Street, the traffic light in front of us changed from green to yellow. He had time to make it through, and normally my father would have speeded up. Instead, he braked firmly, and we came to a stop as the light turned red. I took it as a positive sign, that he had more he wanted to say.

"I believe that God wants to forgive us, Buddy. Hard as we humans may try, we can't achieve perfection. It doesn't mean we shouldn't keep trying. It just means that it's not realistic to think we could live a perfect life. And He knows that! It's not our fault for bein' imperfect. As the Creator, it's God who made us outta the dirt of this earth and gave us all these human imperfections in the first place. We were given curious minds and the freedom to make choices in life. Lord knows, that can be a dangerous combination sometimes. So, I believe that He wants to forgive us when we make bad choices. I also believe that He can forgive people who do something terrible 'cause they were under huge pressure and their brain got all screwed up—like in Daniel's case. It wasn't his fault that something in his head snapped. Do you understand?"

"Yes, sir. It makes sense to me," I said. It was a lie, but one

I felt I could justify under the circumstances. This was complex theological stuff, and even though I couldn't follow exactly how he got there, I liked his conclusion. According to Dad, Daniel had been forgiven. His suicide wasn't his fault. He was safe in Heaven. I was pleased that Dad had been able to figure all that out.

My own fate was another matter. As we turned onto Hazel, I wondered for the thousandth time why I didn't react to the signals Daniel had given. *How could I have been so stupid?* Despite what Dad had said, I still had doubts. *How could I ever be forgiven for what I did to him?* As Dad pulled the Falcon to a stop behind the station wagon in our narrow carport, I was trance-like, a prisoner to those thoughts. It was dark inside the car except for little flashes of light that danced across the dashboard. In that light, I could make out an image of Daniel, revolver in hand with a single bullet in the chamber. As it flickered, I watched him lie down on his pillow, roll onto his side, and raise the gun to his head.

I reached for my father and grabbed his arm as he turned the key to stop the engine. "Dad?" I asked.

"What's the matter?"

"Dad, will you pray for me?"

"Right now?" he asked.

"Yes, sir. Right now. And do it in your own way, please."

"Well, okay," he said. He took a deep breath, closed his eyes, and made the sign of the cross, but with his left hand because I had his right wrist, which rested on the steering column, in a tight grasp with my left hand. After crossing himself, Dad put his left hand over mine. The contact with him felt good, and I loosened my grip. I closed my eyes and, as he had done, crossed myself and invited God into my body.

It was a cold night, but I felt a warmth inside as I thought again of Daniel with Jesus, like my father had talked about in the auditorium. I could see Jesus giving Daniel a tour of Heaven and introducing him to all the apostles and saints.

Abruptly, my prayer was interrupted. Dad jerked his hand away from mine and made his closing sign of the cross. I heard a sniffle as he reached into the hip pocket of his pants for his handkerchief. The headlights from a passing car lit the right side of his face, and I was shocked to see a tear trickling down his cheek. It was the first time I had seen my father cry.

He wiped his face and blew his nose into the handkerchief. "I'm sorry," he whispered. "I guess it's been a pretty tough day for everybody."

He leaned to his right and wrapped an arm around my shoulders as he stared through the windshield into the quiet night. I was tense under his grasp, and I'm sure he felt my confusion. He cleared his throat and searched for the right words to explain.

"In my mind just now, I tried to think of a happy, carefree scene for you, Buddy, but—"

"But what?" I asked.

"It didn't work. God knows all our thoughts, and we can't hide anything from Him. When that happy scene wouldn't come, I got scared. He knows I'm worried."

"About what?"

"I'm worried that it may take some time—maybe a lotta time—for you to put all this behind you and get to that happy, carefree state."

Our front porch light came on, and it projected soft, yellow-white strands of illumination into the darkness within the car. I continued to sit motionless, facing the dashboard, but I let my eyes wander to one side and saw a woman's figure behind the window of our house. Her body was turned sideways toward the carport. When I looked back the other way, I saw sad shadows in my father's face.

"I asked for too much," he said. "Then it hit me right in the gut that my little man is gonna have to experience some pain first, probably a lotta pain, before things can get back to normal. I guess that made me feel like a failure. You see, fathers are supposed to protect their children from pain. I should take the hurt off you, even put it on my shoulders if that's what it takes. But my inner voice told me—*He* told me—that I won't be able to do it, not this time.

"You've suffered a huge loss, Buddy. You're gonna miss your friend terribly, and you're gonna ponder what you coulda-shoulda done different. I know it and you know it. It doesn't matter how many people tell you not to think in those terms. That's just not human nature."

"So, what should I do?" I asked.

"You're gonna have to be strong, Son. Your mom and me, we're gonna help you. But, ultimately, you'll have to deal with it inside your own mind. You'll have to come to terms with all that's happened."

"I wasn't a good friend," I said, choking on my emotion. I had to look away from him, into the dashboard again. "I did some bad things, Dad, stupid things."

"Buddy, don't—"

"There's so many questions swirling around, like you said, inside my mind. I don't think I'll ever be able to stop them."

"You have to, over time."

"And if I can't?"

"That's not gonna happen."

"But if it does?"

"Listen, you're not gonna let that happen 'cause—"

"But if I can't—*answer me!*"

When several seconds passed without a reply, I looked up from the dashboard and our eyes locked. After another silent second, I nodded at him to speak.

He cocked his head and then gave in. "Then I guess the Devil wins." He sighed. "He changes you into something different, something dark and depressed."

I held his eyes for another second before turning my head away. "Great," I mumbled.

"But you're not gonna let that happen," he said, tugging on my shoulder. "You'll work through this in a mature manner, one day at a time."

His optimism was uninspiring. "Yeah, right. Thanks for the vote of confidence," I said.

"Your mom and I will be there to help."

"Thanks," I muttered at the dashboard.

"Talk to us. Let us in when it gets bad."

"Yeah, okay."

"And you have to rely on your faith in God. Talk to Him. Pray to Him. He has a plan for you. I know He does."

Some plan, I thought, but I didn't respond.

"I'm sorry I let you down with the praying and everything," he said, "but I'll do better from now on. You can count on it, Son. I'll pray later tonight that you get safely through this night. Tomorrow, I'll pray that you get through tomorrow. The same for the following day. You know, one day at a time."

In the short silence that followed, I could tell that he needed reassuring. Part of me wanted to make him sweat, make him feel anxious and uneasy like I was feeling about my uncertain future. But I couldn't do it, not to my father.

With as much sincerity as I could muster, I looked up and said, "Don't worry, Dad. I can be strong like you said. I come from pretty good stock, you know. I think I can handle this and, if I can't, I'll tell you, so you and Mom can help me."

He leaned closer. "You promise?"

"Cross my heart," I said and made the sign of the cross with a grin.

Dad grinned back. Then his focus shifted to our house. "We'd better go in now," he said. "Your mother will get all worried if we stay out here much longer."

There was his intuitive sixth sense at work again. He could precisely measure how long it was going to take for the silhouette in the window's curiosity to turn to concern. We were obviously getting close to that point.

"Dad?" I said as he reached to open his door.

"Yeah?"

Using my best imitation of Allie's sweet voice, I said mockingly, "It's okay to cry. It's part of the healing process."

"Why, you little—" he said as he lurched across the front seat at me, his hand raised like he was going to hit me. His quick move surprised me and I recoiled. He laughed loudly.

"You thought I was gonna smack you, huh?" he said. He grabbed me in a headlock and tousled my hair in a rough but affectionate way. It tickled and I chuckled, knowing my comment had gotten to him and made him laugh at the same time.

When he released me, I looked over at him and it just came out. "I love you, Dad."

"I love you too, Son. I know I don't say that very often, but I do love you—with all my heart."

"But why do you love me, Dad?"

"What?"

"Why? Why do you love me?"

He smiled. "That's easy. I love you 'cause you're mine."

"What?" I wrinkled my forehead at him.

"Because you're mine, silly. It's as simple as that. You're a blessing that God Almighty reached down and gave us—your mother and me—a blessing to cherish, to educate, to protect. Oh, you'll grow up someday and you'll leave us, but you'll still be mine. The blood that flows through you and gives you life, it all comes from me and your mom. That makes you ours for life. That's why I'll always love you." He reached over and tousled my hair again as he grinned. "I just hope I like you."

"And what's that supposed to mean?"

"Simple. You'll always have my love, just 'cause you're mine. Period. But for someone to *like* you, well, a man's gotta earn that. You earn people's trust and respect through your deeds, like the way you showed courage and maturity in that meeting this afternoon. Like the time—"

"Dad?" I stopped him mid-sentence. "Do you like me, Dad?" I held my breath as I looked up into his eyes. It's impossible to describe how much I wanted him to like me, how much I needed him to like me after spending much of the day worrying that he might fire me as his son. My entire body tensed as I waited for his reply.

"Yes, I do," he said with a proud smile overtaking his face.

A gentle warmth permeated my body. I didn't want to cry in front of him, but my emotions were heating up again like a pot of water over a flame.

As always, he could sense my feelings. He shifted into a high-pitched, Allie-like voice and said, *"Oh, Buddy, I like you a* lot. *You're such an extraordinary young man.*" We both laughed. He was making fun of me, using the three words Allie had called me—an "extraordinary young man"—just before she left our house. It felt good to laugh with my father. "But your mother's not gonna like either of us," he said, "if we don't get in that house. Now!"

We got out of the car and started walking across the lawn toward the front door. After a few steps, he tugged on my jacket and we stopped. Mom was still watching from the window. "It's probably better," he whispered, "that we don't tell your mom 'bout all that in the car just now, you know, me trying to pray with you and losing composure and everything. That's not like me and no need to get her any more concerned than she is. Okay?"

I raised my eyebrows and sized him up in the glow of our porch light. "How much is it worth to you?" I asked, trying not to laugh.

He made a wicked face and pulled back his fist, but this time I knew he was faking. I broke for the house. He gave chase, but I reached the door three paces ahead. I threw it open and leaped into the house, slowing to a fast walk once inside. Running in the Torrence house was prohibited. It was a rule.

Mom had moved away from the window. When I saw her open mouth, I laughed and said, "Hey, Mom, Dad's trying to hit me!"

"I am not!" he said as he entered the house, continuing the chase.

I glanced over my shoulder. As he passed Mom, he flashed a reassuring smile in her direction. Mom looked utterly confused.

Dad continued after me, but I fast-walked to my room and slammed the door behind me. I plopped down on my bed to catch my breath.

He knocked hard on my door.

"Sanctuary! You can't come in!" I shouted.

"Buddy, I need to have a word with you."

I thought for a second. "Five dollars!"

I heard Dad laugh and Mom say, "What's going on?"

"Shh!" he told her, but she wouldn't be quiet.

"Mac, what in God's name is going on?"

That made both of us laugh.

"Wait a minute. Just a minute, Lon," he said.

It was too quiet. He was obviously up to something sneaky. I heard a noise on the floor in the hallway, and then I saw a shiny penny being pushed under my door. "I'll give you a penny for your thoughts," Dad said, "and not a cent more!" We laughed again.

Mom said, "Mac, tell me—"

"Shh! One minute, please," he demanded.

I walked up to the door. "Oh, Mother, dearest. Would you like to enter and have a chat with me? Would you like to know something about your husband?"

"C'mon, Lon," I heard my father say hurriedly. "I'll tell you all 'bout it." And then there were footsteps walking down the hall away from my room.

I laughed out loud as I picked up the penny. I rubbed it with both hands as I sat on my bed. After a few seconds, I tried to laugh again but nothing came out. Nothing seemed funny. Staring out my window at Marty's house, my shoulders sagged. *Oh, Marty, what are you doing right now? What are you thinking about? What would you think if you knew the truth?* There was no reply, only an increasing sense of how exceptionally quiet it was and how alone I was in this little room.

My thoughts slowly melted into despair. I tossed the idiot penny into my trash can and then took off my glasses. I held my head in my hands and rubbed my eyes. I was exhausted, and I struggled to fight back the tears. Within a few seconds, the struggle was lost.

After Marty, Daniel, and I had become really good friends—like in *The Three Musketeers* and all—I convinced my parents to let them both spend the night at our house on a Saturday. It was a few days before Halloween, and it was the first sleepover I'd ever had.

We had a great time. Mom fixed a special dinner that included her homemade chocolate pecan pie for dessert. After dinner, Dad played Spades with us. He never complained about having to take Marty as a partner and didn't get upset when Marty made bonehead plays. Daniel and I crushed them, three games to none.

After that, Mom told us stories about Hawaii and what it was like to be there when the Japanese bombed Pearl Harbor. I'd heard it all before, but Marty and Daniel were mesmerized. Afterward, Mom went to bed, but Dad told her he was going to stay up and watch some TV with the rest of the boys.

When it was 10:00 and the local news came on, Daniel announced that he had a card trick to show us. He asked Dad to sit in the middle of our family room sofa, flanked by Marty and me. Daniel stood facing us with a deck of cards fanned out, face down in his hands, our long coffee table separating him from the three of us.

He asked my father to select any card from the deck. Dad picked a card randomly from the middle. He showed it to Marty and me, and we all took great care to conceal it from Daniel. It was the jack of hearts, the one-eyed jack with the smug look on his face.

"Remember your card," Daniel instructed my father as he placed the other 51 cards in a tight stack on top of the coffee table, "and put it face down on top of the deck, so I can't see it."

Dad complied. Daniel then picked up the deck and put both his hands behind his back where we couldn't see what he was doing. He shuffled the cards behind him, or at least it sounded like he was shuffling them. He abruptly pulled the deck forward, holding it vertically at our eye level, his thumb on one side and four fingers on the other. We could all see the bottom card—the six of clubs.

He said, "And that's not your card. It's not on the bottom, correct?"

"Right," we all said in unison, the anticipation building.

"Good," he replied and pulled the deck behind his back again, shuffled once more back there, and then extended the deck stiffly toward us in the same manner, showing the nine of diamonds now on the bottom of the deck.

"And, after shuffling some more, that's not your card either, right?"

"Right," we confirmed.

This time, instead of putting the deck behind his back, Daniel set it on the coffee table, all 52 cards face down in a neat stack, and he announced to my father, "Okay, now I will find your card in this deck." But he looked unsure, as though he was worried that his trick had gone awry.

Dad tried to give him some encouragement. "Great, Daniel, show me my card."

Daniel closed his eyes. His forehead wrinkled like he was trying to remember something. It was unsettling.

"Okay, here goes," he finally said. Daniel was clearly nervous as he took a deep breath and then turned over the top card—the king of spades—for us to see as he muttered something low under his breath that sounded like, "One." He dropped the king face up next to the deck. Looking straight down oblivious to our presence, he turned over another inconsequential card and muttered softly to himself, "Two." The same process continued. "Three, four, five, six . . ." It was apparent to me, and must have been to Dad and even Marty, that Daniel was counting the cards down to the place where he had slipped the jack of hearts into the deck when it was behind his back.

What a stupid trick! I expected better from Daniel. I was constantly telling my parents how smart he was in school. This was embarrassing. Poor Daniel.

He continued to softly count. "Eleven, 12, 13, 14 . . ."

But wait a minute! *The 14th card was the jack of hearts.* The one-eyed jack was staring at us from the table where Poor Daniel had turned it over and let it fall on top of the others. The three of us saw it and exchanged quick glances. Daniel didn't see us. He continued to concentrate on the deck. We heard him whisper, "Fifteen." The 15th card was the ace of clubs, and he placed it face up onto the jack of hearts. "Sixteen," he muttered as the three of diamonds was turned over on top of the ace of clubs, the jack of hearts, and the 13 other cards in the exposed pile.

He looked up with a weak smile as he took the top card from the deck—the 17th card—face down into his left hand. He was careful not to expose it as he grabbed a corner of the card with his right hand. Standing ready to flip it over, he announced with cautious optimism, "I'll betcha a dollar that the next card I turn over is your card, Mista Torrence."

"Whoa there, I don't think you wanta make that bet," Dad said.

That's for sure, I thought. Poor Daniel must have miscounted because he held the 17th card in his hand when the 14th card was the one he wanted.

"Yes sir, I do," he said. He extended the card toward my father and said, "I'm pretty sure 'bout this. I'll bet a dollar."

This was painful. I wanted to stop Poor Daniel. Idiot!

"No, Daniel, no bets. But I do think you've messed this one up, son." Dad smiled sympathetically. He was going to mercifully let him off the hook.

But Daniel wouldn't give up. "I'm a big boy, Mr. Torrence." As he spoke, he pulled a wrinkled one-dollar bill from his jeans' pocket with his right hand as he continued to clutch the ill-fated "next card" face down in his left. "I got George Washington here, and he says the next card I turn over is your card." He set the dollar on the coffee table. As he did, he bumped the stack of exposed cards, and we could see the corner of the jack of hearts, the card he needed to be holding in his hand.

"It's a mighty tempting offer but, sorry—no bet," Dad said.

"I'll take that bet!" Marty's mouth was open and he was panting. His eyes darted between the dollar bill and my father like a dog waiting for permission to go fetch.

"Now boys, I don't think you should do this. I don't think it'd be fair." Dad caught himself staring at Daniel. "I mean, I don't think it'd be right."

"Please, Mr. Torrence, please," Marty said.

"It's okay, Mr. Torrence," Daniel chimed in. "I wanta bet. Like I said, I'm a big boy and, well, I'm pretty sure I know what I'm doin'." But he didn't sound so sure.

PART ONE: 9:30 p.m.

My father protested again, but Marty and Daniel were both adamant that they wanted an opportunity to play out this sporting proposition. Dad said something about them being too young for gambling, which hit a raw nerve with all of us. Marty gave him a look that said, *And I thought you were trying to be cool,* and he told Dad in a nice sort of way that he ought to take a closer look around the room. We were growing up. Daniel added that wagering for small stakes could be a good character-builder for young men.

To my surprise, my father caved in. "I'm not gonna stop you boys, but I tell you, I don't like it."

"Great!" Marty said. He started rubbing his hands together like he could feel that dollar between them. "So, it's a bet!" he proclaimed.

"Well?" Daniel asked.

"Well, what?"

"Where's your dollar, fool?"

"I've got it next door. Hey, I'm good for it! Now turn over the next card."

Daniel extended the card he had been holding in his left hand toward Marty. "Okay, to be crystal clear, you and I are betting a buck—one American dollar—that the next card I turn over is the one Mista Torrence picked in the beginning and showed all y'all, right?"

"Right! That's right," Marty said with a confident smirk as he looked at the exposed corner of the jack of hearts.

"Okay, then it's a bet," Daniel announced, and he shook Marty's hand. Showing a newfound poise and confidence, Daniel slowly reached with his free hand into the stack of previously exposed cards next to his dollar bill. He found the jack of hearts, lifted it for Marty to see, and then turned it face down on the coffee table.

We were all silent, spellbound. A grin started in the corner of Daniel's mouth before slowly spreading over his entire face. When he finally spoke, he gave us a long wink, and I swear he looked just like that smug one-eyed jack of hearts. "Things ain't always what they seem, are they?" he said.

After my father realized what had happened, he laughed and shook his head about a hundred times like he couldn't believe how we'd all been sucked in so completely. Marty screamed that Daniel had cheated, but it was obvious, even to him, that he had been outsmarted. Marty eventually gave up his protests and told Daniel that he'd pay him in the morning. With the ledgers settled, Dad retired to his room.

Before I fell asleep that night, with my two best friends in sleeping bags on the floor in my room, I thought about how fortunate I was to have such good friends.

But then, things ain't always what they seem, are they?

Chapter 22

10:20 p.m.

It was magnificent. In the most fundamental sense, it was just a piece of paper. But fondling it, running my fingers over its crisp, green edges, gave me a strange and unfamiliar sensation. Possessing it gave me a sense of power I had never experienced.

I was having second thoughts. I had convinced myself five minutes earlier that I must destroy it, but now I wasn't so sure. *Could there be another way out?* I wondered if Daniel Carter had similar thoughts prior to squeezing the trigger.

It was ironic, in a sick way, that I was trying to compare my feelings about destroying a 20-dollar bill to Daniel's feelings about destroying his life. It laid bare my distorted views about money and the overstated value I placed on it.

* * * * *

The previous summer, shortly after my 12th birthday, we'd taken our first family vacation. We drove the Rambler wagon to Chicago, then to Detroit, and then back home to Beaumont. It was almost 3,000 miles. I got to see and do a lot of neat things on the way like ride a paddlewheel boat on the Mississippi River and walk around on a Civil War battlefield on the very spot where great armies had clashed and brave men had fought and died.

Mom kept a detailed log of every penny we spent, comparing it to the budget she and Dad had prepared for the trip. To do my part to help us come in on budget, I ordered cheap things from the menus in restaurants along the way and drank water instead of Coke or ginger ale.

We spent a week in south Chicago being passed around among our relatives. I felt like a Gypsy nomad, but Mom said we saved a lot of money doing it that way. My parents took me downtown to see the awesome skyscrapers, and we got to go to a beach where I waded in the cold water of Lake Michigan. We also had enough in the budget for my parents to take my cousins and me to an amazing museum with giant dinosaur skeletons, and we saw all the wild animals in the Lincoln Park Zoo. It made me want to live and work in a vibrant city when I grew up.

Then we drove to Detroit. Ames Boudreaux, my dad's friend from work, and his wife, Cherrie, had moved to Detroit that summer. When they found out we were heading north for a family vacation, they invited us to stay with them for a few days. It was great. We toured The Henry Ford, a huge museum where I learned all about technological innovation. And I got to see another one of the Great Lakes. Well, it was actually the Detroit River, but it connected two of the Great Lakes.

The Boudreauxs took us into Canada. It felt weird to stand in a whole different country like I was some high-class world traveler. Mr. Boudreaux suggested that we go all the way to Toronto and spend a day there. He said it was a spectacular city, where we could experience real Canadian culture and see Niagara Falls. I begged my parents, but they said we couldn't go. It wasn't in the budget.

On the way home, we got to stay two nights in a motel in St. Louis. It was in the budget. We also had enough in the budget to take in a Cardinals game at Busch Stadium. It was the highlight of the trip for me. I got to see Bob Gibson pitch, although I couldn't make out his famous scowl or see the fear in the batters' eyes from the left-field bleachers where we sat. When the Cardinals prevailed over the Yankees in the World Series later that year with Gibson winning the seventh game, I proudly announced to Marty, Daniel and anyone who'd listen that I had seen Gibson play *in person*, without disclosing that we sat in the cheap seats.

Going through Arkansas on the way home, Dad got on the

wrong highway. They didn't realize it for quite a while, and then Dad tried to recover by taking a shortcut on a farm road that was supposed to connect with the interstate. It didn't. In all, counting the backtracking, we ended up going three hours out of the way. Mom was unusually hard on him, not for wasting three hours of our time, but for costing us an extra $2.90 in gas according to her precise calculations. Dad got in a big debate with her that it was only $2.50. I would gladly have given them the 40 cents just to stop the arguing, but I didn't have it. I was never paid a weekly or monthly allowance, and I never had any money in my pockets, not a penny. If Mom or Dad gave me money for a specific purchase, they always asked for the change.

In our family, every potential purchase, however modest, had to be analyzed to determine if it was absolutely necessary. Most times, it was deemed to be a "want," not a "need," like the new tennis shoes they determined that I wanted. I told Dad that I really needed new ones because my old tennis shoes were too tight and made my feet uncomfortable when I ran in P.E. class or played sports. Dad said my old ones were just a little snug and could last a few more months. He said that tight shoes were a part of "growing pains" for a youngster and made what he must have thought was a joke, comparing my current shoes to dependable old tires that have another 5,000 miles of tread left on them. I dropped it since I knew we all had to make sacrifices for the family to get by.

When something was ultimately determined to be needed, shopping to make certain we could purchase the item at a bargain price then became the priority. When my old tennis shoes couldn't last another day, the new ones my parents determined that I needed were not the ones with high tops and extra thick soles that made you look taller, gave you more spring, and let you run faster. Those were the ones I wanted. But they weren't a good bargain. The new tennis shoes I went home with, the ones they said I needed, had thin soles and low tops. They also were a half-size too big which made them an even better bargain since they would last longer. I could grow into them. I continued to be one of the slowest boys in seventh grade.

* * * * *

I stood in my bathroom with the door locked and continued to stare at Andrew Jackson's powerful features on my precious 20-dollar bill. Although I knew it was imperative that I destroy the evidence, I couldn't bring myself to tear it up. This was the first piece of currency I had ever been able to call mine.

Well, that may not be entirely correct. Three years earlier, when I was nine and we were living in the trailer, Gary Medina, a new kid in my fourth-grade class, invited me to play at his house after school. It was rare that I got this kind of invitation, and Mom enthusiastically gave her permission.

I took my glove, and Gary and I had a good time talking about baseball as we played catch in the empty lot next to his house. When it started to rain, we went inside. Gary had a Monopoly game. I hadn't played before and was fascinated that you were given money in the game.

Gary had bad luck with the dice, and I won the game. I remember the thrill of holding the crisp Monopoly currency and making purchasing decisions with *my* money. I got a rush of adrenaline each time my good fortune or shrewd investments added to my wealth. I vowed to ask for a Monopoly game of my own, but Christmas was three months off, an eternity to a nine-year-old. I also fretted about whether Santa or my parents could be convinced that I *needed* a Monopoly game.

When it was time for me to go home, I helped pick up the cards and currency used in the game. Gary was looking the other way when I stuck one of the 20-dollar notes in my pants pocket.

When I got home, I went straight to the little bathroom near the back of our trailer and closed its sliding door. I took out my treasure and ran my hands over it. It was green, just like the real money that my parents prized so much. I pretended that it was real and imagined all sorts of things that I could buy with it—not the things I needed, but the things I wanted. I spent ten minutes pleasantly daydreaming until Mom's call for supper broke my trance.

PART ONE: 10:20 p.m.

After my bath, disaster struck. I was removing a clean pair of jeans and a tee shirt from my dresser drawer to wear to school on the following day. I placed my selection on the dresser and turned to find my father standing in the trailer hallway. Mom was close behind. He stared at me without saying anything.

"What?" I asked.

"Where did you get this?" He held up the Monopoly money.

I swallowed hard. My mouth went dry, and my heart was suddenly pounding like a sledgehammer. I had left the bill in my dirty jeans.

"I said, 'Where did you get this?'"

"I found it," I said and immediately regretted it. How could I be so stupid?

"Lawrence, I'll give you a break, although I suspect you don't deserve it. I'm gonna pretend I didn't hear that." He raised his voice as he said, "For the last time, *where did you get this*?"

I looked at the floor. "Gary Medina and me, we were playing Monopoly today at his house. I guess I must've picked it up when we were putting the game away." He waited like I should say more, but I couldn't. I was a no-good thief and my shame consumed me.

"Look at me," he commanded.

When I didn't obey, he grabbed my arm and put his other hand under my chin, forcing my head up. Dad looked hurt, disappointed, and mad as hell, all in one. Mom was standing beside him, clutching her hands against her chest like I'd just stabbed her in the heart. I couldn't bear their looks, and I shook my head as hard as I could. His grip was dislodged, and I buried my chin into my chest.

Dad released me and flung open the hall closet. He ripped my jacket from its hanger and forced my arms through the sleeves. "Lon, get me the address of that boy he was playing with. What was their last name?"

"It's Medina. The boy is Gary Medina. I spoke with his mother yesterday. I've got their address on the table. Why?"

"Buddy and me are gonna pay a visit to the Medinas."

The rest was a blur. My father dragged me out of the trailer and into the car as I wailed at him to stop. Neighbors opened their trailer doors to see what was causing the commotion. It must have been a disconcerting sight. I was barefoot and still in my shorty pajamas, covered only by my winter coat on that cool night. I don't think my father noticed or cared. He was on a mission.

Dad stared straight ahead as we drove the short distance. He ignored my pleas for mercy and kept repeating the words I was to say when they answered the door. When he stopped the car in front of Gary's house, the scene of the crime, he shook me and commanded that I practice my speech, the one he had scripted. I obeyed, speaking in weak, halting segments through my sobs until he was satisfied.

When Mrs. Medina opened the door, I began whimpering my lines before she could say anything. I hoped to end my punishment quickly, before Gary might arrive at the door and witness my degradation. But it was not to be. Gary, looking as bewildered as his mother, peered around her before I finished the first sentence.

I said, "I'm sorry to disturb you. I took something today that didn't belong to me. I'm very sorry and I want to return it."

I handed the Monopoly note to her. Mouth open, she accepted it. But then, seeing my lack of proper clothing and obvious emotional distress, her motherly instinct got the better of her. She handed the note back to me. "Oh, Buddy, it's okay. It's just play money, and we won't miss it from the game. Why don't you keep it?"

Dad jerked the note from my hand and placed it firmly back into hers. His deep voice caught her by surprise. "Ma'am, he will not keep this money. He took it from your son, and that was wrong. Now, he is returning it, and you need to take it back."

She took a step backward with the note pressed to her bosom, almost knocking Gary to the floor as my father added, "We are sorry to have disturbed your evening. Good night to you both. Let's go, Son."

I turned and ran for the car.

When my father got into the car, I was curled into a ball,

cowering in the passenger seat and weeping profusely at my humiliation. "I hope you learned something tonight, boy," he said gruffly, and then he was silent the rest of the trip home. I cried all the way, cursing him in my mind and wishing I had flushed that Monopoly note down the toilet when I had the chance.

Dad continued to give me the silent treatment the following day. He didn't speak to me until the next evening when we said prayers at bedtime. With my parents in their usual places on the edges of my bed, I told God that I was sorry that I had stolen, and I asked Him to forgive me. I promised to never do it again.

Dad leaned over and kissed me on the forehead. "That's a good little man," he said.

Now I was thinking about a different 20-dollar bill—the real one in my hand. Unlike the Monopoly note, I had not stolen this one. I received it from Daniel Carter in a business transaction. He had given me a crisp 20-dollar bill in exchange for one shiny .38 caliber bullet.

Daniel and I were the only witnesses to that transaction, which had taken place in the science lab before school started last Friday morning. Now one of us was dead, a victim of that bullet. I was the only one alive who knew where it came from. If I destroyed the money, there would be no evidence to link me to that bullet. Only the private Hell that was burning in my guilty conscience.

It was on Tuesday, our second day back to school after the Christmas and New Year holiday, when Daniel approached me about selling him a bullet. He had apologized to Marty and me first thing on Monday morning for the incident at his house. He said he was an asshole for attacking me. Best friends shouldn't act like that, and he didn't know what had gotten into him. He thanked me for not taking his Bible. He said those other things he gave away were mere trinkets, but the Bible held sentimental value for his family. It was best that it remained in his family, and he was appreciative that I had recognized that fact. He also seemed genuinely concerned about the injury to my knee and must have said a hundred times that he was sorry for hurting me.

At lunch that Monday, Daniel cracked jokes with Marty and me as we speculated about the various junior high couples that were going steady. Marty entertained us with his rationale for which girls were letting their boyfriends get to first, second, or third base.

According to Marty, none of the seventh graders had come close to getting all the way around to home plate. However, he was quite sure there was an eighth-grade girl who had done a round-tripper, Marty's slang for a home run—going all the way. She was going steady with a high school boy called Snakes, and Marty said it was obvious she was getting nailed. You could tell by the peculiar bowlegged way she walked on Mondays after a busy weekend.

Daniel and I were intrigued by this revelation. During the breaks after fourth and fifth periods, we camped out around the alleged promiscuous girl's locker to observe her comings and goings. We were highly disappointed when we couldn't detect anything unusual about her walk. We reported back to Marty that it must have been a slow weekend.

After school that Monday, Daniel called his cousins and arranged a football game. We played on the big field across from Daniel's house. It was a blast. Some of the black kids from the neighborhood asked if they could play, and we let them. Marty joined us after basketball practice.

We played touch-and-pass until it got too dark to see the ball. I got to quarterback one of the teams since my knee was sore and I couldn't run too well. I was a regular Johnny Unitas that day. Daniel even caught one of my passes for a touchdown. That surprised everyone, especially Daniel. We went a little crazy celebrating after the score, slapping each other on the back with excitement. Then his father came home.

Dr. Carter made Daniel quit. He gave me a cold stare that I assumed meant he was still sore from the Bible-throwing incident. He told Daniel to get in the house and get started on his homework. Daniel protested, but his father told him that he would never amount to anything if he played around all the time instead of applying himself to his studies.

The next day, Daniel got into a first-rate, spirited debate with Sister Anne in social studies class. Sister Anne was not especially qualified to teach social studies. We speculated that her college degree must have been in rosary braiding, the nuns' equivalent of a jock majoring in basket weaving.

She never knew what to make of Daniel. He didn't watch much TV, not like me, preferring to spend his free time reading biographies of distinguished generals, world explorers, and famous statesmen. He had a near photographic memory and was a regular *Encyclopedia Britannica* when it came to all sorts of historical trivia. Daniel intimidated Sister Anne, and she distrusted him after the farting incident. He knew it and liked to call bullshit on her when she got her facts wrong, although he hadn't done it in over a month.

In class that Tuesday, they got into it when Sister Anne said that Columbus thought the world was flat. Daniel kept saying that was ridiculous and wouldn't let her get on with the lesson. He said all learned men of Columbus' time knew that the world was round. They just disagreed on its circumference. Despite the facts that Daniel kept spewing out, she stuck to her guns that Columbus and his men worried constantly about sailing off the edge of a flat world. By the end of the debate, I think it was Sister Anne who thought the world was flat. It was great to see Daniel back to full strength.

After sixth period, the last of the school day, Daniel and Marty would always meet at my locker, and then the three of us would walk down the stairs and out of the building discussing the day's events. Marty and I would walk with Daniel to his bicycle, say goodbye to him, and then go around the corner to the student pick-up area. Mrs. Shannon would be waiting there to drive the two of us home, or she'd make two trips—one for me and one for Marty—on days when Marty had basketball practice like that Tuesday.

As we emerged from the stairwell onto the ground floor, Marty gave a goodbye salute and headed for the gym. Once his back was turned, Daniel abruptly pulled me toward the door to the large room where they held choir and band classes. He opened it and, with his index finger to his lips, motioned with his other hand for me to enter quickly. I accepted his invitation. It seemed like some sort of James Bond game.

Once inside the empty room, he closed the door and came directly to the point. "Hey bro, lemme ask you something. Do ya think you could get your hands on one of those .38 caliber bullets your daddy has—for me?" Daniel knew about my father's pistol. I had told him about Dad going madman last year and wanting to shoot Old Man Washington with his .38 special.

"Why? What you want it for?" I asked.

He gave me an annoyed look and said sarcastically, "So I can kill myself with it, okay?"

"Good, then I won't have to put up with all your cheap bullshit anymore. In fact, I've got a better idea. If that's why you want it, go ask Sister Anne. I'm sure she'd be happy to accommodate you."

We both got a good laugh out of that. But after the laughter faded, he was still looking for a response. When I didn't answer, he asked again. "Well, Answer Man?"

"Well, what?"

"Do ya think you can get a bullet? Just one?"

"Why?"

"Cuz I'm doin' a science project on gunpowder," he said, mocking me like a kid backtalking an inquiring parent. "Hey, what difference does it make, bro? Can ya get one or not?"

I eyeballed him and he looked straight back, unflinching. He wasn't going to be satisfied until I answered the question.

"I don't know," I said slowly. "My dad, he keeps his gun and ammo locked in a cabinet in their bedroom closet. I'd have to get the key—it's on a ring with the car and house keys—and I'd have to get in there when he was gone or wasn't looking. So, that's not too likely." I paused before adding, "Besides, I'd need a reason to want to do something stupid like that, and right now, I've got none, *bro.*" I added that last word in my own mocking tone.

He leaned into my face. "What if I dared ya to do it?"

"Oh, great! What if I dared you to go play in the freeway?"

"I'd probably do it!" he said and flashed that big Daniel-grin.

I smiled back, recalling his performance as the zombie of North Street. I didn't want to smile about that, but I couldn't help it. He drove me crazy.

"Look," I said, "you dare me all you want. You can even *double-dog* dare me like a six-year-old. I don't intend to swipe no bullet from my father. It wouldn't be right. Now, we ought to get—"

"Ya know, that's your problem, man. Right there! That's it."

"*My* problem?"

"Yeah, like Marty and me keep tryin' to tell your sad ass. Your folks have you on a short leash like a little puppy dog. It's a joke! I betcha have to report in on how many times you wipe each time you take a dump. Right? And every other word outta your mouth is, 'Yes, suh' and 'No, ma'am.' It's downright painful." He shook his head at me.

"Hey, what's wrong with you? Why am I getting this ration of shit all of a sudden?"

"Aw, forget it," he said. "You wouldn't understand."

He turned to walk away, but I grabbed his arm and spun him around. "I asked you a question!"

He looked me in the eyes and tried to stare me down. "Okay, ya wanta know what I'm talkin' 'bout?"

"Yeah!" I stared back without blinking.

"Ya wanta know what I'm talkin' 'bout?"

"I said *yes*, you dipwad. What are you trying to say?"

Daniel began walking in circles around me while repeating, "Okay, okay, okay." He did that sometimes when he got worked up. I kept pivoting, trying to stay focused on the moving target.

"It's like this, bro," he said, pounding a fist into his open palm. But then he stopped pacing and his eyes widened as they stared into mine. This new look seemed to say he felt sorry for me. He didn't speak, letting the anticipation build. I wondered if he knew how intensely uncomfortable he was making me feel.

"It's like this," he repeated, only softly this time—lecturing, not threatening. "Do I have your undivided attention?"

"Yeah," I said.

"You should see yourself 'round 'em. It's pathetic, bro."

"Around who?"

"Your parents, man! It's like you're tryin' so hard to be some junior version of Mr. Goody Goody. And it's all the time, no matter how spaced out your dad gets about having to do this and don't do that. I mean, I know they're good people, deep down. Hey, often times I wished I could trade my give-a-shit folks for yours. But *c'mooon*, man, don't ya see what I'm sayin'?" He cocked his head to one side, his face less than a foot from mine.

I hesitated—trying to think, to digest his words.

"I'm right, huh?" he said, not waiting for a response. "I'm right and ya know it. I think it's all those rules of theirs—rules fo' this, rules fo' that, *rules fo' everything*! Where do they get off with all that jive? I mean, you're getting smothered, and you can't even see it, man. You're too busy being the poster child for perfect obedience. At some point, you gonna need to prove to yourself that you can break free and be your own man. Know what I mean?"

I must have been subconsciously nodding as he spoke.

"You see where I'm goin' with this, don't ya?" he asked with confidence.

Our eyes remained locked as I answered. "Maybe. But what's that got to do with me possibly getting my ass in big trouble just to get you a bullet to play with?"

"That's the point, don't ya see?" he implored. "The fact that you *might* get in trouble is what gets you pumped. It's a rush! And don't think you're doin' it for me, cuz you're not." He finished by poking his finger into my chest. "You doin' it for you!"

"If I'm doing it for me, then why don't I take something *I* want—let's say, how about a handful of cookies out of the cookie jar instead of a bullet out of a locked cabinet?"

He looked at me in disbelief. "See? I rest my case. You are so messed up that you think takin' cookies is the same as takin' a bullet. Well, here's the difference in cookies and bullets, my man: Any fool can swipe cookies. But, more likely than not, your momma will notice those cookies being gone and you'll suffer the wrath." He grinned, but then turned serious again. "But you take just one bullet from a big box of shells . . . Now, who counts bullets? Who's gonna ever notice it's gone? I'll tell ya—nobody! Not even your tight-assed old man. Nobody, that is, 'cept you, bro. You'll notice that it feels good to go just a small step over the out-of-bounds line from time to time and not get caught. What can I say? It's a rush, man."

Daniel gave me a wicked smile as he opened the three-ring binder he was carrying and found a plastic pouch, the kind used to store pens, pencils, small rulers, and the like. He unzipped the pouch, and I gasped when he removed a 20-dollar bill.

He waved it in front of me. "I'll betcha this 20-spot that you ain't got the balls to bring me just one of your daddy's shells. Just one!"

"Where did you get that?" I asked.

"You let me worry 'bout that. Point is: I got it and *you*, my young man, can have it. That is, if you can do one simple thing."

"Tell me what you want with the bullet, Daniel."

His face turned angry. "And you let me worry 'bout that too! Do ya wanta make a fast 20 or not? Or do ya wanta be that perfect poster boy all your life?"

When I returned his scowl, Daniel softened, like he realized he was being too harsh, like he knew I wasn't going to seriously consider his request without some assurances regarding his intentions. He threw up his hands and gave me that mischievous jack-of-hearts smirk.

"Look," he pleaded, "it's just a bullet, fo' Chrissake! Ya know what I mean? It's not like some big bad weapon or something. Don't sweat it. Okay?"

I couldn't figure out his game, his angle. Why would anyone give up 20 bucks for a stupid dare? There had to be a catch.

"Is this, you know, like a bet?" I asked. "Do I owe you $20 if I don't deliver the bullet?"

He laughed. "That's a tempting idea, my man. But where

would you get 20 bucks in cold hard cash?" He laughed again. "Nah, it's not a bet. Consider it an incentive."

"Then what's the catch?"

"No catch. I just want me a bullet, and just as important, I want *you*," he said, pointing at me as he said the word, "to step outta your sugarcoated shell and be the one who gets it for me. I want you to feel that rush. Now, what'da ya say, Answer Man?"

Again, I was silent. I was starting to worry that Mrs. Shannon had been waiting for a long time.

"Well?" he asked.

"I'll think about it," I said.

He reverted to the look of disgust. "*Shiiit*, man! Yeah, like hell you will." He returned the currency to the plastic pouch.

"Hey, I said I'd think about it and that's what I'll do!"

He put his face in mine. I felt his breath and smelled the contempt with which he said, "Right, and leopards can change their spots." Then, he shrugged and backed away, adding, "Hey, ya can't help what ya be, bro. It's okay. I apologize. I am *sooo* sorry that I tempted you."

As he walked toward the door, he added in a cheerful voice, "C'mon, I've had enough of this joint for one day. I gotta get home or my old man's gonna raise hell at me. I couldn't stand it if I made him mad at me, *could I?*" As his laughter reverberated in the big room, the dig from that last sentence went right under my skin.

I started the destruction with the top right-hand corner, but it was half-hearted. I could only bring myself to tear a tiny piece from the tip. I carefully tore off each of the other three corners and then held all four pieces in my hand, uncertain, not ready to drop the tiny green triangles into the toilet. I was reasonably confident that my precious 20-dollar bill had not yet been mutilated so badly that it wouldn't be valid currency if I suddenly changed my mind.

I thought about the past Thursday night. I wished that I could go back to Thursday night at 8:00, while Mom was working her second job at the hospital and Dad and I were watching TV. Dad stood up and announced that he needed to walk to the little store on Seventh Street to get a pack of cigarettes. He said he'd be back in three minutes.

I agreed with his time estimate—a minute to walk to the store, a minute chatting with Mr. Carson at the store while he paid for the smokes, and a minute to walk home. It would be just enough time.

It all happened so quickly. I jumped up and looked out the window to see Dad at the end of our driveway. He turned and started down Hazel Street. Like a madman, I didn't stop to think about what I was doing; I just did it. As my heart pounded, I dashed into my parents' bedroom and found his keys on top of the dresser, where he always left them. Standing in their closet in front of the tall filing cabinet, I inserted a small silver key into the cabinet lock. It fit perfectly. A slight turn to the right and the lock popped out.

I discovered the revolver in the middle drawer along with one box of ammunition. The way the closet light danced on the gun, it was almost blue in color. It was mesmerizing, and I stood trance-like for a few precious seconds before reaching in. The weapon was cold to the touch. I was careful to keep my fingers away from the trigger and the barrel pointing away from me as I lifted it from the cabinet. I cupped it in both hands like a fragile newborn baby. It was the first time I had held a real gun, and I was amazed by how heavy it was. The toy guns I had played with as a youngster were so light in comparison.

I gently returned the pistol to the cabinet, careful to place it in the same position as I had found it. I opened the box of shells. It was about three-fourths full, and I couldn't see how anyone would notice if another round was missing. I was certain that Daniel was right—who counts bullets? I removed one and placed it in my pants pocket. I closed the cabinet drawer, locked it, and returned Dad's keys to his dresser.

I ran to my room and hid the bullet deep in the bowels of my desk. I figured that I still had a solid minute until my father returned. I rushed into the family room, picked up the telephone, and dialed Daniel's number. When his mother finally got him on the line, I spoke quickly.

"Daniel, it's me."

I heard him say, *Hey, bro—*

"Listen, I've only got a minute. You remember the dare you gave me on Tuesday after school?"

Sure.

"Can you bring the money to school tomorrow?"

Yeah, but—

"Good. I'll see you tomorrow. Bye."

I hung up, not waiting for him to say goodbye.

The next morning, in the science lab with no one else around, we made the exchange. In about two seconds, I got $20 and he got one shiny little bullet. Eight hours later, that same bullet met Daniel Carter's brain, and he ceased to be a conscious, thinking, feeling human being. I should have gotten 30 pieces of silver.

I slowly tore the bill in half and then, more rapidly, in half again. Now there was no turning back. I tore it into at least 20 separate pieces that all went into the toilet. I was watching them float in the water when I was startled by a loud knock on my bathroom door.

My father's deep voice penetrated from the other side. "Buddy, are you okay? You've been in there a long time."

"Cons'terpation. You remember, right?" I giggled, thinking about that idiot Stoddard, but Dad wasn't amused.

"Quit playing 'round, Son. It's late. It's time for your prayers and lights out, and your mother and me have some things to talk 'bout—with you. Get finished with your business, right now. Understand?"

"Yes, sir."

"Good."

I heard him walk away. With a sigh, I gave the commode handle a firm pull. I gazed into the bowl to watch the pieces of my 20-dollar bill spin in a circle, like the now-tattered pieces of my young life, and then get flushed down the toilet.

* * * * *

Here's a riddle for you: *Which comes first, the bullet or the gun?* Be careful. It's a trick question.

I thought a lot about it that morning when I was by myself in my room and again late that night before I started thinking about Allie and all that other stuff. It's a question that has relentlessly hounded me over the years that have followed.

I know what I did was wrong. But, *C'mon*, I've tried to tell myself, *it's not like you gave Daniel Carter a gun.* With what I knew about my friend, if I'd given him a gun—say my dad's .38 special—and he'd gone home and used that gun to take his own life . . . Well, that's a different story! There is absolutely no excuse how anyone could be such an idiot as to give a gun to a 12-year-old—even another 12-year-old. If I had given him a gun, I would deserve to rot in jail for the rest of my life and then burn in Hell for all eternity. End of discussion.

But a bullet? A bullet is vastly different from a gun. A bullet is a small, lightweight, inconsequential thing that, in and of itself, can't hurt anyone. What did Daniel say? *It's just a bullet, fo' Chrissake!*

A bullet is not a weapon, not like a gun or a bow or a cannon. Bullets, arrows, and cannonballs, these things are merely projectiles. They are not weapons. They are merely instruments for the powerful weapon to use, things designed for the sole purpose of piercing and tearing the flesh and taking life away from previously healthy organisms.

I didn't give him a gun! Everyone knows that guns are dangerous. I gave him a bullet, a small projectile that slammed through his skull and splattered his brain all over his pretty little pillow and neatly folded towels.

Do you see what I mean about it being a trick question? *It's just a bullet, fo' Chrissake!* And yet, it's *everything*.

Chapter 23

11:00 p.m.

My father flicked the light switch and closed the door behind him. I was suddenly surrounded by darkness. I rolled over to look at the illuminated face of my clock radio. It was 11:00, an hour later than my normal bedtime.

When Mom and Dad were in my room, I had felt mentally drained and physically exhausted. Now, I was scared. I wasn't afraid of the boogie man or any monsters of the night. I was afraid to be alone in the dark with my own thoughts. I didn't want to think any more about Daniel Carter and the things that I should have done differently. I needed a respite from those guilt-ridden, introspective reflections. I needed something to divert my mind from the serious life-and-death issues that I'd been struggling with all day, something to help me relax so sweet unconsciousness could have a chance to overtake me.

So, I thought about Mom and Dad and how lucky I was to have them as parents. After I had said farewell to my dismembered 20-dollar bill and emerged from the bathroom, Mom had come to my room to tuck me into bed. Dad followed and said he wanted to tell me about the meeting at school. It was late, and he only hit a few of the high points that M Squared and Allie had covered. It took all my energy to act like I was paying close attention when I had heard all this—live and in person—a few hours earlier.

Dad's primary focus was on the things he had said in his speech at the end of the meeting. He talked about Daniel's wiring getting messed up and how it caused him to behave in a manner that was abnormal for him and for human beings in general. He said it wasn't Daniel's fault. I had heard it before, but I liked hearing it again, particularly the part about Daniel up in Heaven with Jesus. The three of us held hands and said a prayer for Daniel and his family. Then they kissed me and left me in the darkness.

I tried to turn my thoughts to God and Jesus, but that didn't work at all. Theology, including *my* potential fate in the next world, was far too deep a subject so late at night.

Then I had it. Of course! I would think about the only pleasant thing that had happened to me during the 16 long hours that I'd been conscious that miserable day. I would think about her. I would think about the most beautiful woman in the world. I would think about Allie Masterson.

I lay on my back and stared at the black ceiling. I held my own hand, trying to recapture the way she had touched me as we were introduced. I recalled the modest look on her face when she overheard Sister Mary Margaret whisper to me, "She's every bit as intelligent as she is beautiful."

In my mind, I replayed the sweet sound of her voice when she told me that I could call her by her first name. I saw her smile as she joked about our names being similar. She had said the words, "Allie Larice Masterson." I repeated them under my breath, and the soft sound filled the darkness in my room. I whispered it again.

I thought about the intelligence and compassion she had displayed, first in our family room and then in the school auditorium. She spoke to the parents, all of them considerably older than her, in an easy and confident manner. By the end of the meeting, it was clear that she had gained their respect and trust.

Allie had been so easy for me to talk to. Under more pleasant circumstances, I felt like we could spend hours just sharing each other's company. I had a crazy mental image of us sitting at a quaint sidewalk cafe, holding hands while we sipped our afternoon tea and chatted nonstop about a myriad of interesting subjects.

I remembered her saying that she would be at my school for a few more days of counseling. I was confident that I would need more counseling tomorrow. The prospect of seeing her again so soon was both reassuring and exhilarating. Yes, I was likely to need a lot of counseling.

These were the pleasant thoughts I had been searching for. I was starting to relax. I felt the tension leaving my body. In its place was an inner warmth and excitement that made my ears radiate.

I thought of how statuesque Allie appeared and how her perfect face could reflect a wide range of emotions: sadness, sympathy, contemplation, and compassion. Of Allie's many prominent features, her hazel eyes were the most striking. They twinkled when she laughed, and her silky brown hair bounced on her shoulders and sparkled in the overhead light.

As I was thinking about the way that Allie and I had said goodbye in the family room, I was distracted by an uncomfortable constriction in my pajama bottoms which were twisted around a fully erect stiffy. I raised my hips and tugged on the pajama shorts to get some slack into the afflicted area. With my other hand, I reached down to free my Leaning Tower of Pisa from the clothing that was forcing it to list to the port side. I pulled it forward, so it was pointing at a more comfortable angle. I don't want this to sound pornographic and all, but the pressure of my hand felt good. So, without really thinking about it, I left it there.

When we stood to say goodbye, Allie had stepped toward me and said, "I'm so sorry about Daniel, Buddy," and then she reached out and gave me a consoling hug. But it wasn't a quickie like M Squared and Sister Katherine had done. Allie held me in a firm embrace for a couple of seconds. It was like the way Mom held me when I brought home a good report card.

Allie's smell was different from Mom's. My mother wore perfume that wasn't unpleasant but had a sweet fragrance. Allie's smell was much more subtle, not at all sweet. It was inviting and made me think of wildflowers in springtime.

Allie was five or six inches taller than me, plus she was wearing two-inch heels. When she reached out for that goodbye hug, my head naturally cocked to the side to fit under her chin, and her soft hair fell forward and brushed the side of my face. We came together so naturally. There was nothing awkward about the way she draped her arms lightly over my shoulders and her hands cupped my shoulder blades, pressing me gently to her body. Being shorter, my arms instinctively went lower, circling her waist and resting on her skirt at the place where the slope of her hips began.

The old springs under my mattress creaked softly, and they seemed to say, "A-lee, A-lee" as my hips involuntarily rocked back and forth. It was like an inviting voice whispering to me as I focused my mind on the most exciting part of our embrace.

My head was tilted downward so Allie could rest her chin on top of it. As a result, my right cheek was pressed against her skin at the point of the "V" in her sweater and my mouth came to rest lightly on her sweater, over the gentle slope of her right breast. When she didn't immediately release me, I rubbed my head very gently against her—just once. I couldn't help myself. Moving my cheek against her sweater, I could feel the contour of her breast within the low-cut bra.

When Allie finally loosened her grip and I did the same, her hands moved to her hips, and she cocked her head slightly while looking directly into my eyes. I was concerned that she had noticed my subtle facial movement and was angry. I thought I had blown it. But she whispered, "You're an extraordinary young man, Buddy Torrence." She had said it softly, but it was loud enough for my parents and the others in the room to hear. Then she turned to say goodbye to the group, walked to her car, and drove away.

Allie hadn't called me a boy. Rather, she viewed me as a young man. She had said that I was extraordinary. My imagination went wild. Were her words a signal to me, an invitation?

The chanting of the springs intensified as I fantasized about a more intimate relationship with her. I remembered the long look I had down her sweater at her exquisite breasts straining against the lacy bra. I had never touched a girl on the breasts, except Allie with my cheek (through her sweater). I was fairly sure that didn't count. I wondered what second base felt like with my hands instead of my cheek.

I recalled the way Allie periodically crossed and uncrossed her long legs while sitting in the recliner, how the sheer stockings tightly enveloped her perfectly proportioned thighs and calves. I thought about her skirt high on her thighs as she climbed from her car. Her legs had splayed open for me to see her panties and the straps that held her stockings. I wondered what third base would be like, how it would—

That's when it happened. I don't want to get into a big description, but it was something completely different from anything I'd ever felt. I was suddenly lightheaded as intense shudders racked my body. My heart rate instantly doubled, and if I could have spoken, I would have cried out to my parents that I was having a heart attack.

Beads of cold sweat formed across my hot forehead, and I felt frightened, dizzy, and disoriented all at once. The spasms passed, but my heart continued to pump like a full-on firehose and my breathing was heavy.

During the next minute, 60 of the most confusing seconds of my life, I tried to process what had just happened as my breathing and heart rate gradually returned to normal. Coach Peters had discussed masturbation in a health class for boys that we took as part of P.E., and Marty had offhandedly talked about jerking-off and his joystick. But I never quite understood, never fully got it—until that moment.

I sat up on my bed and felt the cold stickiness of my cotton pajamas on my groin. I was strangely pleased with myself as this no doubt meant that I was now a man, with the power to impregnate a woman. But the euphoria that came with my newly discovered manly power quickly faded, to be replaced by new doubts and fears, not the least of which was how a man like me actually went about impregnating a woman. I was unsure about the intricacies of the physical act and equally distressed wondering how I was supposed to find someone who wanted to do it—with me. What were you supposed to say to them—before, during, and after?

I stood up slowly, slouched over because of the weight on my shoulders from all the questions with no answers. I tiptoed out of my bedroom and into my bathroom, quietly locking the door behind me. I searched between my legs to make certain my equipment was still intact and there was no visible damage. My penis had returned to its normal flaccid state, and I tried as best I could to clean myself and my clothing. Back in my room, I changed pajamas. I hid the stained ones in my closet and vowed to further assess the degree to which they had been soiled and try to better clean them in the morning light.

I was incredibly tired and fell asleep as soon as my head touched the pillow.

Chapter 24

11:55 p.m.

When I awoke suddenly from the nightmare, it was almost midnight. I was disoriented and wet with sweat. I ran, confused and terrified, into my parents' room. I spent that first night curled in the fetal position as I lay between them, afraid to fall back asleep. Over the years that followed, my folks and I came to refer to it simply as "the Daniel dream."

For the next two nights, I slept in their room. It didn't stop the Daniel dream. It just gave me two pairs of comforting arms to fall into when I awoke screaming. Mom and Dad were scared shitless. It made me even more uncomfortable that I couldn't tell them everything about the dream.

I discussed it with Allie, or at least certain aspects of it. She said that recurring dreams like mine were natural after a traumatic experience, but I wondered what she would have said if I'd been totally honest with her. It didn't matter. I loved discussing things with Allie. I saw her twice that first week (at school) and once a week thereafter for five weeks (in her office)—not as patient and shrink, but as two very close friends. At least, that's how I remember it.

She always seemed delighted to see me and never tried to pull any shrink tricks. She never used psychobabble when we talked and never treated me in a patronizing or condescending adult-to-kid manner. In fact, we hardly ever talked about Daniel. We just talked. She was my new best friend, and I was her extraordinary young man.

Allie Masterson was the main reason I didn't give in to my deep depression during those first few weeks after Daniel's death. I lived to share her company and show her how extraordinary I could be. When I moved out of my parents' bed to confront the terror on my own, it was to show Allie my strength and maturity.

I ended my bedtime prayers each night by asking, "Dear God, please let me have good dreams and sleep well tonight." My parents would force a smile and nod at me in a reassuring manner but then glance apprehensively at each other. They would kiss me goodnight and leave me with some encouraging words. On most nights, after a couple of hours tossing and turning, fighting with myself to try to relax my tense body and make my mind go blank, I would finally fall into a restless and apprehensive state of half-sleep.

And then it would happen. Nothing helped. I experienced the Daniel dream almost every night for the next two months. I came to accept it as my punishment, a burden that I was destined to bear for all eternity. I learned to stay reasonably calm after waking in a panic and how to eventually coax myself back to sleep.

A year after Daniel's passing, I was only having the dream about once a week. By the time I graduated from college, it was only about once a month. But the randomness was its own cruelty. Each night before I fell asleep, somewhere in my final thoughts was the chilling uncertainty of whether I would be terrorized on that particular night by *the Daniel dream*.

The boy is thin and has a handsome face. He and I are standing in front of St. Christopher School in the paved area that contains the bicycle racks. He walks to his bike, a red Schwinn. I give him a goodbye wave and start to walk around the school building. He shouts, "Hey, bro!" I turn and he says, "Thanks for everything." He winks at me like we share a secret.

I frown, pretending not to understand what he means. He leaves his bicycle and steps forward until he's standing in front of me. All I can see is his angelic face. He speaks with a soft despair, "Nobody really cares. I know you tried but—" He doesn't complete the thought, just repeats, "Thanks for everything." As he says the words, he embraces me and whispers, "Goodbye," into my ear in a way that has an unsettling finality to it.

I draw back, surprised by his uncharacteristic show of emotion. I want to say something, to confront him on this strange behavior, but my vocal cords are frozen. I can't speak, but my mind is thinking the unthinkable.

The boy walks back to his Schwinn and I follow. I need to know what he is talking about. I need for him to explain why he is thanking me and why he's saying goodbye in that voice.

He must be clairvoyant because, with one hand on his bike, he reaches out with the other to draw me close and hug me again. He whispers into my ear, "I'm free, bro." As he pulls back, I look at his face, only inches from mine. Why does he look so serene, like a cloudless sky? I feel weak, disoriented. Before I can withdraw, he whispers, "You the gravy now."

His breath is warm and moist, and it sticks to my face as he begins pedaling off. This time, instead of turning my back on him, I follow. I'm chasing after him but in slow motion. I can't keep up. So, I spread my arms wide like two wings, and I spring into the air. I am flying! It's a bit awkward at first. I drift down and then soar upward like a kite on a windy day, and in no time I've mastered flying. A dip of my left arm while tilting my head in that direction allows me to turn left and vice versa.

I make lazy circles over the boy with my arms outstretched. His head is down, and his legs are pounding on the pedals. He's in a hurry and doesn't look up. I continue to follow, effortlessly gliding above him.

We arrive at his house: a simple two-story, red-brick structure. The boy jumps off the bicycle. In a fluid motion, he puts down the kickstand, takes out his key, and walks to the front door. He opens it, oblivious to my presence overhead. I swoop down and swish sideways, flying over his head in a flash of speed, making it into the house just before he closes the door and locks it behind him.

Inside, I explore the house, arching my back to fly up to the second floor and then tilting my head downward to descend back to the ground floor. I complete my tour, flying from room to room. No one else is home.

I hover over the entryway as the boy comes down the staircase with blanket, towels, and pillow in hand. He meticulously spreads and smooths the large blanket on the hardwood floor just inside the front door. I see a flash of metal and a plastic pouch in his hand as he fluffs a pillow at the head of the blanket and then arranges several hand towels neatly on top of the pillow. I turn my body vertical, perpendicular to the floor, and descend slowly until I'm sitting in a lotus position at the foot of the blanket, arms outstretched with my palms up.

The boy seats himself in the middle of that blanket, facing me. With one hand, he reaches into the pouch, the one that used to hold a 20-dollar bill, and he extracts a single bullet. He carefully loads the bullet into a chamber of the .38 caliber revolver that he holds in his other hand. Then he looks at me, acknowledging my presence for the first time since coming home. He says the words again, unemotionally, "Nobody really cares. I know you tried but—" He smiles, then says, "Thanks for everything."

I am frozen. Try as I may, I cannot speak and I cannot move. I'm an observer, not a participant in this drama, there to witness what happens when you don't care enough, don't try hard enough.

In a single motion, the beautiful boy raises the gun to one temple while he lowers his body so that the other side of his head rests on the towels and pillow. I hear him whisper, "Goodbye."

There is an explosion.

I awaken with a scream.

THE OUTSKIRTS OF REDEMPTION

* * * * *

I banished myself at 12 years old
To atone for my acts and omissions;
So close to Hell, yet it's always cold
Here, at the outskirts of redemption.

I failed a friend when he needed me most;
Now he's gone to another dimension
While I mark time in a desolate post
Alone, at the outskirts of redemption.

Dreams haunt my nights, where he whispers goodbyes
And I'm helpless in black recollection;
It hurts deep inside where I live with my lies;
I hide in the dark and I try not to cry;
Alone in my room, I ask why, dear God, WHY?
Here, at the outskirts of redemption.

Please tell my mother I can't come home;
Hands outstretched, my soul in prison
I'll live out my life—here, all alone
At the outskirts of redemption.

- Lawrence J. Torrence, 1965

Chapter 25
BE SOMEBODY

When I was only 11 and still an innocent little child, I asked my father why the first thing that grown-ups always wanted to know about me was what I wanted to be when I grew up. He said it was just adults' way of trying to engage children in an adult-level conversation. I asked him how I should respond.

"You should tell the truth," he said. "Tell 'em what you wanta be."

"But what if I don't know?" I asked.

He frowned at me and narrowed his eyes. "Don't ever say that, Buddy. You need to have a plan for your future. Even at 11 years old, you need to have a plan."

"So, what should I be?"

"That's for you to figure out, but—" He paused.

"But what?"

"You should set your sights high, Son." Without specifically telling me what I should be, he talked about choosing a vocation that would be worthy of respect and provide a good living for my family. "That's important. That's why you need to go to college, so you won't end up like me. I want you to *be somebody* when you grow up, when you become a man."

I thought a lot about what he had said, and a few days later I made a momentous decision. I would set my sights on becoming president of the United States. What the heck! So what if times were tough and we were living in a trailer? Abe Lincoln grew up in a log cabin, and it didn't stop him from becoming president. In 1960, I had watched the presidential debates on television and stayed up late at night on Election Day, following the returns with an all-consuming fascination. I had wavy brown hair and a good smile, just like John F. Kennedy. And I was from a big state with lots of electoral votes. *This is America, the land of opportunity, where anything is possible*, I told myself. Besides, I was confident that just saying I wanted to be the president of the United States would make my father proud of me.

But the first time I announced my career intentions—on Saturday at the barbershop while Dad and I were getting our haircuts—the barbers and adult customers laughed at me. They made wisecracks about laws I could propose to reduce the price of trailers and used cars, about all the derelict kids in the neighborhood who could serve in my cabinet, and on and on.

I shot a desperate glance at my father in the next chair. He was sitting more erect than usual and staring straight ahead as Mr. Jimmy worked on his sideburns between chuckles. I knew he could see me out of the corner of his eye. He must have known I was looking at him for help. But he just sat there, unwilling to come to my defense, as if he was testing me, waiting to see if I could deal with the situation in a presidential manner. They continued to taunt me until Mr. Jimmy motioned for them to stop. He could see a tear rolling down my cheek.

On the way home, Dad talked about not setting my goals quite so high. I listened respectfully and tried to make him believe that I wasn't serious about the president thing, like it was all a joke. I promised to think some more about my future and come up with a *real* plan. But inside, I was certain that I had disappointed and embarrassed my father. I was crushed.

The next day, while Dad was outside washing the car after Sunday Mass, I asked my mother the same question. "Why do grown-ups care so much about what I want to be when I grow up, Mom?"

"I think it's because people place too much importance on what you do and not enough on who you are," she said.

It sounded deep and didn't fully sink into my 11-year-old brain. "So, what should I tell them?"

She stared into my eyes and said, "Why don't you tell them, 'When I grow up, I want to be *a fine person.*'"

I laughed. I couldn't help it, even though I knew she was being serious. I tried to keep a straight face as I asked, "Do I need to go to college for that?"

"If the knowledge you'll get from a college education will help you to be a better person, then you should definitely go. Otherwise, what's the point?"

I was surprised by her irrefutable logic and unable to come up with a reply other than a slow affirmative nod. After a few seconds, she gave me a big smile and said she had a lot to do. She told me that she loved me, planted a kiss on top of my head, and then went back to her housework. I marveled at her simplistic approach to the meaning of life, but I also recall wondering if mothers have any idea how frightening it is to be a young boy who knows he must grow up someday to *be somebody*—to become a man.

PART TWO

1973-74
The Aftermath

Chapter 26
LARRY

I couldn't appreciate it when I was 12 years old, but time does have a healing effect. By 1973, the year I turned 21, the painful memories of Daniel Carter, my overwhelming guilt, and all the unanswered questions had slowly, inexorably faded from my conscious mind. That's not to imply that everything turned out all rosy for me. It's just that, with time and maturity, I learned how to block those memories and feelings and force them down into my subconscious. There they would simmer just below the surface until some everyday catalyst—seeing a cop who looked like that Officer Don fellow, watching a TV show where some kid began acting strangely for no reason, or reading a book where suicide was part of the plot—would cause them to boil over and come flooding back.

I paid a high price for my carelessness and insensitivity toward Daniel Carter. My childhood abruptly ended on January 11, 1965. From that day forward, unlike most adolescents, it was impossible for me to plan or dream about my future because I was a constant prisoner of my past. Don't get me wrong. I'm not complaining or trying to score sympathy points here. I don't need anyone to feel sorry for me because I know I deserve everything that's happened to me since that time. I've grown to accept it as my fate.

After I finished seventh grade at St. Christopher School, my parents decided it would be better for me if we moved out of Beaumont, out to the country. They picked China, Texas, a sleepy little goat-roper town 15 miles west of Beaumont, where no one interesting lives and nothing exciting ever happens.

When we moved, I insisted on being called Larry to sound more grown up and to try to distance myself from Buddy and all his baggage. I never wanted to be Buddy again.

During the succeeding years, my relationship with my parents changed dramatically. For 12 and one-half years, they had been like two giant helicopters hovering over me to cater to their precious only child's every need and actively participate in every little thing that was happening in my life. After Daniel's death, I began establishing no-fly zones designed to protect my privacy and keep them at bay. Whenever they ventured into my space, I would take pot-shots specifically targeted to hurt their feelings or make them dislike me so they would retreat and leave me alone. I couldn't afford for them to get too close for fear that I might slip up and do or say something that would reveal my secret.

My behavior outside the home also changed in order to accommodate my darker psyche and more fragile self-confidence. I lost interest in participating in competitive sports. I quit Boy Scouts. The summer I turned 14, I quit going to church. My parents were disappointed and hurt by each of these decisions. They would plead with me to explain, but I couldn't have an intimate conversation with them about my feelings. "I just don't want to" was all they would get from me. Once, they accused me of being mad at God. I wasn't, but I didn't argue with them because I didn't want to get into a big theological deal. I didn't blame God for what happened between Daniel and me, but it was impossible to say a prayer—any prayer—without thinking about Daniel and wondering about his fate in the next world. As a result, I stopped praying.

What little gratification and self-esteem I derived during those years came from consistently making the best grades in my class. Schoolwork had always come easy for me, but I became a compulsive perfectionist. Fear of making a careless mistake became a paranoia, compelling me to over-study for exams and double-, triple-, and quadruple-check everything I did.

That paranoia spilled over into my personal life, making me hypercautious and suspicious around other kids. When I did interact with my peers, my cynical attitude and caustic tongue made me about as pleasant to be around as battery acid. I had a spattering of classmates who periodically took an interest in me during my high school years but never for long. Each potential pal, buddy, and semi-friend quickly melted away like cotton candy in the mouth. Even during college, when I had roommates in the dorm and study-buddies, I never had another really good friend—that close, special kind of friend like Daniel and Marty—the kind that everybody needs. During all those formative years, I never had a serious girlfriend. While everyone else was going on dates and "doing it," I spent my evenings at home or in the dorm and studied, read, watched stupid TV programs, listened to the radio, or played my records.

After I was old enough to drive and have a little spending money from a part-time job, I went to see films. I saw every popular movie that came out—by myself during the day, mostly Sundays, when the theatres were almost empty. I told myself it was better like that, so I could concentrate on the story and not have people there to distract me. I thought of myself as one of those fascinating James Dean characters—a mysterious, thoughtful, brooding sort of loner. But "loner" is a derivative of the word "alone," the place where I spent most of my time. They don't show that part in the James Dean movies because it's too depressing.

My parents coped with my moodiness and withdrawal by not being judgmental and giving me time and space as I struggled with all my hang ups. My father still maintained his rules, but they evolved and became less rigid as I got older and began asserting my independence.

My father called on the community telephone for my floor at Shivers Hall, the dormitory at Lamar University in Beaumont where I lived during my first semester of college. I heard him say, *Larry, you're comin' home this weekend.* It was odd the way he said it, more as a command than a question.

"Yeah. That's what I'd planned."

I need to talk to you 'bout this report card we got in the mail.

"Give me a break, will you?" I rolled my eyes. "It's not a *report card*. Those are just midterm marks, not the real—"

His voice was firm and left no room for negotiation. *Son, we need to have a conversation. I'll talk to you when you're here on Saturday morning.*

"Yeah, okay," I mumbled into the phone, and then we hung up.

Lamar had a policy of mailing midsemester grades to the parents of freshmen. It was their way of trying to get parents more involved and hopefully reduce the first-year dropout rate. At mid-term of my first semester in college, I had two A's and four B's—not bad, but hardly what you'd expect from a high school valedictorian. Eighteen years old and living away from home for the first time, I may have been doing some slightly immature and possibly misguided things like not focusing as much as I should on academics and experimenting with grass.

The roommate they assigned to me that first semester was Ray Donner, a junior from Galveston who was majoring in marijuana. He knew everything there was to know about marijuana. I didn't know anything. Ray kept trying to get me to smoke with him, but I told him I didn't want to get hooked or anything. He said you couldn't get hooked on grass. But, if he was any example, I didn't believe it. In a moment of weakness, I told him I'd give it a try, just this once. Wouldn't you know, Teddy Richards, the dorm dick for our floor, popped into our room just as I was beginning to float up to the ceiling.

The dorm dick had a master key and could let himself into your room if he suspected something improper was going on. I thought we had constitutional rights to protect against uninvited entry like that, but Teddy set me straight on that issue. He said the Constitution didn't apply to college campuses after all the riots in the Sixties and especially not to drug addicts—like me—on college campuses. Teddy, who took his chickenshit responsibilities far too seriously, headed for the community phone on our floor to call the campus police and have us arrested and kicked out of school.

Ray and I gave chase. I was scared shitless. My first time to smoke grass and great waves of destruction were about to come crashing down upon me if I couldn't somehow stop this madman. "But Teddy," I pleaded, saying the first thing that flashed into my mind, "I wasn't smoking it—not really. I mean, I wasn't inhaling."

Teddy looked at me like that had to be the stupidest thing he had ever heard. He shook his head in disbelief, and soon neither Teddy nor Ray could hold back their gut-splitting laughter. Because I had come up with that ridiculous excuse and made him laugh, Teddy said he wasn't going to turn us in—this time.

Later that night, Teddy and Ray confessed that they had staged my bust for their mutual amusement. Teddy was actually a marijuana major, just like Ray. After that, each time Teddy saw me around the dorm or on campus, he'd point at me, say, "I'm not inhaling," and break into uncontrollable laughter.

Maybe I wasn't applying myself to my schoolwork as seriously as I should, but I resented the way my father had summoned me home. It was demeaning, considering that I was now an adult and living on my own. I spent two days working on my speech, how I would explain that college was different and harder than high school, how I'd let him have it for his inflated expectations. To make certain I would feel appropriately adult for my interrogation on Saturday morning, I spent Friday night drinking beer until closing time at The Little Brown Jug, a dive close to campus on Railroad Avenue. Wanda, the bartender, called me "Cutie" and never hassled me over my pathetic fake ID. I had become a regular.

* * * * *

"Sit down," Dad said after I'd finished a little chitchat with my mother. I took a seat across from him at our dining room table.

"I'll be in the laundry room if you boys need me," Mom said. She flashed a nervous frown at Dad as she left.

"Let's talk 'bout this," he said and set the official-looking report on the middle of the table for me to see. As usual, he went straight to the point. I was mildly disappointed that he hadn't first commented on the fact that I didn't show up until 2:00 when his summons had been for Saturday morning.

"That's fine with me," I said. My head was pounding from the hangover, but I was ready for anything he had. There was no way he was going to intimidate me. Not this time.

"Do you see this?" He pointed to a box on the form that read, "Major: UNDECIDED."

"Yeah. So?"

"So, you will not be 'Undecided.' Your mother and I are happy to pay for your schooling, but you will develop a plan for your college education and for your career after graduation. I don't care if you change it each and every semester, but you will *always* have a plan. Are we clear on that?"

"But the freshman curriculum is pretty much the same no matter what. I told you I wasn't sure what I wanted to major in, remember?"

"And you'll remember that I've asked you 'bout this at least a half-dozen times. You need to make a decision."

"Right—and I will."

"You're damn right you will! I've lost my patience on this, Lawrence. By the end of next week, you will be majoring in something other than Undecided, and you'll have a plan for your life. Now, are we crystal clear on that?"

There was no point in arguing. I could easily come up with something to appease him. Besides, my head felt like it would explode each time the blood pulsed through my temples. "Yes, sir," I said.

"Good," he said calmly, satisfied. "We'll meet back here next Saturday—in the morning if it's not too much trouble for you—and you can tell us what you've decided. If your mom or I can be of any help in that process, you let us know."

"Yes, sir."

"And one other thing."

I gave him a nod.

"I want you to know that I'm proud of you for going to college. I have confidence in you and know you're gonna do real well, Son. You'll be the first college graduate ever in our family."

"Thanks," I mumbled.

"You know, some kids, they don't transition well to college or so I hear. They have problems adapting to being on their own without their parents 'round. They come from small towns where they made good grades in Podunk high schools, but they never can achieve those same levels in college, where it's a lot tougher and the expectations are so much higher."

Here we go, I thought. "What's that supposed to mean?" I asked. "Do you think I should be doing better than two A's and four B's? Is that it?"

"I can't say."

"What do you mean, you can't say?"

"I mean, I can't—I don't—speak for Larry Torrence anymore. You're 18 years old, Son, and that's a question you'll have to answer for yourself. But if you aren't doin' your best and livin' up to your potential, you'll see it staring back in the mirror each morning and, well, frankly, I don't think you'll like the looks of it."

"And what if this is the best I can do—two A's and four B's?"

He never hesitated. My father leaned across the table and locked his eyes on mine as he said, "Then I'm proud of you, Son—for doin' your best. You see, you don't have to *be* the best to make your mom and me proud. You just have to *try* your best. The only thing we're asking is that you have a plan for yourself and you try your hardest to achieve that plan."

"That's it?" I asked.

"That's it," he said and leaned back into his chair.

"Nothing more?" I asked.

"Nothing more," he said, and we sat in silence. I hated the silence.

He smiled at me. I hated the smile. I wanted to argue, to fight. "And what if I decide not to try my hardest? What if I decide to coast through college doing just enough to get by? What then?"

His expression changed to stone, and he took his time before answering. "Then the Devil wins," he finally said.

"Yeah, right, and I lose my soul, huh?"

"Something like that," he said, continuing to look through me with his stare. "You'll lose your own self-respect, and that's the same as losing your soul."

Again, there was silence as our eyes maintained the connection across the table. After five seconds, I couldn't take it any longer. I lowered my head and stared at the tabletop. I had to swallow hard to choke back the bile that had risen into my throat, mixed with last night's greasy food and cheap beer.

Several more seconds passed before he spoke with that deep, authoritative voice. "And next Saturday, be here to talk 'bout your plan."

"Yes, sir," I said softly.

My head was still bowed as he got up from the table. He patted me on the back before he left the room. I walked into the bathroom and threw up.

The following Saturday morning, I told him I was going to major in English, that I wanted to be a writer, maybe a poet. I expected that to shock him, but if it did, he never flinched. My father listened attentively to my rationale without offering any encouragement, but he didn't try to talk me out of it either. When we had thoroughly discussed the subject, he congratulated me on having a plan and urged me to put all my energy into learning as much as I could about literature and writing so I could excel at my chosen profession.

I lasted about a week as an English major. When I seriously thought about my future, my logical, analytical side overpowered my pensive, literary side. I changed to an accounting major and immersed myself in learning about debits, credits, and how to achieve precisely balanced books of account. My father tried to be his usual unemotional self when I told him, but I'm sure he was pleased. There was a lot of demand for good CPAs. The ones he knew drove Cadillacs. Writers, particularly the struggling young ones, borrowed their parents' car, talked constantly about truth and love, and were Democrats.

Mom must have said a hundred times that she was proud of me, and she just wanted me to major in something that would make me happy.

* * * * *

I worked hard, as diligently as I had ever applied myself to anything in my life, and I pulled my grades up to straight A's by the end of that first semester. I got a different roommate the following semester, a guy who was majoring in business. He was a dork, but a smart dork, and we pushed each other academically. Wanda at The Little Brown Jug forgot who I was.

Accounting, economics, and upper-level business subjects came naturally to me. After three and a half years at Lamar, I was poised to graduate with a Bachelor of Business Administration degree on December 22, 1973—*summa cum laude*, first in my class. I had bright career prospects with a job waiting for me in Houston with one of the top accounting firms. I had gone over a month without the Daniel dream to disrupt my nights. The planets and stars were perfectly aligned, and my horoscope was predicting great things. "Top of the World," another mindless, upbeat little ditty from the Carpenters, had just completed its second week as the number one song in the nation. I should have been on top of the world.

But things spun out of control in my life in December of 1973. Marty Shannon suddenly reappeared, coming back into my life after an eight-year absence but this time with a big black suitcase full of problems. After Daniel's death, Marty was the only person I could confide in. I told him the truth about how Daniel was able to shoot himself. He screamed obscenities at me and called me a murderer. He said I had killed the only *true* friend he ever had. That was my low point, the time when I seriously contemplated the manner and the means by which I could bring about my own suicide.

But the next day, Marty said he was sorry and didn't mean to blame me. He said that I was just stupid, and he knew how easy it was to get tricked around Daniel. With all the sincerity that he could muster, he said it wasn't my fault. I wondered whether he really believed the words he was saying, but that didn't matter. My good friend knew my secret and had forgiven me. I felt like living once more, and I knew at that moment, as he allowed me to find solace in his 12-year-old arms, that I wasn't going to let the Devil win. I could tell that the physical contact was uncomfortable for Marty, but he didn't complain. When I finally stopped crying, he shook my hand firmly in a very serious and grown-up fashion, looked me in the eye, and promised that my secret would be safe with him. He said he would take it to his grave. And he did.

Chapter 27
MARTY

He startled me. The lanky young stranger with closely cropped hair and a short black beard opened the door and jumped into the passenger seat of my little Volkswagen bug. "Long time, no see," he said.

"What the hell—"

"Don't tell me you don't remember."

He wore faded blue jeans and a plaid coat. He shut the door behind him and scrunched into the seat as though he didn't want anyone to see him.

"You don't remember, do you?" the stranger said. He blew hot air into his hands to warm them from the nippy December afternoon and tilted his head sideways to give me a better view of his face.

Then I knew it was him—the same guy who had been sitting alone when I arrived for an early Sunday dinner at the Burger Chef near the Lamar campus. The sun was low in the sky, and a cold front was sweeping through Beaumont. I'd ordered a nutritious double cheeseburger and fries, a staple in every college student's diet. There were only a few other diners scattered in the restaurant, and I took a secluded seat near the door. As I ate and thought about upcoming final exams, I had this strange, eerie feeling that he was watching me. He looked scroungy and I didn't want to make eye contact, so I ate quickly and left.

"I can't believe you don't remember, Buddy boy," he said.

"Marty?"

"At your service."

"Jesus, you scared the shit out of me, you big turd. Why didn't you just—"

"Yeah, and I'm thrilled to see you too," he said.

"It's been a long time, man. I didn't recognize you with the beard."

"And I thought you were giving me the cold shoulder in there 'cause you didn't love me anymore." He grinned at me, but then his tone became serious. "Look, I'd love to sit here and shoot the breeze, but can you start this thing up and get outta here?"

"What's the matter?"

"Just drive, Buddy. They probably think I went to the john, so let's go, okay?"

I didn't like the cloak-and-dagger stuff. Who the hell was he talking about? But it was cold and I was ready to go, so I played along. I started the car and pulled out of the restaurant parking lot onto Railroad Avenue, which runs along the eastern border of the Lamar campus. Marty remained crouched in the passenger seat as I worked quickly through the four gears. Maybe it was some perverted game he played. After all, I hadn't seen him in over eight years.

"Where to, Mr. Bond?" I joked.

"That depends."

"On what?"

"Tell me if a big gray Lincoln with two goons in it is following you."

I glanced in the mirror. "No, nothing back . . . Wait a minute. Yeah, Marty, a big Lincoln and, yeah, it looks like two guys. It's pulling out of the Burger Chef."

He raised his head and took a quick look behind us, between the two bucket seats. "Shit!" he said. "I thought—"

"Marty, what's going on here?" This suddenly didn't feel like a game.

"Buddy, try to lose them," he said.

"In this piece of shit? Get real," I said.

"Maybe you can turn on a side street and give 'em the shake."

"Look, what the hell's going on here? Who are those guys?"

"I'll tell you later. Just step on it, okay?"

"You tell me now or I'm stopping right here," I demanded.

He looked up at me. "Don't do that, man." I heard the fear in his voice and saw it in his eyes. I smelled it invading my car. "These are bad dudes, Buddy. I think they wanta hurt me."

"What?" I shrieked at him. "Cut the crap! Right now, man!"

"Hey, I'm sorry I got you into this. But they were parked on the other side waiting for me to leave, and you gotta believe me—I didn't think they'd see me gittin' into your car."

"So, what do I do?" My voice trembled as I pushed on the accelerator. The Lincoln was getting larger in my rear-view mirror.

"Speed up."

"I'm trying, but they're gaining."

"Then turn off," he said. "No, stay on this street—it's busier. Oh, shit, I don't know, just do something!"

Marty's fear was contagious. I fought to stay focused as adrenaline swept through my body and made me lightheaded. The traffic light at the busy intersection with Lavaca Street was five or six blocks ahead. It gave me an idea, something that had worked during a car chase I'd seen on a TV show. The light was green, but I took my foot off the accelerator.

"What are you doin'?" Marty said.

"Shut up! I'm going to try something."

My heart was beating like a jackhammer. The Lincoln had closed to within 50 yards before the traffic light cooperated by changing to yellow. I downshifted to first gear and rested my right foot lightly on the brake so they could see that I was stopping. Through the mirror, I watched the Lincoln jerk to a stop behind me. When my light changed to red and the cross traffic got their green light to enter the intersection, I counted to two—just like in the TV show—and then let off the clutch and pushed hard on the accelerator. My little VW sailed through the intersection.

Unfortunately, so did the Lincoln. The driver must have seen the same show as me because he stuck like glue to my rear bumper as horns blared and tires squealed from the cars braking on either side of us. The Lincoln roared into the open lane to the right of me and pulled alongside before I reached third gear.

Marty was more on the floorboard than the seat. "Whatever you did, did it work?" he asked.

"Not too good," I whispered.

"Are they still following us?"

"Yeah. Now stay down and shut up," I said through clenched teeth so the men in the Lincoln wouldn't see that I was talking to someone.

I swallowed hard and forced a weak smile onto my face as I looked to my right. The driver was a big guy, probably in his 40s. He had a fat face, big ears, and greasy black hair combed straight back. He looked like he ate kids like me for breakfast. He shook his index finger at me like a father would do to a misbehaving son. Then his eyes narrowed, and his expression turned to anger.

I looked away but could see from the corner of my eye that he was signaling for me to look at him. When I continued to focus straight ahead, ignoring him, he swerved the big Lincoln into my lane. My heart went into my throat as I jerked the wheel to my left to avoid contact. The Volkswagen bounced hard when its tires hit the train tracks that run down the center of Railroad Avenue and separate the north and southbound vehicles. My head hit the ceiling as the two left tires jumped the rail and we careened down the wooden slats. I fought to keep the car steady as I looked over my right shoulder. The Lincoln had fallen back and the lane to my right was open. So, I pulled hard at the wheel to free my car from the teeth-jarring tracks, and we returned to the smooth pavement.

The Lincoln pulled abreast, back in the outside lane. I looked across at the driver and tried to mask my terror. "Are you crazy?" I screamed.

We both had our windows up, so he couldn't hear me, but he could read my lips. He reached in his coat, and with his right hand, he removed a large gun and held it to the window for me to see. "Yes," I saw his lips move, "I'm crazy." He gave me an icy stare as he motioned with the pistol for me to pull over.

I looked away and covered my mouth with my right hand. "Marty, he's got a gun," I said.

"Oh, shit!"

"I think there's a police station about a mile up Railroad. Maybe we can make it there."

"No, for God's sake, don't get the police involved," Marty said.

"Well, what then?"

"I don't know! Think of something!"

The muscles in my chest were so tight I could feel my lungs being squeezed as I fought for breath. I tried to concentrate and not let my panic completely take over. As we passed side by side through the green light at Washington Boulevard, I heard a whistle in the distance. I looked up to see the lights from the engine of a train traveling toward us. I eased off the accelerator. I had another idea.

Freight trains lumber up and down the active tracks on Railroad Avenue within a few yards of the parallel automobile traffic on either side. It's like the trolleys that ran for years through the streets of Brooklyn or the cable cars that share the busy streets of San Francisco with faster-moving automobiles.

I downshifted and made a frantic wave at the Lincoln. "Okay, okay, you win," I mouthed at the driver. He nodded and tucked the pistol back inside his coat.

"Hold on," I whispered to Marty. When the oncoming train was only 30 yards ahead, I turned sharply to the left. The Volkswagen bounced roughly over the two sets of tracks, and Marty and I both screamed as the train horn blasted at about a thousand decibels directly in front of us. We crossed the tracks just in time to avoid the train, and I kept pulling on the steering wheel to complete the U-turn. We slid across the inside lane on the opposite side of the tracks before I regained control of the car. Screeching tires and an angry blast from the horn of a delivery truck welcomed us to the southbound traffic.

I had cut it close, and I knew there was no way the Lincoln could make the same U-turn from the outside lane. My right arm shook as I shifted through the gears. I looked over both shoulders and then checked the mirror. The Lincoln was nowhere in sight as I sailed back through the light at Washington. The freight train that separated us was only moving at about 20 miles per hour, and it was growing smaller in my mirror. I made a quick right turn and wound through several residential side streets until I was sure that we had lost the Lincoln.

"Okay, you can sit up," I said.

Marty moved from his animal-like crouch on the floorboard into the passenger seat. He looked out into the twilight to get his bearings as I made yet another turn and checked the mirror again.

"Was that a train we almost hit?" he asked.

"Yeah," was all I could manage to say. A wave of nausea was flooding over me. I pulled to a curb, opened my door, and leaned over to deposit my double cheeseburger, fries, and soda onto someone's yard. After I finished heaving, I took several deep breaths and tried to convince my trembling hands that our ordeal was over.

Marty was shaking his head from side to side. "Holy shit, Buddy. Are you okay?"

I gave him an angry look.

"Are you sure you've lost 'em?" he asked.

"Yeah, but I don't think that big guy was very happy about my bat-turn."

"No, I wouldn't think so," he said and chuckled to himself.

"Marty?"

"Yeah?"

With a stupid Ricky Ricardo impression, I said, "You got some 'splainin' to do, man."

That made him laugh out loud. "Yeah, I know," he said.

"Are you sure those guys don't know you live here? Can't they trace you here?" I shouted at the closed bathroom door in the hallway.

I heard the muffled sound of a toilet flush. "No way!" Marty responded as he opened the door and walked back into the entry room where I'd been standing. "I just moved here a couple days ago 'cause my last place got too hot. I gave the landlady a false name and paid cash for the first month." He gave me that boyish grin that I remembered, but it looked strange surrounded by a man's beard. "It's cool. Don't worry, man," he said. Then he winked at me, just like in the old days, before he turned his head skyward and poured the last half of a beer down his throat.

I sighed and took another sip from my beer bottle. The cold liquid felt good, washing my dry throat and slowly calming my nerves.

Marty belched loudly. "Ah, that was a good one, about a six on the old Richter scale. You ready for another beer, Buddy? It'll help get all that puke taste outta your mouth."

He hadn't lost his way with words. Before I could answer, Marty disappeared through an archway that I assumed led to his kitchen. On one side of the archway, there was a hole in the drywall about the size of a fist. The letters "B.S." were etched below it in brown-red ink (or was it dried blood?).

The sound of a refrigerator door opening made me recall Marty's question. "No, I'm still working on the first one!" I yelled in his direction. "Besides, I've got to go real soon. I've got final exams coming up, and I need to finish an economics paper that's due on Tuesday."

"Yeah, I hear you're quite the scholar—graduating Make me Cum Loudly or something like that. Congratulations!" he shouted from the next room.

"Yeah, I'm a goddamn genius. That's how I get into situations where guys with huge guns chase me all over town!" I shouted back. I heard him snicker and then the popping sound of a cap coming off another bottle of beer. "And how would you know about my academic accomplishments?" I asked.

He walked into the entry room and said, "I've got my sources. I know a lot about you." He flashed that grin again. "In fact—"

"Listen, I don't want to talk about me. You keep changing the subject. If you don't want to tell me what that was all about, you know, with Luca Brasi back there, then, hey, it's okay. I'll just be leaving."

He walked over to clang his fresh bottle of Schlitz against mine. "Cheers, bro," he said. "I owe ya one. That was some drivin' you did."

"Yeah, I'm a regular A. J. Foyt. You'll probably see me in the Indy 500 next year," I said.

"Sure," Marty said with a laugh, "as lead driver for Team Volkswagen, right?" He took a swig of beer and then plopped down on an off-white, terry cloth sofa. The springs creaked and the sofa sagged as his butt landed on the cushions. "Sit down, man. Get comfortable," he said and gestured toward the sprawling mush of a gigantic beanbag chair.

Besides the sofa and that chair, the only other furnishings in this drab room were two end tables, one on either side of the sofa. One was littered with empty potato chip bags and beer bottles. The other supported a couple more empty beer bottles, a deck of playing cards, and a *Playboy* magazine opened to the centerfold gallery. No TV, no stereo system, no pictures on the wall. Spiderwebs stretched around the overhead light fixture, and their shadows cast an intricate pattern across the ceiling. The room's only window was covered by a makeshift dark curtain.

I hesitated. Part of me wanted to leave, to get out and never return. That part had had enough excitement for one night. But another part was curious to find out what was going on.

"Okay," I said as the curious part won, "but I can only stay for a few minutes." I glanced at my watch to let him know I was serious.

"I'm gonna tell you about those guys, but you can't tell anyone else," Marty said.

"Don't worry," I said, annoyed at his admonishment as I dropped into the massive chair. The stuffing retreated from the weight of my body, even more as I thrashed around trying to level myself. I wound up seated an inch off the hard floor with my legs fully extended. It was cold this close to the floor and intensely uncomfortable. It only increased my keen desire to get out of this depressing place.

"No, I'm serious," he said. "If you tell anybody, then I'll have to kill you."

"What?" I said weakly.

"If you blab about any of this, I'll have to kill you," he said, and he reached under a sofa cushion and withdrew a snub-nosed pistol.

I got a sudden jolt of adrenaline, just like earlier in the evening when the Lincoln driver had brandished his weapon.

Marty laughed. "Hey, it's a joke. I'm kidding, okay? Jesus, man, don't you watch gangster movies? I swear, all that education and you're still as gullible as ever."

I wasn't amused. "Well, that gun's no joke," I said. I hadn't touched a gun of any kind since I was 12, and I was counting on my high draft number to keep things that way.

"It's not loaded," he said. Then his eyes got big. "Wait just a minute," Marty said as he opened the gun's revolving cylinder. "Yeah, I see you in there. Come to Papa," he muttered to himself, slowly extracting a single bullet from one of the six chambers. He slammed the cylinder shut, and I jumped from the sound. Marty smiled at me. "Now it's not loaded," he said.

I stared at him with a morbid fascination. "Why was there one bullet in there? What's going on?"

He shrugged and set the gun and single bullet on the sofa. "I was a little wasted and, you know, it's just pretend. It's just something I think about."

I must have looked confused.

"Maybe you should have another beer," he said.

While Marty was in the kitchen fetching two more beers, I kept thinking about something my father had said, a warning he had given me regarding Marty when I was 13. It happened on a Saturday, four weeks after the beginning of my eighth-grade year at a new school, China Junior High. It was a small public school deep in the sticks, which had yet to be integrated with the impoverished black community living on small farms and in shanties south of town. My new school was populated by segregationist racists at every level—administration, teachers, and students—who freely used the "n" word as a part of everyday conversation. There were only about 20 students in eighth grade—gawky boys whose main interest was the local chapter of

Future Farmers of America and homely girls who flunked math and excelled in home economics class.

My teachers had reported to my parents that I wasn't adjusting to the new environment. When translated, that meant I wasn't making any friends. I refused to discuss it with them. How could they understand? I still missed Daniel, and now I was surrounded by guys who detested black people and only wanted to talk about the rice crop in the lower 40 or the size of the balls on the bull they were raising for some FFA competition.

Contrast that to Larry Torrence, who spent much of his time fantasizing about living in a futuristic country that the United States had morphed into: *Equarinity*, a combination of the words "equality" and "serenity." Inhabitants of Equarinity were mostly tea-colored because for centuries there had been no shame in loving and having children with someone of a different race. It was also common for people ten years apart in age (or more) to fall in love and marry. There was no racial, age, or gender discrimination, and people were judged by their character and their deeds. Women who wanted to work were able to find good jobs, and some were even in positions of great responsibility like store managers. Women held one or two of the elected seats at all levels in government and helped the men pass laws that were fair to all. Medical science had been able to eradicate most diseases, including mental health disorders. People lived long, healthy lives, free of depression and suicidal thoughts. New inventions, like fuel-efficient cars that automatically took you safely to your stated destination and clean factories that never spewed black smoke into the air, made Equarinity a very clean and pleasant place to live.

That's why I got upset with my mother that Saturday afternoon. I was trying to figure out how people in Equarinity could stay in constant contact with one another using Dick Tracy-like watches, while she kept ragging on me. "Why don't you call someone to play with?" she asked, like I was a little kid, as if teenagers like me fondled and "played with" each other.

I ignored her and continued to make notes and doodle in my Equarinity notebook.

"Why don't you call Marty? Your father said that Marty called again last week. Why don't you invite him to come spend the night out here with us? We'll go into town together and pick him up. That'll be nice, won't it?"

"No, it wouldn't be nice," I said, getting up from the sofa to increase the volume coming from the TV.

"But why, honey?"

"Because I don't want to."

"But he was such a good friend. Don't you miss him?"

"No," I said as I sat back down. It was a lie.

"Buddy, you should—"

I looked up and gave her the most outraged scowl I could conjure up.

"Oh, I'm sorry, honey. I meant 'Larry.' Larry, you should call Marty. You should keep in touch."

I ignored her.

"*Pleeease.*" She stretched it out like some super-special request that I wouldn't be able to resist. "Your mother would like to know how he's doing." She smiled so sweetly that it looked like a sugar cube might spring from her lips if I didn't intervene and wipe it off her face.

"Then why don't you tell my mother to call him because *I'm not going to!*" I shouted at her, picking up my pen and notebook and rising from the sofa. "Now, you need to shut up about Marty, and stop bothering me. Get off my back!" I turned to leave her but couldn't stop myself from looking back and rebuking her again. "You don't know anything about me, and I don't want you interfering in my life. Got it?"

I turned and stormed off to my room. When I got there, I slammed the door behind me, hard enough to be sure she heard it. I found my Rolling Stones album, the one I knew she despised, and cranked up the volume as I placed it on the turntable.

Twenty minutes later, my father returned from his weekend errands. I relaxed on my bed and waited patiently, trying to mentally prepare myself. I felt good, like a young ram ready to butt heads with the leader of his herd. Maybe I could take him this time.

When I didn't reply to the knock at my door, he opened it and walked in. I looked at him and mouthed the words with Mick Jagger, "*I can't get no, no sa-tis-fac-tion.*"

"Turn that off," he commanded.

I frowned at him. Rather than antagonize him too much—just yet—I slowly reached over and picked up the needle. "You didn't knock," I said.

"Oh, I knocked," he said.

"Then I must not have heard you. I was really getting into the music."

"You heard," he said matter-of-factly. He waited to see if I would compound my lie. I opted for the silent treatment. "Now make sure you hear this, too. Are you listening?"

I rolled my eyes up to the ceiling. "Okay, shoot," I said.

"I don't care if you ever call Marty Shannon again. I don't care if you piss on the only good friend you've ever had. That's not—"

"You mean the only good friend I've got left!" I shouted.

He stared at me. "Maybe," he said, "but that's not the point."

"Then what *is* the point?"

"The point is that you will at all times be respectful to your mother. Is that simple rule too much for you to remember?"

"Even if she harasses me and says something stupid that doesn't deserve my respect?"

He put his hands on his hips. "How is it possible for a 13-year-old to ask a question that dumb?"

"Well?" I asked, not wanting to retreat.

He walked to the edge of my bed and glared down at me. "Aside from the fact that she's the person who gave you the gift of life, you ungrateful smartass, don't you ever forget that she's *my* wife. She's the woman that I love, and I don't tolerate any man on this earth being disrespectful toward my wife. *Nobody!* Especially you."

He sounded like vintage John Wayne, and no one wins when they lock horns with John Wayne. I was beginning to feel queasy.

He continued, "Even if she suggests that you call the man

in the moon, you can decline, but you will *respectfully* decline. Do you understand?" His face was red and the veins in his neck were pulsating.

"I guess," I said.

"Is that completely clear to you?" he asked.

"Yeah, okay. You don't have to get so emotional about it."

He knew he had won. His voice softened as he went for a final humiliating blow. "Making a woman cry doesn't make you a man, Larry. It makes you a punk. And we don't tolerate punks in this house. Is that okay by you?"

"Yes, sir." I lowered my horns.

"Good," he said. "I'll give you five minutes to think 'bout what you're gonna say to apologize. Then I want you outta this room and in there with your mother."

"Yes, sir."

He turned and walked toward the door. As he was about to shut it behind him, he stopped. "Larry?"

"Yes?" I said to the ceiling.

"Look at me." When I complied, my father said the words that were haunting me—eight years later, there in Marty's little duplex apartment. He said, "Marty Shannon's basically a good kid, Son. Oh, he's not real intelligent, not like you, but he's got a big heart and he tries hard. But that combination makes him vulnerable, easy to manipulate. He needs a friend like you, someone to help him make good choices. And lord knows, you could use a friend too. I wish you wouldn't shut him and everybody else outta your life. But *that's your business*, and I'm not gonna pry. I'm just afraid that someday you'll look back and wish that you'd kept up with Marty, but by then it'll be too late."

He didn't give me a chance to respond. He closed the door with his words ringing in my ears.

Marty told me all about the McCarthy brothers. He referred to them as small-time hoods and took delight in explaining how he conned them into believing he was a "player." So, they sold him 30 pounds of marijuana and two large bags of cocaine—on consignment. That meant that Marty had to sell the drugs on the street at a price high enough to cover the $10,000 cost plus the egregious daily interest charges that were accruing.

"What are these guys—dope pushers or loan sharks?" I asked.

"Yeah, that pretty much describes them," he said, managing a weak laugh.

Marty explained that steep interest was the price you paid for not having capital, for having to do the deal on consignment. "It's pure economics," he said, and then he began lecturing me on the time value of money. As he droned on, I gazed into space, trying not to think about how uncomfortable I was in that damned beanbag chair and wondering why I had once considered him such a prized friend.

To regain my wandering attention, Marty announced that he would show me his stash. He leaped from the sofa and dashed out of the room. When he returned, he was lugging a large, beat-up black suitcase. He had a gleam in his eye like a six-year-old about to show off his new birthday present. He returned to his seat and hoisted the case onto his lap. It made me nervous as hell. I was only two weeks from graduation. You went to jail, not commencement exercises, for being around illegal drugs. Still, I was curious. I couldn't take my eyes off the suitcase.

Marty inserted a small gold key into an opening near the handle. He turned it ever so slowly until there was a loud pop. He smiled when I jumped at the noise. Then, with painstaking care, his thumbs flipped each of the two snaps holding the top in place. All the while, Marty stared at me—smiling, watching my reactions, and taking great delight in my obvious anxiety. I felt like an underage kid watching his first striptease.

With the suitcase facing him in his lap, Marty lifted the top until it totally blocked my view. I stretched my neck, but I was hopelessly too low to see around the case. All I could see was the top of Marty's big head as he stared into it. Finally, he raised his head and rested his chin on the lid of the case. Our eyes locked for a second before he arched his eyebrows and broke into an ear-to-ear grin. I was annoyed, but before I could speak,

Marty exclaimed, "Behold!" and he rotated the suitcase—very slowly because of its weight but also to prolong the tension. When it was completely facing me, he leaned forward, dipping the case so I could admire its contents.

I was immediately struck by the sheer volume of dope crammed into the suitcase. "So, out of the original ten grand's worth, how much have you sold?" I asked.

"Oh, it's been a little slow since my car broke down last week. But I'm doin' okay."

"Yeah? Well, how much have you sold?" I asked again.

"Some guys I know at Lamar—on the football team, no less—they took six dime bags of grass. And a senior over at South Park High, he took two, and some friends of his, they took three. Then yesterday, the girl on the other side of this duplex bought one."

"And?"

He raised his hands palms up and shrugged his shoulders.

"That's only $120," I said.

"Actually, a little less 'cause I gave the girl a discount. Man, is she a fox!" He rolled his eyes at the ceiling and whistled. "You should see her, Buddy, she's—"

"Marty, that won't even cover a week's worth of interest. What the hell are you doing?"

"I'm branching out," he said. "I've got the kid at South Park on commission now. He thinks he can move a couple pounds of grass for me. And I've got lots of other prospects. There's—"

"But that's all you've sold, right?"

"Yeah, but I've—"

"And how long have you had this shit?"

"Not long. Just a couple weeks or so." He grinned at me. "I've also been takin' some for my own account," he said. "It's like a fringe benefit. You wanta try some? This is Acapulco Gold, my man. Or, at least, that's what they told me. Anyway, whatever it is, it's really good stuff." He reached into the suitcase and picked up one of the plastic bags. "How 'bout I roll us a number?"

I ignored him. "What happens when you can't pay those goons?"

"Oh, that's not gonna happen. Like I told you, I've got some real hot prospects, particularly for the coke. And those guys who bought so far, I think they'll buy more. It's what they refer to as *a client base.*" He smiled.

"Marty?"

He dropped the bag of marijuana back into the suitcase and slouched into the sofa, hiding from my view behind the open lid.

"Marty?" I said again, stronger.

He slowly closed the lid and slid the case off his lap onto the sofa. "Well, it's not like they'd kill me or anything. Not for a lousy ten grand," he said.

I gave him a skeptical frown. The driver of the Lincoln, the one waving the gun, didn't look like he would have any patience—or mercy—with a deadbeat like Marty.

"Anyway," he said with a sigh, "what could they do to me that I'm not already doin' to myself, huh?" He gave a pathetic little laugh. "I mean, look around."

"What's that supposed to mean?" I asked.

"I don't know, man. It's just my life, it's so fucked up right now." He smiled like it was no big deal.

"Don't you have any friends?"

"Sure. Of course," he said.

"Like who?"

"Like the people who've been buying from me."

"Who else?"

"Well, let me think." He rubbed his chin and then his eyes lit up. "You know, I was pretty tight with the McCarthys and some of their friends," he said proudly. "At least, until here recently."

Was he serious or just pulling my chain? I shook my head and couldn't help but grin, it was all so surreal. Marty seemed pleased that I was smiling, and he grinned back.

"How 'bout another cold one?" he asked.

I didn't think about the apology I had to make to my mother. For five minutes alone in my room, all I could think about was Marty. It was so complicated. After Daniel's death, Marty tried to act like nothing had changed between us. The moodier and more withdrawn I became, the more jovial he became. Acting undaunted and carefree may have been his way of coping, but it wasn't mine. I couldn't stop thinking about things I should have done differently, and my guilt was reinforced on most nights by that cursed Daniel dream.

I could tell that Marty was genuinely concerned about me those last few months of seventh grade at St. Christopher. I was always tired and missed a lot of school from January to May with a variety of real and invented ailments. To make me feel better—despite my protests—Marty fixed me up with Janey Miller, a cheerleader and one of the most popular girls in school. We were a real item for a week. She was the first girl I ever kissed. Actually, *she* kissed me and it was only on the cheek, but I think that still counts. When we were sitting together, she liked to hold hands with the back of my hand resting over her crotch. It was exhilarating.

But she was always asking how I was feeling—about Daniel and everything. It didn't take me long to figure out that Marty was playing on her sympathies behind the scenes, telling her I was all downhearted and she would be doing a great service—like the Salvation Army—if she could lift my spirits. Like an idiot, I confronted Janey in an angry way, embarrassing her. In about the time it takes to give someone the middle finger and tell them, "Grow up, you weirdo," she dumped me and never spoke to me again.

Marty and I got together three or four times after my family moved out of Beaumont that summer of 1965. On those occasions, we never talked about Daniel, but it didn't matter. I felt Daniel's presence every time I was with him, and depressing thoughts of Daniel Carter would fill my mind for days after he'd left. I couldn't escape the fact that Marty knew my secret. He never said anything about it—that I was the uncaring idiot who provided the means for Daniel to take his own life—but *he knew it*.

I wanted to remain friends with Marty, but it wasn't the same. Each time we got together that summer, I felt on edge and despised myself even more. It was pathetic, but at 13, I knew that my desire to avoid painful, self-loathing memories was going to win out over my desire to maintain his friendship. I was too selfish and too scared of those memories, and I resolved at 13 years old that I never wanted to see him again.

I went into my bathroom, washed the tear stains from my cheeks, and washed Marty Shannon from my mind. I blew my nose and even combed my hair. I wanted to look my best when I apologized to Mom.

"Oh, Buddy." Marty sighed, then repeated, "Buddy, Buddy, Buddy," in rapid fire. He managed a weak grin.

I wanted to let him know I was now "Larry, Larry, Larry," but I let it pass. His mood had turned melancholy. He was on his fourth beer.

"It looked so easy in the movies," he said.

"How so?"

"In *Easy Rider*, man. They sell that dope at the beginning, take the money, and then get on those choppers and *r-i-d-e*." A peaceful longing came over him. "They just ride off to discover America." He took another long swallow from his beer bottle.

"That's the movies, man. That's not real life. Besides, they both get blown away in the end."

He leaned closer. He had a look of euphoric bliss. "Yeah, but what a way to go, right?"

I recoiled into the soft chair, unable to respond.

"Besides, that's why I got this protection," Marty said, his hand moving over the short barrel of the pistol. He sat back but kept stroking it as he spoke. "I just get all bored and depressed sometimes—a lot lately. I think about playing that game, wondering if I have the guts for it."

"You think it's a game?"

"Yeah, one bullet and one roll of the dice." He brought the gun up to his temple, pulled the trigger, and shouted, "Click!" as the metal hammer clanged against one of the six empty chambers.

I jumped. I couldn't help it.

"Or it might be: 'Boom!'" he said loudly.

I jumped again.

"But I'd probably never hear it. Or, at least, I'd never remember hearing it, just like Daniel, right?" He set the gun on the sofa, by his side and next to the lone bullet.

All I could do was shake my head slowly. It was getting too bizarre for me. "Marty, I've got to go. All the car chases, guns, dope, and Russian roulette—good luck with all that. I'd love to help you, man, but I've really got to go." I pushed downward to get up, but my hands just sank into the chair.

"No, you wouldn't," he said.

"What?" I stopped struggling with the chair. "What are you saying?"

"You know."

"No, I don't. I'm not sure what any of this means. I wish I could help you figure all this—"

"Quit sayin' that!" he demanded.

"Saying what?"

"That you wanta help me. That's a crock! You don't wanta get involved. It's not your nature." He continued to run his right hand over the revolver like it was some sort of idiot pet of his.

"I'd say I was pretty involved this evening when your business associates were chasing us."

"I'd say you didn't have much of a choice," he scoffed, "and I'd say you woulda rather been anywhere on earth back then, rather than on the firing line tryin' to help an old friend. I'd say you can't wait to get outta here right now, and you hope to God that another eight or nine years go by before you have to see my sorry ass again. That's what I'd say." He stared down at me from the sofa with a contemptuous look.

Why does the truth hurt so badly? I suddenly felt claustrophobic. The beanbag chair had engulfed me, wrapping itself tightly around my hips and torso. I slid my outstretched legs to the side and heaved my upper body forward, struggling to free my ass from its grasp. My arms flailed the air in a spastic breaststroke that took me nowhere.

"I can't believe you're saying that!" I said in my most indignant voice, turning my body sideways and rolling out of the mush onto the cold floor.

"The truth hurts, doesn't it?"

What? How does he know what I'm thinking? My mind was reeling as I got to my feet.

"You don't wanta help me, Buddy," he said.

"Hey, I came here—"

"Or should I call you *Laarrry*?" he asked, stretching out my name in a mocking, high-pitched voice. "What a candy-ass name. What's the problem? Was Buddy carrying too much baggage for you?"

I took a step toward the sofa. My fists were clenched. "Look, man," I said, "you talk like you know all about me. Well, you don't! You may have known me once, but you don't know anything about me now."

He stood and glared at me, and the heat of his pent-up hurt and anger easily outshined and deflected mine. We were only two paces apart. He was about five inches taller, and he looked down at me, into me.

"Oh, I know all about you," he said as I took an involuntary step backward. "Like I said, I've got sources. Ever since Daniel put that gun to his head with your daddy's bullet in it, you've been afraid—afraid of feeling. That's why you didn't wanta have anything to do with me after you told me your dirty little secret. I reminded you of how Mommy and Daddy's perfect little angel fucked up really bad, didn't I?"

Ouch. I looked longingly at the door. "That's not true," I said. "That's ancient history. It's all behind me now."

He shook his head. "Why can't you be straight with me—with yourself?"

"You don't know what you're talking about."

"I don't? Then answer me this, Answer Man. Back in high school, how many kids there ever asked you over to their house on weekends? Like I always did?" When I didn't reply, he added, "How many were as good a friend as I was?"

I stared blankly at him. He already knew the answer.

"And why did those other seniors hold up that poster of a turkey at your graduation ceremony, you know, while you were delivering the commencement address?" he asked.

"How did you know about that?"

"I was there—with my mother."

"What?" When he continued to smirk without replying, I added, "Why didn't you say something, come see me?"

"We sat in the back. We didn't wanta bother you or your parents in your moment of glory. Then, after it was over, we felt too embarrassed for you. My mother didn't think you'd wanta see us after that."

"Well, those guys got punished for that prank," I said.

"Oh, right! What're they gonna do to graduating seniors?"

"They put a full report in their permanent record," I said. "It's there for colleges and future employers to see."

He laughed. "I bet that taught 'em a lesson."

"Marty—your mom, how's she doing?" I asked with a smile, hoping to relieve some of the tension between us.

"She's dead. Died last year. How sweet of you to ask."

I looked down. "I'm sorry. I—"

"Save it," he said. "You didn't care enough for eight years to ever ask about us, so there's no need to act like you care now."

"That's not fair. Your mother, she was a special person and, hey, I *am* sorry, man."

He let out a skeptical snicker.

It was too much. I felt trapped. I needed to get out of there, to get some fresh air. "Look, if that's how you feel, I need to—"

He stepped forward, his face six inches from mine. "And how 'bout the fact that you're afraid of chicks? How 'bout the fact that you're 21 years old and still a virgin?"

"I am not!" I said and stepped backward. This was ridiculous. Where was he getting this crap?

"Okay, then who have you ever made it with?"

"A gentleman does not discuss these sorts of affairs," I said in an aristocratic voice, trying to make light of his disturbing accusation.

"Then how many?"

"How many what?"

"How many girls, lover boy? How many girls have you made it with?"

"Well, let's see, there was one in high school and at least a couple more since I've been in college," I said.

"Wow, I didn't realize you were a track star in school." He paused for a couple of seconds to take in my puzzled expression. "You were a broad jumper, right?"

"What?"

"A broad jumper. You were a broad jumper. Oh, forget it. I suppose Sheryl Williams, she was one of your conquests, hey?"

"Maybe," I said cautiously. Sheryl Williams was a freshman at Lamar, a sociology major, and a very liberated young woman. She had made it with a dozen guys who lived in my dorm, and she sought me out one day to explain in a brazen way how she liked the mature, intellectual type—someone unafraid to explore new horizons with her. Just the mention of her name was likely to give me heart palpitations. "What do you know about Sheryl Williams?" I asked.

"I know she's a free spirit." Marty gave me that idiot wink of his and added, "And I know she had the serious hots for you back in October."

"She sure did. She sure did," I said with a sly smirk.

"And?"

"And, like I told you, I'm not going to name names, but—"

"But what?"

"It seems like you may have figured one of them out," I said.

"Is that so?" A grin started slowly and eventually stretched across his entire black beard.

"That's right," I said. "Guilty. What can I say?"

He stepped forward again and spoke in a singsong, mocking voice. "The way I heard it, the only place you creamed was in your jeans. That you only lasted a few seconds the time she put her hand on you."

"What?"

"And that you didn't know the geography down there—on a woman."

"What?" I said, holding my ground and maintaining eye contact so he wouldn't see how intimidated I was by his knowledge.

"Yeah, lover boy," he said. "Sheryl told me she wanted you bad, but all you did was fumble around under her skirt."

"What?" It was all I could say.

"She said you ruined *the moment* when you kept rubbing her tummy and then tried to stick your finger up her bunghole." Marty had to put a hand over his mouth to stifle his laughter.

"That's absurd!" I said as I retreated another step. My ears and cheeks were burning. I felt lightheaded and my eyes darted around the room. Where the hell was the door to this dump?

"At first, she thought you were kinky," he said, gulping for air between guffaws. "But then she figured out that you didn't know what you were doin'. That you didn't know the terrain, if you get my drift."

"That's not true! You don't know what you're—"

"And Sheryl, she said she tried to give you some . . . I think she called it *constructive criticism*." He crossed his chest with his arms to hold the laughter in. "But she said you got all tensed up and left. Now that doesn't sound like an experienced broad jumper to me."

"Well, she's a liar!" I shouted.

He grabbed my right hand, pulling it toward his face. "Let me smell that finger," he said. I jerked back my hand as he inhaled. "My God, man!" he said in disgust, covering his nose as he staggered backward. He was immensely enjoying himself, punishing me in his crude way for my insensitivity toward him.

The last thing I saw before I slammed the door behind me was Marty falling into the sofa in a ball of hysterical laughter. The weight of his body hitting the cushions caused the pistol and the single bullet to spring into the air, and they tumbled onto the cold floor, landing with an ominous banging sound.

I was asleep in my dorm room dreaming about Sheryl Williams. Just as we were getting friendly in the back seat of her Dodge GTO, the dream-fantasy was shattered by a frantic knock on my door. It was Fat Freddy, the pimple-faced freshman who lived across the hall. The kid looked frightened and said, "It's a guy named Marty. He's on the phone asking for you, talking crazy. He sounds all messed up, Larry."

"Shit!" I said, reaching for my jeans.

When I finally got to the community phone on our floor, the connection was still open. I tried repeatedly to elicit a response from the other end, but there was only silence. So, I hung up. "Are you sure his name was Marty?" I asked Fat Freddy.

"Yeah."

"Are you sure he was in trouble?"

"Yeah, that's what it sounded like."

"Shit!" I said as I wheeled around and walked quickly back to my room.

* * * * *

It was a few minutes past 11:00 when I turned off Avenue A onto Terrell Street, wondering for the umpteenth time if I'd lost my mind. I had a final exam, my first for the semester, at 8:00 in the morning. I was well prepared, so I'd gone to bed early. *So much for that plan*, I thought.

The rathole apartment that I had stormed out of three nights earlier was on Terrell, a couple of blocks ahead on my right. As I got closer, I noticed a late-model Buick sedan parked across the street and down just a little from Marty's duplex. It looked out of place in this low-rent neighborhood. As I approached the car, two crew-cut, middle-aged men in the front seat each raised their hands to protect their eyes from the intensity of my headlights. *Sorry guys, just passing through*, I thought. I continued past them for a block before taking a right onto Avenue D.

I drove another three blocks before pulling into a church parking lot. I locked my VW and set out on foot through the residential neighborhood, working my way back toward Terrell Street. Corner streetlamps provided lighting—too much for my liking—and I tried to stay in the shadows in the yards and sidewalks. The two guys in the Buick had made me nervous. And cautious. My pace increased as I cut through Roberts Park, which provided more cover. Darting between the trees and children's swing sets, I scanned the area for signs of activity. It was a quiet night, and the park and surrounding streets were deserted.

Questions swirled around inside my brain: *What kind of trouble was Marty in this time? Was he in his apartment; is that where he'd called from? Who were those guys in the car, and did they have something to do with Marty? Why was I getting involved in things that didn't concern me?*

A block before reaching Terrell, I diverted down a parallel street, then up a driveway and through a back yard that bordered Marty's duplex. My mind was reeling as I put my ear to Marty's back door. When I couldn't detect any sounds or light coming from the other side—what I was reasonably certain was Marty's kitchen—and no one answered when I softly called his name, I swallowed hard and tried to turn the doorknob. It was locked. I loosened my grip on the knob and knocked, tentatively at first.

When there was no answer to my repeated knocks on the back door, I peeked around the corner, the side where Marty's bedroom was situated. There was one large window on this side of the building, and light from within the apartment cast a faint glow into the darkness outside the window.

I saw the Buick parked in the shadows across Terrell Street. It was positioned so the men inside could view both the front and this side of the duplex—Marty's side. I prayed that they were bored and wouldn't notice me as I hugged the side of the building, creeping forward until I reached the window.

The closed curtains inside were thin enough to let some light out but too thick to see through them. "Marty," I said several times in a loud whisper. Again, no answer. I tugged and pushed from every angle, but the window wouldn't budge. It too was locked.

So, I slinked back around the corner. As I stared at the back door, wondering for the hundredth time if Marty was inside, I noticed a quarter-inch gap between the door and its frame. The bolt, an inch-thick piece of steel that was denying me access to the apartment, was visible in that thin gap. I removed a heavily laminated student ID card from my wallet and stuck it in the gap, onto the bolt. This little trick worked on my dorm room door on those occasions when I left my key inside. With my right hand, I pushed hard on the ID card—down and to the left. With my left, I pulled back on the doorknob with equal force to avoid friction between the bolt and its sheath. As the bolt slid from the safety of the frame, I pulled and the door popped open.

The stench of dirty dishes and stale beer hit me as I stepped inside. The kitchen was dark, and the only sounds were my footsteps on the linoleum floor and the cockroaches scurrying for cover. I walked slowly through an archway toward the light ahead and tried not to step on the articles of clothing strewn on the floor.

The light was coming from inside an open door, down a short hallway and past a bathroom. I wasn't prepared for the sight as I came to the door. There was no furniture in the dingy bedroom, only a mattress in the middle of the floor. A telephone cord extended from the wall and disappeared into a thin blanket, which partially covered Marty's body. He lay face up, sprawled across the mattress. My first thought was that he was dead. I walked to him, knelt on one knee, and began shaking him.

"Hey, stop it," he mumbled, semi-conscious. "What's goin' on?"

"It's me, you idiot. Why'd you call me?"

Marty opened one eye and then quickly closed it. He brought a hand up to shield his face from the ceiling light and then squinted the eye open again. His arm was tangled in telephone wire, and his movement had pulled the receiver close to his ear. I leaned over him, unwound the cord, and placed the phone back on the cradle to stop the annoying bleating noise.

"You came," he said.

"Yeah, I came."

"So, how does it feel to rescue someone?"

"Tiring. What am I rescuing you from?"

"My heart, man. I got scared. It started beating funny for no reason."

I doubted the part about "no reason." An empty Jack Daniel's bottle, marijuana roaches in a nearby ashtray, and scattered white powder on the floor by the mattress all seemed like plenty of reasons.

"What's going on, Marty? All this?" I pointed at the remnants of his party.

He sighed heavily. "I had a friend over—that kid from South Park and a friend of his. They're gonna move a lotta shit for me." He laughed. "I guess I kept the party goin' after they left. I get so, I don't know." After a long pause, he added, "Thanks, man, you know, for comin' over."

"Marty, there's a car parked out front with two guys inside."

His eyes fully opened for the first time. "The guys that followed us on Sunday?"

"No. I only got a quick look, but these dudes were in a Buick and seemed clean-cut."

"Was the license plate white?"

I thought for a second, replaying my headlights on the front of their car, trying to get a glimpse of the plate in my mind. "Yeah, come to think of it, I think it was."

"Then they're cops or detective dicks, something like that."

I nodded in agreement. New license plates were required each year for private vehicles in the state of Texas. The state issued black plates with white letters in odd years and white plates with black letters in even years. But government vehicles always maintained the same white plates. That made them easy to spot every other year.

"Why are they out there?" I asked. "Do you think they're onto you?"

Marty rolled on his side. "Don't know. My head's killin' me, man. Everything's spinnin'," he said, slurring his words. "Help me sit up."

I stood up. As I pulled him upright so he could tuck his legs under him for support, I saw the handle of his pistol protruding from under the pillow. "What the shit, Marty?"

"Oh, it's just there for protection. You know, there's lots of bad guys out there."

I wasn't amused. I dropped to one knee beside him and picked up the gun. My heart sank as I opened the revolving cylinder and saw a single bullet resting in the second chamber from the hammer.

"Goddamnit, you did it again, didn't you?"

He lowered his head into his hands. "I just get so depressed," he said.

Holding the gun, I launched into what I intended to be an uplifting lecture right out of *Father Knows Best*. It was all about not getting down on yourself or something equally patronizing. But I stopped mid-sentence when Marty looked up. The expression on his face was pathetic: hopelessness on his brow, emptiness in his bloodshot eyes, and surrender hanging open in his mouth. On his cheek, I could make out the trail of a tear. It ended in some drool that had solidified in his beard by the side of his mouth. He hadn't been listening to me, and the cold reality of the situation finally hit me.

"It doesn't matter," he said, wiping at his cheek. "Pretty soon, none of it'll matter." His lip quivered like he wanted to smile, but his body refused to comply.

"Oh, man," I said softly. I set the pistol down and reached out to him. I wrapped my arms over his shoulders and pulled him to me, just as he had done with me when we were 12.

My embrace took him by surprise. For a split second, he was tense in my grasp, and then I felt a complete release in his body and spirit. His arms and hands pressed into my back as he lost control of his emotions.

"Thanks for comin'. I'm sorry, but I didn't know who else to call. I just needed somebody to . . . Hey, I still can't believe you came. Thanks, man," he babbled in my ear between sobs.

I didn't reply, just held him until, after a minute or so, he released me and announced, "Buddy, I think I'm gonna be sick."

A single thought kept whirling through my mind as I helped him into the bathroom and watched him submit to Ralph, the porcelain god. If, against all my instincts and better judgment, I was going to get involved, if I was going to seriously try to save my old friend, I was going to need some professional help.

Chapter 28

ALLIE

I could remember everything about my last visit with Allie in 1965: the pastel cotton dress she wore with matching shoes, her perfume, her natural beauty, her perfect smile, and how she laughed out loud when I said something funny. We talked nonstop for an hour and then I left, bedazzled and euphoric. I was confused about a lot of things back then but never regarding my feelings for her. There wasn't a single day during the almost nine years that followed when I didn't think and fantasize about her. I always knew that we would meet again, and she would come to understand, as I did, that we were destined to be together.

* * * * *

Thank God for the *Beaumont Yellow Pages*. I found her under "Therapists," the only Allie listed there, although with a different last name. When I called, the receptionist was a bit crotchety and didn't like my inquiries about Allie's age and what she looked like. But she answered enough to confirm that it was definitely *my* Allie, working in a firm located downtown on Pearl Street. When the receptionist wouldn't put me through to talk to Allie without first providing my entire life story and submitting to a psych exam, I showed up at her office that Thursday morning without an appointment and nervous as hell. It was the day after my late-night visit to Marty's apartment and with only three final exams to go before graduation.

"Larry Torrence," I said. "I don't have an appointment, but I'd like to see Allie Masterson about a potential case. I understand she works here."

"Mrs. Parker?" the receptionist asked in a rebuking tone. She was an elderly lady who looked like she'd forgotten how to smile.

"Oh, that's right. I'm sorry. Is she in?"

"Do you have children?" she asked.

What a strange question, I thought. "No, heavens no." I laughed.

"So, are you a patient?"

"No, just a good friend from before she was married."

"Really?" she said without trying to hide her curiosity. "You and Mrs. Parker? That's odd. Are you the one who called this morning wanting—?"

"Is she in?" I asked in my politest voice.

She turned her back to me and picked up a phone. After a short conversation that I couldn't hear, she turned around, got up, and led me back to Allie's office. She lingered as Allie greeted me with a warm smile and handshake. Allie was wearing a white silk blouse and a black skirt hemmed a couple of inches above her knees, and she kept repeating how happy she was to see me after all these years. She made me blush when she called me handsome. Then she thanked the receptionist, who gave me a shriveled-up, squinty look as Allie closed her door.

In the flesh, standing so close, right in front of me—Allie was even more beautiful than I had remembered. I noticed two other important things. First, I was now an inch or so taller than her, and second, she wasn't wearing a wedding band.

We sat down across from each other—only a few feet apart—and she crossed her long legs and leaned forward as I began telling her about Marty. She remembered him from St. Christopher and said she was sorry things weren't going well for him. I told her about his alcohol and drug abuse, how he felt like he didn't have anything to live for, and how he was always saying depressing things, just like Daniel Carter had done. I asked her to help me get him out of the deep, dark pit that his life had become before he hurt himself or someone around him. She asked several questions, and I was truthful for the most part, although I may have left out the gory details. When she seemed reluctant and said her specialty was children and teenagers, not young adults, I begged her.

"Please, Allie, I don't know what to do. I need your help."

"Yes, and I can refer you to a therapist who specializes in—"

"No, you don't understand," I pleaded. "It's got to be you."

"Why me?"

"He doesn't trust *anybody*. But he'll remember you—from school."

"Oh?"

"Yeah, in a good way, okay? You were so kind, so helpful back then. He'll trust you. He'll talk to you." I added, "If you don't help him . . . He's so depressed, I know something terrible will happen."

She didn't say anything, just looked deep into my eyes. My God, her hazel eyes with the green flecks were amazing, intoxicating—just like in my dreams.

Put me under, I thought. *Do anything you want to me. Just let me be near you—forever.*

She finally asked something, but I can't recall what it was or my reply. I must have answered satisfactorily because she said, "Okay, it doesn't matter because I've got some *pro bono* time accumulated and can use it for this case."

"So, you'll do it? You'll help me? I mean, help me to help him?"

"I can't promise anything, Larry. But yes, I'll see Marty, and I'm hopeful, working together, that you and I can help your friend. But I need to get started right away. Can you bring him here tomorrow afternoon, say 1:00? I'll have to confirm with Dr. Shapiro, but I think that'll work."

Allie had no idea what she was getting into. I took Marty to see her the next day and to each of his three appointments the following week. The first one was the longest, almost two hours, and included a doctor-looking fellow in a white physician's coat. Each time, I waited outside her office, studying for finals or reading a magazine, until they emerged. Marty always wore a big grin and winked when he saw me, like they'd been doing something naughty behind closed doors. Allie usually had a strained look that betrayed her concern.

I spoke with Allie on the phone after Marty's first visit and again in the middle of the following week. She never discussed anything they talked about, but she gave me advice on things to say to him and topics to avoid. She reminded me to make sure he was taking the medication that had been prescribed for him. She also asked each time how I was doing and seemed genuinely interested as I talked about final exams, graduation, Christmas shopping for my folks, and other things.

Allie and Marty both came to my graduation ceremony on Saturday afternoon. They sat with my parents. I saw them all standing and clapping when I received an award for the highest GPA in the graduating class and then again when I walked across the stage to receive my sheepskin.

Afterward, the five of us went for ice cream, and I was able to sit next to Allie. We shared stories about our college experiences, talked about my bright future as an auditor, and she gave me some details about a big research project she was doing with preteen girls. She smiled constantly and even threw back her head and laughed out loud at one of my sarcastic comments about accounting professors. Each time she looked at me, my heart raced in my chest. It was a special evening, marred only by Allie's anxious words to me as I walked her to her car.

"Larry, stay with Marty tonight. Don't let him be alone."

"Why?"

"You should go to a movie. Do something fun with him."

"A movie?" I asked, thinking about the McCarthy brothers. I was running a risk each time we left Marty's apartment together. They knew my car, although I took some comfort that there were a thousand Volkswagens just like it in Beaumont. Taking Marty to his appointments with Allie, taking him to Lamar for my graduation—it was dangerous. Going out on the town wouldn't be wise until we could make peace with these gangsters in a manner that wouldn't involve a choice between knives or guns.

"Just do it," she said. "I'm quite concerned by the way he's been acting tonight. You've been on center stage, and he's been distant, brooding, and quiet." Then she added, "Call me at my house in the morning. Let me know how he is."

"Okay."

"And there's something I need to talk to you about tomorrow. It's very important."

"Okay."

"And make sure he's taking those pills."

"Yeah, okay."

But rather than a movie or somewhere public, I took Marty to my parents' house in China. We watched TV for a couple of hours, and then Mom and Dad convinced him to spend the night on their living room sofa.

The next morning, traffic was light as I drove Marty back to Beaumont. In the car, we talked about inconsequential subjects, avoiding the metaphorical elephant on both our minds. As we approached his duplex, I promised to come over that night for a serious talk. We hadn't seen any cops since the night of the Buick stakeout, but we both knew they were onto him. And the McCarthys were out there—somewhere. They weren't going to just fade away when he had their merchandise and owed them money. Continuing to sell dime bags here and there while always looking over his shoulder was bound to end badly, and Marty had to have known it. I sounded like my father as I told him we'd discuss all his options when I returned that evening, and this time we'd agree on a definitive plan for his future.

"Yeah, whatever. It's cool," he said as he surveyed the street before stepping out of my car and hurrying inside.

After leaving Marty, I drove to a pay phone a few blocks away and called Allie. I told her Marty was fine and back at his apartment. She said that we needed to meet and suggested a quiet cafe she knew downtown. *She needs to see me*, I thought. My emotions were bubbling over with excitement and anticipation as I returned to my car.

When I arrived, she was already seated at a small table out of earshot of other patrons. I had hoped for a big hug like the previous night, but she stood and quickly shook my hand, all very perfunctory. There were no cheery smiles and no small talk. She was all business.

"Sit down. I want to tell you some things, Larry, and you need to listen and understand, okay?"

"Sure. All ears," I said.

"Be serious," she said. "Now, you didn't tell me that Marty was selling drugs when you came to see me two weeks ago."

"Well, yeah, but I did tell you—"

"It was a statement, not a question."

I nodded, then folded my arms over my chest and sunk deeper into my chair.

"Good. Now, please understand that psychologists—therapists like me—we are here to help people who feel broken by life's circumstances, who are confused or maybe feeling hopeless. And those who are going through a rough patch in their lives—like Marty. We lend them an attentive, professional ear, and we get an earful in return, much of it not so pretty. People aren't perfect, Larry. We're all dented cans, and therapists don't sit in judgment. We look for ways to help the broken ones to fix themselves and for the ones in the rough, dark patches to navigate through it to the sunshine. Does that make sense?"

"Yes," I answered.

She leaned in. "But there's a limit," she said slowly, enunciating each word as she locked her eyes onto mine with an intensity that rivaled my father's. "Marty Shannon is selling drugs, including to high school children. Seventeen, eighteen-year-old kids, Larry, and that crosses the line for me, for any licensed therapist."

She shook her head and raised her hands in a *What can I do?* gesture. "You know, if therapists put up a sign that said we only took patients who'd never done anything immoral or illegal, well, we wouldn't have many patients. But I can't abide certain things. I can't have him sit across from me," she said and shook her finger at me, "knowing that once he leaves my office, he's out there selling illegal drugs to kids at South Park High. And that's what I'm going to tell him tomorrow."

When I didn't offer a response, she continued, "I wanted you to hear it straight—from me." Her voice softened. "Marty doesn't have any family members for me to turn to for help, so it's just you and me. Do you understand?"

"Of course."

"You and I are the only ones who can get him through this rough patch, and I'm going to be gone on Monday if he doesn't agree to go to the police, tell them everything, and surrender the drugs."

"No way!"

She winced from the volume of my voice and whispered, "Quiet," as her eyes moved around the cafe.

"Sorry," I said, leaning closer to her. "But Allie, he's not going to go to the cops under any circumstances."

"He has to, Larry."

"He can't. If he turns that suitcase over to the police and ends up in jail, he'll be a sitting duck for big-time payback. He won't last a week in jail and he knows it. Didn't he tell you about the McCarthy brothers and how much he owes them?"

"Okay, okay," she said.

I studied her face and wondered why she'd given up so quickly. My reaction didn't seem to surprise her; it had to be the same thing Marty would have emphatically told her in therapy. Yes, *in therapy.* So, it was her way of confirming something Marty had told her without revealing those confidential conversations to me. It was our little dance.

"Then there's only one other alternative," she said.

I leaned forward.

"Marty has to return that suitcase, give it back to those pushers."

I smiled. I couldn't help it. "Allie, did he tell you what they're likely to do to him if he shows up after all this time with weed missing from the case and no money?"

"Look, I know it's not an easy answer, but it's the only one that I can accept if he won't go to the police. I have ethical standards to follow. He's engaged in illegal activities, and I can't continue to see him if he doesn't stop—immediately."

"Allie, do you like Marty?" I asked.

"That's not the point."

"I know, but do you like him? Tell me."

She exhaled and closed her eyes. When she opened them, the tension was gone, and she said, "I want to help him, I truly do, if that's what you mean. He's funny. He has such an easy, innocent manner. He reminds me of my younger brother, who I love dearly, and who drives me crazy, by the way." She smiled, just slightly, before continuing. "Marty deserves a do-over, and I'd like to help him get it. Does that answer your question?"

"So, what do we do—you and me?"

"When you see him later today, don't mention this conversation and what I'm going to say on Monday. I'll cover that with him. Do you understand?"

I gave her a nod.

"What you need to do—*today*," she said, "is convince him to return all the unsold drugs and, in the process, make some arrangements with the McCarthys so he's not looking over his shoulder. Do you agree?"

I gave her another nod.

"Look, I don't want to put you in a situation where you could get hurt, Larry, but maybe you could act as a go-between. Maybe?"

"Yeah, maybe. But Marty's got to agree. It's got to be a good plan that he'll agree to," I said.

And so, we talked for 20 minutes about setting up a payment plan with the McCarthy brothers, like a couple of bankers. We talked about helping Marty to find a good job with a steady income. In hindsight, it all sounds incredibly naive. We should have known that Marty had a different plan, especially me. He made jokes and tried to act carefree, but behind the façade, his self-esteem was subterranean. The world had beaten Marty down and convinced him that he was scum. That's how he'd come to refer to himself—as scum. Then, just like Daniel Carter had done, he'd say he was kidding. I should have known better. Despite all the encouragement that Allie and I provided and behind all the smiles he gave us, he'd given up.

Marty wasn't completely honest with Allie in their private

sessions. He never told her about his gun and his games. And he lied to me about wanting to find a way out of this mess and come clean. He told us repeatedly that he was taking the antidepressants and was feeling better about himself, but I'm certain now that it was just another lie.

I spent a lot of time with Marty during those two weeks, and I saw his external and internal demons converge on him. Paranoia consumed him. He must have felt like he had no control over his own life, except for one final solution. In the end, when he needed me most, I abandoned him to those demons, and Marty Shannon resigned himself to a dark, morbid fate: that scum must eventually give way and be eradicated. When he finally emerged from his apartment that Sunday, it was in a body bag.

Allie was a wreck. She'd never lost a patient before and she felt awful, like she must have said the wrong things and thereby failed Marty in his desperate time of need.

Marty had no family, and Allie said she wanted to help with the funeral arrangements, so we both went to see Monsignor Jerrard at St. Anne's on Calder. He had performed the funeral service for Mrs. Shannon, and we pleaded with him to give Marty a Catholic funeral. I knew that's what Mrs. Shannon would have wanted.

A recent Vatican pronouncement had softened the Church's position on denying funeral rites to those who take their own life. Grave psychological disturbances, anguish, and fear of hardship, extreme suffering, or torture were described as reasons that could diminish the responsibility of a person committing suicide. Special language had been adopted into the Catholic Order of Christian Funerals that was to be used for suicide victims.

The old priest was skeptical whether the exception applied in Marty's case. I argued that Marty clearly had a fear of hardship when he took his life. The monsignor noted that it was probably because he feared being caught by the police and sent to jail for selling drugs. I wanted to protest his characterization of Marty's activities, but Allie motioned for me to let it drop.

Allie pointed out in a clinical way that learning about the death of his natural mother at his father's hand and his father's subsequent suicide must have caused psychological trauma to Marty. Surely that would qualify as a grave psychological disturbance, Allie argued.

It had been difficult for Marty to recount what his dying mother had confessed about his father, Frank Shannon. How he had been a successful attorney with a seemingly perfect life and a seemingly perfect wife. How she'd been unable to have children and how sad and distant this made him. How he developed a middle-aged weakness for the ladies and the bottle. How he stayed late at the office one night to drink and contemplate a desperate and painful situation, and in a fit of alcohol-induced depression, he started playing with a loaded pistol. How he had been startled by a young Mexican woman who worked in his office and accidentally shot her through the heart. How the following morning he had turned that gun on himself. How his suicide note had disclosed that this young woman, who had no family in this country, had borne him a son two months before she was killed. How the grieving widow, Mrs. Shannon, had adopted that boy and raised him as Martin, her own son.

But the monsignor said that happened over 20 years ago, when Marty was just a baby. Even though he had only recently been told all the details, he didn't see how it could be used as an excuse for Marty's actions as an adult. The old priest also was distressed by Marty's failure to attend Mass and show any remorse for his actions by making a confession prior to taking his life.

The best we could do was to get the monsignor to agree not to give us an immediate "No," but to reflect on our request. He called Allie the next day to say he had prayed over the matter and had even spoken with his bishop. They were sorry, but Marty could not have a Catholic funeral.

Allie arranged for a retired Methodist minister she knew to say some words over Marty's closed casket at the funeral home.

He didn't know Marty, and I didn't pay much attention to what he said. I couldn't help thinking how heartbreakingly sad it was that Marty had no relatives in attendance for the short service. Allie had made a phone call to the AMA to try to locate his psychiatrist uncle, but I couldn't remember his last name and it was hopeless.

Besides my parents, Allie, and me, just six other people came. There were three scroungy-looking guys and their groupie chick, who said they knew Marty from South Park High, and there were two suits who never introduced themselves. They looked like Sergeant Joe Friday and his partner from one of my favorite TV shows, *Dragnet*. After the service, I exited quickly through a side door into the small courtyard outside the chapel to get a better look at the suits. As they stepped outside, they both brought their hands up to shield their eyes from the bright sunlight. That's when I realized I had seen them before, and I understood why they were there and why they'd been staring at me throughout the service.

Thirty minutes later on that cold Friday morning—December 28, 1973—we laid Marty Shannon to his eternal rest in the cemetery on Pine Street in a simple grave beside his mother.

After the funeral, Allie made it clear that our sexual encounter at her house on Christmas Eve, the day after Marty took his life, was a one-night affair. There would be no repeat performance. We had talked about it on the phone after Christmas, and she never said that she regretted that night, the most wonderful night of my young life, and I was at least thankful for that. In fact, she said that it seemed so right, so perfect—*at the time*. All the pressures in her life—her husband, Tom Parker, developing a bad case of the seven-year itch and leaving in October, the anguish and loneliness she had to suppress beneath the happy face at work, the holiday season, and the way we both became emotionally drained trying to save Marty—had intensified to a crescendo. After sharing all her frustrations, a few tears, and a bottle of Scotch with me, it just happened. Allie said that no one had loved her in a long time, and I think she desperately needed a night off from an uncaring world, particularly on the day before Christmas. She found it for one long loving night in the shelter of my arms.

And it wasn't some pathetic *Summer of '42* charity case between a beautiful, grown woman and a goofus schoolboy. We were two adults sharing intimacy and a passion for each other on an adult level. At least, that's how I remember it.

But Allie wasn't interested in an ongoing sexual relationship with me and all the complications that it would inflict on her life. When I called her on New Year's Eve from my parents' house, she even hinted that we probably shouldn't see each other going forward.

I asked, "So, are you doing anything tonight?"

And I heard her respond, *No, I'll probably just turn in early.*

"Yeah, I'm not doing anything either."

Silence.

"So, maybe we should get together to say goodbye to 1973. It sure has been a strange year, and we could—"

I don't think that's such a good idea.

"Why?"

I like you, Larry, but I'm in a really messed up place in my life right now.

"I know. We talked about it."

Silence.

"And I think you need a friend, Allie—someone to talk to, someone you can just, you know, relax around."

I heard a snicker before she said, *Just talk?*

"Sure"

And just relax?

"You know what I mean."

Look, I'm going to be brutally honest, Larry, and every therapist would tell you the same thing here, in our situation. After two people have sex, the urge for a repeat performance—an encore, if you will—is so great that it dominates their relationship from that point on. And I don't want to go there. I'm not ready for that.

"Am I in analysis now?"

No, but I understand these things. I've studied this aspect of human behavior, particularly how it affects young people. I understand how difficult it is for a male and a female to have a purely platonic friendship after they've been sexually intimate. There's always an uncomfortable tension there. It's a fact.

"Always? So, I'm just a statistic. I'm *young people* now—a raging-hormones schoolboy that you've prejudged—"

No, that's not—

"And pigeonholed into a neat little behavioral category."

No, you don't understand.

"Allie, how well do you know me? I mean, *really* know me?"

Silence.

"Well, I don't think you know me very well." Pause. "If you did, maybe you'd see that I don't fit that stereotypical profile in your textbook. Maybe what I'm looking for right now is a friend—someone I can talk to, hang out with, and just *relax* around. But relax like friends. I'm sure you've noticed that I'm a little short on friends just now."

Yeah, me too.

"And maybe you've prematurely and *unfairly* judged me."

Silence, like she was thinking.

"Maybe you and I can be more mature about this, not like those generic *young people* textbook situations."

Yeah, maybe.

"Allie, we both could use a friend. I'm ready to be your friend, and I only want your friendship in return. Can you accept that and *please* be my friend?"

A short pause, then, *Yes, and I'm sorry. This is just a very confusing time for me. You know—you have to know—I'm extremely fond of you. I enjoy talking to you, being around you. You know that, right?*

"Hey, don't get all mushy on me."

I heard her chuckle, then, *I just don't want there to be any—*

I recalled my father telling me, *If they say they're buying, then you need to stop selling and close the deal.* So, I interrupted, "My mom's made black-eyed peas for tomorrow. Can I bring some over to you, you know, for good luck?"

Yes, I'd like that. I could use some good luck. Thank you.

"About noon? Unless you're doing something."

No plans. I heard her laugh. *I never seem to have any plans.*

"Me either. Maybe we could watch the Cotton Bowl game, cheer those Longhorns on."

Yes, it'd be nice to have someone to watch the game with. See you then?

"Yeah, see you then."

I hung up with a heavy sigh of relief and headed for the refrigerator and a cold beer to help shake off the stress of that call. My father had said on many occasions that, no matter how hard we may try, men are incapable of understanding women. Why Allie believed those desperate lies about only wanting to be friends—after I'd tasted her lips, held her naked body, and experienced the pure bliss of loving her—was completely beyond my comprehension.

I phoned Mr. Collingsworth, a senior partner at Arthur Andersen & Co. in Houston, and told him that I wouldn't be able to report to work in mid-January as we had originally agreed. I apologized profusely for not honoring my commitment to him and the firm. I was nervous on the call, and I'm sure it showed. In a rambling dissertation, I explained that I had some personal issues to work out and had decided to return to school to pursue an MBA degree.

His response made me feel great. I had feared that he would blow me off, considering that my accounting degree was from Lamar. It was a mediocre little school in a blue-collar refinery town, far from the bastions of knowledge like Austin and Houston, where he typically went to recruit worldly and brilliant young graduates to become high-powered Arthur Andersen auditors. Students from other universities in Texas disparagingly referred to Lamar as "Pecker Tech" after the school's Redbird mascot and reputation for attracting students from the local area who were unsophisticated and better suited for a vocational, technical, or correctional institution.

But Mr. Collingsworth said that I was one of the top graduating seniors that he'd seen that year. He assured me that there would be a place for me whenever I was ready to begin my career, and he encouraged me to keep him informed on my activities in the meantime. I was ecstatic.

I was able to enroll at the last minute in the MBA program at Lamar, and I signed up for three classes for the spring semester. I couldn't get my old job back—keeping books for the student center—but I persuaded Dr. Ellison, who taught taxation, to let me be his grader. The job paid the $2.00 per hour minimum wage for ten hours per week, a fixed stipend that Lamar granted to each grader who assisted a tenured professor. Dr. Ellison also helped me get a job working about 20 hours a week at $4.25 an hour for a local practitioner doing tax law research and preparing returns.

I rented a one-bedroom apartment in a little complex that was close to school and super cheap because I had to share it with a colony of large rats. I was able to get rid of the rodents with the help of some chemicals that my father secured from the plant where he worked. Dad strategically placed the toxic solution throughout my apartment for maximum effectiveness. After a few days, I no longer had any worries about rats. Instead, I worried about whether I'd become sterile.

My parents were very understanding of these sudden changes. I was able to assure Dad that I still had a solid, long-term plan for my life. It was just a little different now. I explained how the MBA could be useful and valuable in the future. I told him I was going to get the degree within two years and then begin my CPA career in Houston with Arthur Andersen and good old Mr. Collingsworth, who loved me. Mom asked why I was only taking three courses for just nine credit hours, and I told her it would give me more time to study for the formidable CPA exam, which I planned to take in May. I also said that I wasn't ready to take on a heavy scholastic load after all the turmoil in my life with Marty's tragic death and everything. She immediately concurred with my impeccable logic and suggested that I consider an even lighter load.

My parents agreed to pay for tuition, books, and rent like they had during my three and a half years working on an undergraduate degree. The money I earned from my part-time jobs would be sufficient to cover food, gas, and other modest living expenses. I was amazed how well everything had worked out.

I never questioned whether I was doing the right thing. I had to stay in Beaumont to be close to Allie. I was hopelessly in love.

I also had some unfinished business with the McCarthy brothers.

Chapter 29
BAD GUYS

It all came to a climax on Sunday, January 13th, exactly three weeks after Marty had taken his life. It was the day I was sure that I too had died. I still can't believe what I did—something dangerous and completely out of character. But I know why I did it.

By getting involved in Marty's life and trying desperately to help an old friend, I had stepped out of my passive-loner persona. I was crushed when Marty killed himself, but my guilt, grief, and sadness, painful as they each were, at least made me feel alive. I know that I failed Marty, but the fact that I had tried so hard to help someone else—for the first time in a long time—in a shameful way, made me feel good about myself. By getting involved with Allie, I had felt love and intimacy with a woman. I had an overpowering need to continue to do things that no one would expect from the old Larry Torrence, that I wouldn't expect myself to do. And so, while everyone else in Beaumont was glued to their TVs that Sunday afternoon, watching the Miami Dolphins whip up on the Minnesota Vikings in the Super Bowl, I had a date with Buster and Lefty, the McCarthy brothers . . . and they were late.

I wasn't thinking clearly when I went to the police station immediately after Marty's funeral. I was a madman that afternoon with a single, all-consuming objective—to make the bad guys pay—and I didn't care about the consequences. The uniformed officer I spoke with at the front desk led me through a maze, back to a bullpen area where three suits were sitting at metal desks. He stopped in front of the first one.

"This kid was asking about you, Joe," the officer said. "Said he saw you earlier today and had something he wanted to tell you."

The suit stood up. He didn't show any emotion as he said, "Detective Stuart." His handshake was firm, as I'd expected.

"Yeah, I'm Larry Torrence. But I think you know that."

"Sit down," he said and pointed to a chair opposite his desk. "What can I do for you, Mr. Torrence?"

I came directly to the point. "I just dropped by to see if you knew anything about the McCarthy brothers, Detective."

Curiosity seeped through his poker face. After looking me over for a few seconds, he said, "Yeah, we know all about those lowlifes and that your little friend was selling drugs for them."

When I didn't respond, he asked, "So, tell me, *Larry*, why are you here?"

"Did you find any drugs in Marty's apartment?"

A question in response to a question. He tried to stare me down without speaking. Finally, he responded with another question, "Why do you ask?"

I shrugged my shoulders. "Oh, I'm just curious. But I'm guessing that you didn't."

"Yeah, well I'm guessing that's because *you* have them."

"Me?"

"Sure. You two were awfully chummy."

I didn't respond, just locked eyeballs with him like my dad would have done, and I tried to stay calm.

After a long pause, he spoke with a stronger voice, "That's enough of this cat-and-mouse bullshit, son. You need to answer me—*right now*. Why are you here asking about drugs?"

"Well—" I cleared my throat. "If you didn't find anything . . . Then, if you've got a really tall guy—at least as tall as Marty—and he puts the toilet lid down, stands there on his toes, and moves a couple ceiling tiles right over the commode, he'll probably find a black suitcase and a little gold key up there."

"Oh, really?" he asked, raising his eyebrows. "And what if we've already found that case?"

"It doesn't matter to me, either way."

"And why's that?"

"Because I've got an idea how we can use it."

Allie lived in a nice home on a cul-de-sac in the more affluent west side of Beaumont. I arrived a few minutes before noon, and she greeted me with a hug. During the New Year's Day Cotton Bowl, we talked about the game and not much else as her beloved Longhorns left their offense in Austin and lost 19–3.

I got up to leave, but she said that we should first take a walk, stretch our legs. As we slowly meandered through her neighborhood, she became serious, and we talked about the strange twists and turns that life can take. Allie got a little emotional talking about the tragedy of suicide and the scars it leaves on friends and relatives—even on therapists.

"Marty's the only patient I've ever had who—"

"I know. You told me that night, remember?"

"Oh yeah," she said.

"It's okay, Allie."

"It's not okay. You don't understand."

"Try me," I said.

"Well, it's just that I want so badly to help my patients. To do that, I try to relate to each one of them, to truly understand and feel what they're going through, to see things through *their* eyes. But, at the same time, I have to stay objective and professionally detached. It's a difficult balance. I don't know, maybe I'm too sentimental for my job, like a surgeon who gets squeamish at the sight of blood. What do you think?"

I didn't hesitate. "I think you have to care about the people who come to you for help. If you don't, if you're *detached*—" and I said the word like it was leprosy, "—they'll figure it out, even kids. They'll think you don't care. And you have to care, Allie, or what's the point? It doesn't matter if it's a patient like Marty or a good friend like me. You can't go through life detached from people around you. It's unnatural."

I was shocked by my own words and how easily they had flowed from my brain to my mouth. Was that the James Dean loner talking about getting involved with people? I also was surprised to be the one dispensing advice. I was afraid that it had sounded like some amateur mixtape, a compilation of greatest hits from my mother (*You have to care or what's the point?*) and my father (*You can't go through life . . .*). But she gave me a big smile and said I was right.

After a while, she got around to asking how I was coping with Marty's death. I lied and said I was okay. I talked in a mature manner about how she and I did everything we could and how some people just can't (or won't) be saved. I had checked out a book at the library on suicide bereavement. It was mostly common-sense stuff, but I'm sure it helped me convince her that I was experiencing the typical stages of grief and dealing with them in a satisfactory manner.

My instincts told me if I confessed what really happened with Marty and let her know how utterly guilt-ridden and cowardly I felt, she would, at worst, have me committed to a mental institution or, at best, immediately commence intense analysis and psychotherapy on me. Either way, I would become a patient at that point and lose all hope for a more substantial relationship with Allie, since therapists can't screw their patients, at least not in the way that I was thinking about.

The truth was that I couldn't stop thinking about what I should have done differently on that Sunday, Marty's last day. I couldn't bring myself to tell Allie that I was with him at his apartment on that final night. I was the only one who knew how it all went down, at least the only one alive.

Marty was nervous as we sipped our beers on his sofa. I kept explaining how he had only one option: Return the suitcase and make amends with the McCarthy brothers. I had volunteered to act as a middleman to arrange surrender terms, to work out a payment plan with them. He didn't argue, but it also didn't seem like he was paying close attention. Every two seconds, he'd get up and peek through the dark curtains to check the street in front of the duplex.

When he saw the gray Lincoln pulling to a stop, he shouted, "Oh, shit!" He made a beeline back to the sofa, yanked me up, and pulled me across the entry room and through the kitchen. He opened the back door and pushed me out.

"What the hell, Marty?" I kept asking.

"It's them. They found me. I knew it!"

"Let me talk to them," I said.

"No, you've got to go!"

"We can work this out."

"No, I don't want you involved."

"Okay, c'mon then, let's get out of here!" I pleaded. "Both of us!" I pointed in the direction of my car, parked a couple of blocks away. I nodded and smiled to tell him that the two of us could be cruising down the road in less than a minute.

But he stood inside with a peaceful, resigned look on his face. "I'm sorry, but I can't hide anymore, and you can't get caught in here with scum like me. You've got a life, Buddy boy. Go live it." Then he winked at me and slammed the door shut. I heard it lock from the other side with his last words—"Now, run!"—ringing in my ears.

I protested at the closed door, but it was half-hearted. After standing there for a couple of seconds like a deer caught in the headlights, I did as he said. I ran like the gutless coward that I am, even harder after I heard a single gunshot echo through the night. All I could think about was that big Marty-wink he gave me before he closed the door, something he had to have known I'd remember for the rest of my life.

Detective Stuart had it all planned, every detail. First, he arranged for the McCarthys to find out through some back channels that a certain Lamar student had a black suitcase in his possession that was filled with drugs—their merchandise—that had been on consignment to the late Marty Shannon. The case was taken from his apartment just before he shot himself.

Armed with that knowledge, Stuart was certain that the brothers would seek to make my acquaintance. He was right.

They grabbed me after my afternoon class on Thursday, January 10th, as I was about to get into my car. Detective Stuart, who had predicted all this, said I should act surprised and scared. I had no trouble with that part.

Lefty, the burly, bull-necked one, manhandled me like I was a little girl. He reached around my back and stuck his hand in my armpit while tightly holding me beside him with his other hand. He quick-walked me through the student parking lot and then behind an old dormitory that had been closed for several years. Each time I struggled or tried to slow the pace, he dug his fingers in causing excruciating pain as he whispered in my ear, "You're comin' with me, kid. If ya scream, I'm gonna hurt you—*bad*."

Buster, the slender, balding one, was waiting behind the building. They were an odd-looking pair, and I wondered if they were really brothers. They shared none of the same physical features, except for a ruthless countenance. They wore dark suits that were offset by colorful, silk shirts open at the neck to expose nests of gnarly black chest hairs. Their ensembles were accented by several pounds of gold jewelry around the neck, wrists, and fingers. Lefty had a chaw that protruded in one cheek while Buster twirled a toothpick between his lips.

They dispensed with all the usual pleasantries and went straight to the part where Lefty pins me against the wall while Buster waves a switchblade knife in my face and threatens to cut off my balls and stuff them down my throat if I don't return their property.

"I'm sorry!" I cried, my heart pounding.

"You're about to be *real* sorry," Buster said.

"Thought ya could make a quick score," Lefty said, "with our product, hey?" He spit a mouthful of brown liquid a couple of inches from my shoe.

"Yeah, but I realize now it was a big mistake. A huge mistake."

"You're damn right!" Buster shouted, his face just inches from mine.

"The case, it's still full. I didn't sell anything. I didn't know where to start," I said, my eyes darting from one of them to the other as Bobby Radley walked around the corner of the building and stopped, about a dozen paces from us.

"Oh, hi," Bobby said in a cheery voice. "How y'all doing?"

Bobby was Stuart's guy. He'd been shadowing me around campus for the past couple of days. He was young and could pass for a college kid. He was tall and wiry like a wide receiver. His shirttail was out, I assumed to conceal the handgun he always tucked into his jeans behind his back.

"Beat it!" Lefty shouted.

"We're fine, just having a little conversation," Buster added in a more cordial tone as he lowered the hand holding the switchblade and moved his face away from mine. He semi-smiled at Bobby and said, "Just need a little privacy."

While they were talking and looking at Bobby, I made eye contact with him and nodded a couple of times and winked to let him know I was okay.

"Hey, no need to get hostile," Bobby said. "I'm just walking here and I thought—"

Lefty released my arm and started walking toward him.

"Hey big guy," Bobby said, as he stepped backward. "It's none of my business whatever you guys are up to, you know, standing so close back here."

Buster said, "That's right. It's none of your business, so get lost." He spit the toothpick in Bobby's general direction.

At the same time, Lefty grabbed his crotch as he advanced and said, "You wanta get close to this, asshole?"

Bobby raised his hands in surrender, then quickly turned and walked back around the building and out of sight.

"Blow me!" Lefty shouted at him before he returned to me.

"So," Buster said, "where's the suitcase?"

"It's safe. It's locked and hidden in my room at my folks' house," I said, just like Stuart had instructed.

"And where might that be?" Buster asked.

"In China. China, Texas."

"And it's full?"

"Yeah, Marty, he only sold a few bags. And there's about a hundred dollars in cash in there—the money he took in."

Buster gave me a sinister smile like he thoroughly enjoyed playing gangster with kids half his age. He twirled the knife in front of me. "Then you're going to take a ride with us, a fast boat to China, to get our property."

"But—" I said.

"But what?" Lefty said, as he pulled on my arm to drag me away.

"But how am I going to explain you guys to my parents?" I asked.

Lefty loosened his grip and looked at Buster. When neither of them responded, I kept talking. "My father will be home from work by now. If I show up on a Thursday afternoon—all unexpected, you know—my mom and dad are bound to be suspicious. Sir, I think you should know that my father, he used to be a police officer before we moved to Texas." It was a lie, but I said the words with sincerity and conviction, like I had practiced.

"A regular Wyatt Earp, hey?" Buster said.

I liked his choice of words. I gave Buster a grin and said, "Yeah, you've got it, and he's—"

But I didn't get to finish my thought. Buster backhanded me across the mouth, causing my head to snap back against the wall and my glasses to go flying. The jarring pain and the blood I felt seeping from inside my lip were cruel reminders that this was not a game. I needed to be more serious. And more persuasive.

"I'm sorry. But they'll want to know who you are, why I'm there on a school day, what's in the suitcase, how it—"

"Shut up!" Buster yelled into my face. "We get the picture, punk." He looked at his brother and asked, "Well?"

"I say we cut his nuts off, right here and now," Lefty answered.

"But what about the case?"

"Fuck the case!"

"Will you get serious?"

"I am serious!" Lefty shouted. "This little turd has totally pissed me off." He turned his head and spit again. Then he leaned over me, his grip tightening on my arm. "I told ya I was crazy, kid—ya know, when ya gave us the slip on Railroad." He pulled back his coat with his other hand to expose the pistol in a holster under his arm.

"Look, can you be rational just for once?" Buster asked him.

I swallowed hard and tried to clear the fear from my throat. Looking at Buster, I whispered, "Can I make a suggestion?"

"Oh, please do, college boy," he said.

"You see, I told my parents I'd be home this Saturday." It made me feel like a ten-year-old, but I added, "Mom's going to do my laundry."

"That's sweet, but so what?" Buster asked.

"So, I'll get the suitcase this weekend and return it to you on Sunday, after I come back to Beaumont."

Buster stared at me as he contemplated my offer.

"I don't want it. Really." My voice was cracking. "Marty made me take it. I can't imagine what I was thinking." I looked down at my glasses, and he motioned that it would be okay to pick them up.

As I bent over and reached down, I heard Lefty, on my other flank, say to his brother, "You aren't seriously thinkin' 'bout trustin' this kid?"

"Well, it's an option," Buster answered. "I think he knows what'll happen if he tries anything funny." He looked at me and shouted, "Right?"

"Right. Absolutely. Yes, sir," I said. I looked from one to the other. "No problems, I promise."

Lefty leaned against me and whispered, "So, if we let ya go and trust ya 'til Sunday—?" He paused until I nodded that he had my complete attention. "Ya ain't gonna blow your brains out like that sick friend of yours, are ya?"

I sank back against the wall with Lefty's laughter ringing in my ears. I despised him. I hated both of them.

"Bumble-fuck amateurs," Lefty muttered.

For the next two minutes, they debated the merits of trusting me for a rendezvous on Sunday, storming my house that afternoon, or castration here and now. It reminded me of the good-guy/bad-guy routines that I'd seen on *I Spy* and other TV shows, only this was more like bad-guy/worse-guy. Pushing back against the wall helped to control my trembling as I bent my glasses back into shape and licked my wounded lip.

Eventually, Buster's logic prevailed, and they decided to wait until Sunday. Lefty fumed as Buster put away his knife and then took down the address for my apartment. He said they would follow me home, just to make sure. Then Buster launched into a tirade while pounding his right fist into his left palm like he was practicing for a workout on my face. "And don't even think about a double-cross with the cops, punk. We've got lots of friends, and they'll know where you live." He stopped punching his hand long enough to jab a finger into my chest. "Do you understand me?" He jabbed again as he asked, "Do you?"

"Yes, sir. Yes, sir," I said.

"You can't hide from us," he said and jabbed me once more. His eyes were glazed, and frothy little bubbles of white foam gurgled out of the corners of his mouth.

"I know. I believe you."

"Even if you're a real dumb shit and run to the cops and—"

"I'd never do that," I said.

"You better not!" Buster said, and for good measure he quick-punched me in the ribs. The sudden bolt of pain took my breath away.

He threw his hands into the air. "Now, see what you did," he said.

I doubled over and clutched my side, gasping for short breaths. "I'm sorry," I said. "I won't do it again."

I saw him nodding in approval. "You're a smart kid. You got manners."

"Hey, kid!" Lefty said.

I turned my head, teeth clenched in pain.

"Be cool, play this straight, and ya may get to keep your balls. But try anything uncool, *anything* . . . and I'm gonna enjoy makin' you pay," Lefty said with a sick smile.

PART TWO: BAD GUYS 321

* * * * *

I called Stuart on Thursday night on his private line. I said, "So, it's all set."

And I heard him say, *Bobby told me about your little get-acquainted session with the boys.*

"Yeah, my new buddies were on either side, focused on me. But I was looking out and saw Bobby across the field. Well, I could see part of his head sticking out behind a dumpster."

You know you were safe at all times, right?

Yeah, right, I thought, but I let it pass. I gave him the details for the handoff on Sunday afternoon at my place. I'd set it up just like he'd told me. Stuart seemed pleased and commented that our plan had worked to perfection so far. I hung up the phone thinking that was an interesting perspective considering my busted lip and bruised ribs.

The McCarthys were late. Rocking on the porch swing in front of my little apartment, I was in agony. I hadn't slept for three nights and my nerves were shot. I had gone to St. Christopher Cathedral that Sunday morning and lit three candles—for Daniel, Marty, and me. I couldn't control my shaking hands as I knelt in front of my votive offerings, cursing myself for coming up with this stupid payback idea.

I was sitting on the porch swing trying to slow my racing heart with long, deep breaths when the big Lincoln rolled to a stop in front of my apartment. Lefty McCarthy, with his hulking frame, stepped out wearing a black suit. He looked like he was headed for a funeral. The afternoon sun reflected off the gold jewelry dangling around his neck, and I watched helplessly as he waddled up the sidewalk, careful to avoid putting his freshly shined wingtips in the puddles left by a recent rain.

I stood to greet him, the black suitcase resting on the swing by my right hand. To my left was the door to my apartment, cracked open ever so slightly. As he approached, my anxiety got the better of me, and I called out, "Hey, Lefty, where's Buster?" like he was some long-lost friend. I instantly regretted my words.

Lefty didn't reply until he was on the porch, right on top of me with his belly pushing against mine, forcing me a half-step backward. "Why do ya wanta know, punk?" he asked as he looked up, down, and across my street. He peered over my shoulder, looking through a small window into my apartment.

"No reason," I said.

"Ya thought we'd both show up, huh?"

"I didn't think anything. I just assumed, you know, that you'd both—"

"Ya thought we'd just march in here together. Well, we're not stupid, ya little thief," Lefty said.

"Of course not," I said.

"And who'd ya talk to 'bout that assumption?"

"What?"

"Ya heard me," he said, and he grabbed my shirt collar and pulled me to him. I put my right hand out for support and could feel the pistol through his jacket, in its holster under his armpit. "Don't play dumb with me, college boy," he hissed. "Did ya tell the narc pigs our little secret? Did ya?"

"No."

He motioned down the street. "Are they out there waitin' for us?" he asked.

"No."

He glanced at the door. "Are they in there?"

I shook my head and for the third time told him, "No."

He continued to squeeze my shirt tighter with his stubby, sausage-like fingers. "Maybe they'll come runnin' to save your ass when they see me wring your scrawny neck, huh?"

"No! I'm no fool. I swear I didn't—"

"You were a fool when ya took that suitcase."

"I know, but now I'm smart. Now I just want to give it back."

"So, why're ya waitin' out here with it, Einstein, out where every Tom and Harry Dick in the city can see ya?"

I was petrified. This wasn't the way it was supposed to go down. I could barely breathe with the back of his fist wedged into my windpipe. "I was inside, not out here," I said. "But you guys—I mean, you—you were late, so I came out here to wait." I gasped for air. "I didn't mean nothing by it, I promise! I just want to get this over with."

He gave me a cold stare.

"Please," I said, "take the case. It's not locked. It's right there." I pointed at the swing.

Lefty stuck his face into mine so that our foreheads were touching. "No, *you* take it, Einstein. I don't wanta touch it, not just yet. You pick it up and let's go see who's inside this dump." His breath smelled like raw meat and tobacco. As he slowly released me, I swallowed hard and tensed my diaphragm to keep from puking in his face.

"Sure. That's cool," I said.

He motioned toward the door.

"Sure thing. Whatever you want, it's all groovy," I said. I straightened my shirt and tried not to let my eyes drift across the street as I picked up the big suitcase. Every nerve inside me screamed at my brain to end it here, to signal to Detective Stuart in the apartment across the street. But my brain reminded those quivering nerves that Lefty hadn't taken the bait yet. They wouldn't be able to put him away for coming over to my place for a little chat. And where was Buster? No, if I stopped now, they'd be back someday and I'd have to pay—big time. I had shitty cards, but I had to stay in the hand. Folding at this point wasn't a viable option.

When we got inside, Lefty closed the door, pushed my nose into a wall, and frisked me from head to toe. I said a silent prayer of thanks that I'd refused to wear a wire. Stuart had almost called off the sting. He said these guys were unpredictable. He thought it would be too dangerous if he couldn't hear what was being said. But I convinced him that it would be okay because I would conduct the transaction on the porch in plain sight. So, he gave me the briefcase. Was I brilliant or what?

While I wondered whether Stuart and the cavalry were going to come to my rescue or leave me to play out the hand, Lefty took a slow tour of my place. He peered into, around, and under everything in the little apartment. While he was in the bedroom, I peeked out the window and made a quick "Okay" sign with my thumb and index finger at the two men emerging from the apartment across the street. They hesitated for a second and then nonchalantly turned as though they were out for a leisurely stroll.

From my bedroom came a loud pop followed by a booming, "Son-of-a-bitch!" It made me jump, and I moved away from the window.

"Be careful of the mouse traps!" I yelled.

Lefty returned to my little kitchenette/living room. He was rubbing two fingers on his left hand. "I'll remember that," he sneered. He went to the window, the same one I had signaled from, and he pulled a two-way radio unit from the inside pocket of his jacket.

"Is there a back way outta here?" he asked.

"No, sir."

Lefty pressed a button on the side of the walkie-talkie. "Come in, Buster," he said into the device and then released the button.

Buster's voice filled my apartment. "Yeah, I'm here, and don't use my name, you asshole." The volume was high, and Buster must have had his unit close to his mouth. When he used words with the "s" and "k" sounds, they crackled through the air like fingernails on a blackboard.

"We talked about that, remember? Use the codes. Over," Buster said.

"Sorry, Rebel One. Where are ya?" Lefty said as he gazed out the window.

"Down the street where you dropped me, just to the north of you, Rebel Two. Over."

Lefty's cautious eyes looked from one side of the street to the other. "Right," he said.

"It's clean out here," the Buster-voice said. "Nothing going on 'cept two queers taking a walk. Everybody must be inside watching the game. Over."

"I don't like it!" Lefty shouted into the radio.

"Take it easy. You don't like what, Rebel Two? Over."

"The kid was outside. It smells," Lefty said.

"Hey," I pleaded, "I told you I—"

"Shut up!" he commanded. "I'm not talkin' to you, college boy."

I recoiled against the door. There was a long pause while Lefty stared open-mouthed at the radio waiting for a response. When the scratchy Buster-voice finally came over the device, it was still loud and shrill and said, "You're supposed to say 'Over' when you're finished, Rebel Two."

Lefty rolled his eyes and shot the finger at the radio unit before pressing the talk button. "So sorry," he said mockingly. After another pause, he lifted the radio back to his mouth and said, "So sorry. *Over!*"

"Quit clowning around. Is it clean in there? Over."

"Roger that," Lefty said. "It's clean, but I don't like it." There was another pause of a few seconds with Lefty staring into the radio until it finally came to life.

"Damn it, Lefty, you've got to say 'Over,' or I don't know when you're finished talking."

"And you just said my name, dipshit. Now everybody on this channel knows who we are," Lefty said.

After a few seconds of silence, the Buster-voice, deep with frustration, said, "Forget about it, okay? Maybe the kid likes fresh air. I don't know. Is it a go or not? Over."

"Look," Lefty replied, "I told ya that I don't like it. I got a bad feelin' here. *Over goddamnit!*"

"But you said it's clean, right? Over," Buster said.

"Yeah," Lefty said.

"Well, if it's clean out here and it's clean in there, I say it's a go. Over."

Lefty looked right through me with his piercing eyes, sizing me up. After a few seconds, he licked his lips like he was getting ready for dinner.

"I said, 'Over.'"

"I know what ya said," Lefty barked into his radio unit. "I'm thinkin', damnit!" He lowered the radio and continued to stare at me for several seconds, but then cringed and cursed under his breath. He lifted the radio and said, "Over."

"What?" came the reply.

"I said, 'Over,'" Lefty repeated.

"I know, but did you say something before that? Over."

"Yeah, I said, '*Over, goddamnit!*'" Lefty screamed into his walkie-talkie.

The Buster-voice tried to remain calm. It whispered, "Look, I say it's a go. That piss-ant kid knows we'll have his gonads if he's squealed. What do you say, Rebel Two? Is it a go? Over."

Lefty didn't answer. He turned his radio off, just as Buster was starting to speak again. He'd clearly had enough. He'd made up his mind about something. He slipped the device into his inside jacket pocket and then reached behind his back. The entire time, his cold eyes peered into mine, his expression turning more menacing with each passing second. The temperature in the room was suddenly subzero. It gave me chills and made my knees weak.

"Ya know, college boy, he's right. You're a real piss-ant, a stupid little piss-ant," Lefty said, moving toward me.

"I know," I said, staring back at him but trying frantically to locate the doorknob with my hands behind me. "And I'm truly sorry for any inconvenience that—"

"And ya know what happens to piss-ants?" he asked.

I found the knob, turned it quickly, and pulled to open the door, but his fist came down hard over my head, banging it shut as he answered his own question. "They get crushed!"

When I looked back at him, I saw the blade of a knife in his other hand. He waved it in front of him so I could get a good look at it.

"Oh, Jesus," I said.

"That's good, you talkin' to Jesus." He grinned at me. "'Cause now you're gonna get to meet him."

I tried to bring my arms up, but he was too quick. The hand with the knife shot forward in a blur, straight into my chest at the base of the sternum. I crumpled to the floor, unable to breathe. Lefty kicked me out of his way and reached down to pick up the suitcase. I heard him say, "That's what happens when ya mess with the wrong people, smart guy." Then I felt his spit hit my face just before I lost consciousness.

A statue of Mirabeau B. Lamar, second president of the Republic of Texas, mass murderer of the frontier Indians, and namesake of Lamar University, stands in the open quadrangle at the center of the Lamar campus. The tons of bird shit that have been deposited over the years onto his head have fossilized, and it's no longer possible to tell what Mr. Lamar looked like, other than he had an enormous head. Standing next to that statue at 10:00 on Monday morning, right where he said he would be, was Detective Stuart. I was glad he was dressed casually in blue jeans and a sweater. Still, his crew-cut hair and middle-aged face looked out of place among all the young people moving through the quadrangle on their way to classes.

"How's the chest?" he asked as I walked up.

"Nothing broken, just a deep bruise. That's what they said at the hospital."

"Hurt?"

"Only when I breathe," I said.

"Yeah, I understand. I got popped in the chest once by a pool cue. Couldn't breathe. Thought I was dying."

"So did I. I thought he'd put that knife into my heart."

"I'm really sorry, Larry. We thought you were okay in there."

"I know. Don't worry about it."

"He just wanted to scare you with the blade," Stuart said.

I raised my eyebrows. "Well, he did a damn good job," I said.

"He must've turned his hand as he brought his fist forward. Hit you hard with the butt. He wanted you to think you were stabbed. It's the intimidation factor that hoods like him prey on."

"Yeah, it's just . . . Oh, I don't know—"

"What?" he asked.

I hesitated. I didn't know this guy well, and what I was thinking was personal and probably would sound corny. But

New Larry decided to open up, and I said, "It's just that once you think you're dying, when you wake up alive, it puts a new perspective on the rest of your life. You know what I mean?"

Stuart didn't reply, but he gave me a slow affirmative nod.

I was noticing all sorts of things that I'd overlooked or taken for granted before, little things like the sweet smell of freshly mowed grass that permeated the air that morning and the energy that radiated from the students who passed us on their way to classes. The night before, after I was released from the hospital emergency room, I'd stood alone outdoors in the cold. I had gazed upward for at least 30 minutes, until the pain in my neck became unbearable, searching for the constellations that my father had pointed out so long ago and contemplating the enormity of the heavens. Afterward, alone in my apartment, I watched television. All night long, I kept jumping up and down like a yo-yo to change channels, not wanting to miss anything, until all three channels had gone off the air and there was nothing left to watch.

Then I tossed restlessly in bed until dawn. I couldn't stop thinking about Daniel and Marty—and Allie. I couldn't decide which was the greater tragedy: Daniel's sudden death or Marty's wasted life. Or maybe it was my own pathetic insecurities and hopeless infatuation with an older woman.

I had looked back with disillusionment at the way I'd lived my life to this point. I'd been a miserable, joyless person for a long time. Surviving this affair gave me a sudden resolve to be a different person—someone that I would like more—going forward. At the same time, I worried how long that resolve would last without someone special in my life to motivate and encourage me to be that different person, to keep the brooding loner from taking over again.

"So," I said, forcing an upbeat tone into my voice, "you said on the phone that everything went fine, Detective, just like you'd planned."

"That's right."

"Then why'd you want to meet? Isn't it dangerous for us to be seen together?"

"No," he said, "it's okay. Let's walk."

As we marched in slow, aimless circles around the quadrangle, Stuart told me about the bust. How, ten minutes after leaving my apartment, a black-and-white Beaumont Police Department patrol car had approached from the rear and signaled for the Lincoln to pull over on Calder Avenue, near an old warehouse where the McCarthys maintained an office. How they took off with the black-and-white in pursuit. How the chase ended after only six blocks when a slow-moving freight train just happened to cross Calder on the First Street tracks, right in front of the Lincoln. How Buster and Lefty were cornered by four police officers, two from the car that had tried to stop them plus two officers from a police unit that just happened to be in the area. Outnumbered and outgunned, they surrendered.

After they were handcuffed, the patrolman who had originally signaled them to pull over showed them a busted taillight on the Lincoln, explaining that it was the reason for the stop. He said that he just wanted to give them a warning. But it was a lie. He didn't tell them that he was the same person who had broken the taillight earlier that day when the Lincoln was unattended in the parking lot of Don's Seafood Restaurant. He had poked a thin screwdriver through the outer glass and into the bulb while Lefty was preoccupied stuffing his face with boiled shrimp and raw oysters. As the hard-luck brothers looked on, the cops opened the big black suitcase in the back seat and feigned total surprise when they saw that it was filled with illegal drugs.

It was a long story with lots of details. I had a class soon. I interrupted him, "The McCarthys, are you sure they bought it? And please—" I stopped walking. When Stuart also stopped and we made eye contact, I nodded at him and said, "Just the facts, Detective."

He leaned forward, squinted, and gave me an *I can't believe you said that* look. But then he smiled, just a little. "Cute," he said.

"I watch *Dragnet*. I've been wanting to use that line for a long time," I said.

"Yes, *funny boy*, they bought it—hook, line, and sinker. The narcotics officer who took them to the station said they almost killed each other in the back seat of the patrol car, each one blaming the other for not stopping, for being so stupid."

"Wait a minute. You used narcs for the bust?"

"Yeah, but they were dressed in Beaumont PD uniforms. For your sake, we had to make the McCarthys think it was regular traffic cops they were dealing with, not narcotics officers. But believe me, those were well-trained professionals in the field yesterday, not local yokels." He laughed.

"What's funny?" I asked.

"When I interrogated them, I told Buster and Lefty I was pissed because the local flatfoots were getting credit for a narcotics bust."

"Thanks for handling it that way," I said. "You know, so they don't think I set them up."

"Hey, that was our deal, right?"

But I wanted more assurance that the last part of our plan—where Stuart misdirects the bad guys and keeps them from ever knowing about my betrayal—had been successful. "And you're sure they don't suspect me, that I was part of it?" I asked.

"No way, kid. When I questioned them about the suitcase, they never even mentioned your name."

I wasn't convinced. "But they've got to be thinking it may have been a setup. Lefty was real suspicious yesterday."

"They just think they're a couple of unlucky bastards." He laughed again, and this time I laughed with him.

"That they are," I said.

"Yeah, and in case you didn't notice, these guys aren't too bright."

"I guess I was too busy being scared shitless to notice much else," I said.

"Well, you don't need to worry. They've got two priors from their days in Fort Worth. This time, they'll be going away for a long time."

"Yeah, but what if they make bail before they go away? And what about their friends?"

"That's the main reason I wanted to meet with you, Larry, to assure you that we've done everything that's humanly possible to protect you."

"And?" I asked.

"And my people can be trusted. They know how important it is to keep your involvement confidential. We don't want to have to fight off some bullshit entrapment defense. So, you just keep your mouth shut—don't you tell *anybody*—and there won't be any leaks."

"Hey, I remember the plan, everything we talked about. My lips are sealed, so—"

"Look," he interrupted, "we're going to continue to shadow you, just for a couple more days."

I shot an apprehensive glance at him.

"Bobby will be discreet. You'll never see him."

It still made me uncomfortable.

"It's just a precaution," he added. "The McCarthy boys are mad as hornets right now. But they're pretty much freelance operators—running an auto parts warehouse that fronts for a chop shop and moving drugs on the side—without a lot of friends in Beaumont as far as we can tell. That's probably why they took a chance on a nobody kid like Marty Shannon, who'd stolen some cars for them."

"I guess," I said.

"And there's one other thing working in our favor here." He paused to give me a grin like he'd been saving something good to tell me.

"Yeah, what's that?"

"When Buster finally broke and gave up the name of their supplier—a real lowlife group that we've been after for some time now—well, it turns out we've recently been able to place an undercover officer inside this gang. She's out there spreading the word about how unlucky the McCarthys were. How BPD fell into the bust. How it was all just a coincidence. Given the McCarthys' room-temperature IQ, I'm sure the supplier will buy it."

"She?" I asked. "A lady narc?"

"That's right. And don't you dare talk about that. Not to anybody! You hear?"

"Yes, sir."

"I only mention it to show that we're looking out for you. And—" He waved his finger in my face as he spoke, "To say: you never know who's working for the good guys. So, keep your nose clean, kid."

"Don't worry," I said.

"Anyway, with the evidence she's been able to uncover on the inside plus the McCarthy boys' testimony, we're going to be able to move another step up the food chain."

He seemed highly satisfied with himself, and we walked in silence for another half a minute. I was pleased that he had been so open and trusting with me. I was satisfied that he was making a real effort to protect me like he had promised, and I figured there wasn't much more to say. But Stuart stopped walking and took my arm. I turned to face him.

"Thanks, Larry," he said, looking into my eyes so I could see his sincerity. "You're bright and you've got a lot of courage. Not many young guys would've had the guts to put themselves in that situation, to volunteer it no less."

"Thanks, I guess I'm an extraordinary young man."

"What?" He stared at me, expecting a further explanation, but I just shrugged my shoulders.

"It's an inside thing," I said and started walking again, back toward the statue. I looked at my watch. My class was starting in five minutes.

"That's about it," he said when we reached the statue, "except for one thing."

"What's that?"

He smiled. "Tell me, how does it feel to help get the bad guys off the street?"

I didn't return the smile. My chest hurt. I was tired of him and this whole ordeal. "I don't know," I said softly. "I haven't had much time to think about it, but it feels good to make them pay for what happened to Marty. To put them away so they can't corrupt another kid."

PART TWO: BAD GUYS

"Larry, your friend, Marty . . . Hey, I'm sorry, but he was on a destructive path. We had him in our sights and he was going down. The McCarthys just forced the issue. I only wish we could've gotten to Marty first."

"You know what, Detective?"

"What?"

"I don't think the outcome would have been any different."

Chapter 30
BEST FRIENDS

My friendship with Allie got off to a slow start. After that Cotton Bowl game at her house to kick off 1974, I saw her only one more time over the next six weeks: a brief rendezvous in early January for coffee, where I gave her a Marvin Gaye tape that I'd made with his *What's Going On* album on one side of the cassette and the *Let's Get It On* album on the other—a subtle, subliminal message, I'd hoped.

It was an eternity, made bearable only by the telephone conversations that we had once a week during that time. I planned these calls for days in advance. She seemed glad to hear from me, and we would have lengthy conversations. As desperately as I wanted to see her, to be near her, I remained patient and didn't press her for anything but a friendly ear. I talked to her about juggling work and classes. She gave me updates on the big research project she was working on. We talked about Nixon and the Watergate scandal. I gave her tax tips. I wrote down jokes to tell her when the conversation dragged, and then I waited to hear her laugh. My God, how I loved her laugh.

By February, my phone conversations with Allie had started to become humdrum and too predictable. I worried that she was losing interest. When we were kids, Marty had said that women love it when guys ask for their opinion, especially about personal things. So, I made up some girlfriend trouble and asked for her advice. Allie asked a lot of questions about this fictitious relationship, but I was able to keep my story plausible and interesting. She clearly enjoyed getting involved, and best of all, I could tell that she was trying to be helpful as a friend, not from some professional psychoanalysis angle.

I heard Allie ask, *Okay, so are you two, you know, doing it?*

And I said, "Give me a break."

C'mon, I want to know.

"Maybe. So what?"

Oh, it makes a big difference. After you have sex, you have to pay even more attention to little things, or she'll think that you've gotten what you want, and you don't care about her because she's her, but only about her for her body.

"What? Oh, never mind. What if all I care about is her body?"

Larry!

"Well?"

Does she have a nice body?

"Absolutely."

Look, now don't take this the wrong way, but is she very experienced?

"At what?"

At sex, you silly.

"I guess, but it's not like she's a whore or something."

Of course not. That's not what I meant. But if she's experienced, she'll expect certain things from you.

"And I'm prepared to give them to her."

I know, but seriously—

"Don't worry. I remember everything you taught me."

Hey, I'm pleased to have been of service, but there may be some other things you should be thinking about if this girl is as experienced as I think she is. The way I see it . . .

What Allie said after that was fascinating, but I listened with indifferent ears. I couldn't stop thinking about that night with her—the way she had instructed me on when to kiss, where to touch, when to remove the various articles of clothing, how to know when she was ready. And how to know when she was ready again. About the only thing she hadn't instructed me on was how to hold her afterward, with my arms and legs wrapped tightly around her body, our flesh pressed together, and my hands gently caressing her neck and cheeks as she continued to moan softly. I did that instinctively, out of pure love.

I had to end the imaginary relationship when Allie suggested that we get together so she could meet my girlfriend. Frankly, I was glad to get rid of my make-believe lover. She was breaking my real-life heart.

* * * * *

On Allie's 34th birthday, February 20th, I brought flowers to her office. I gave them to the new receptionist, who started making chitchat about how pretty the flowers were and asking how I knew Allie. I was about to leave when Allie happened by with several thick files in her hands. What happened next was straight out of a dream.

Allie set the files down and gave me a huge hug as she said, "What a surprise. It's so great to see you." She pulled on my arm, toward the reception desk. "Larry, meet Patty. Mrs. Adams retired last month, and Patty's been here since then. Patty, this is Larry; he's my dear friend."

Patty, who was probably 25 but looked like she was 15, couldn't contain her curious grin as she shook my hand, holding it a second too long before releasing it.

I looked back at Allie and said, "Happy Birthday."

"Yeah, Happy Birthday, Mrs. Parker. You should've told someone," Patty added.

"I just came by to drop off some flowers," I said.

"And a card," Patty added.

"I didn't want to disturb you, just leave a little present and go," I said awkwardly, still surprised to see her.

"Oh, thank you. You're so thoughtful," Allie said.

"And he's cute," Patty added.

I blushed as Allie looked at her watch. "Larry, let's get some lunch. I know a—"

"No, I know you're busy and—"

"I insist," Allie said, "I have no plans for lunch, and we should go somewhere and celebrate my special day."

This was unexpected. "Aw, shucks. Well—" I said as I looked away toward Patty's desk.

Patty mouthed the words, *Go for it.*

"Okay," I said.

"Smashing!" Allie said with a big smile. "I'll put these files away and get my jacket. Hang onto those flowers, please, Patty."

"Don't you want to read the card?" Patty asked, but Allie didn't hear her. She'd already picked up the files, turned her back, and started walking away. "I'll bet it says something sweet," Patty added softly as Allie turned a corner. She looked up at me and added in a low, throaty voice, "Smashing."

I gave her a *Gimme-me-a-break* look, and she gave me a wink.

It was a beautiful, cloudless day. Allie and I sat outside on the patio at Treehouse Restaurant and talked about whatever came into our minds. After lunch, we ordered hot tea. As we sipped from our cups and talked some more, she stroked the top of my hand in a lazy, unmindful way as it rested on the table.

It almost exactly replicated the fantasy scene that had played in my mind as I lay in bed on that night—January 11, 1965—after we first met. About the only differences between that fantasy and this reality were that I didn't come in my pants and she insisted on paying for lunch. She said that lunch had been her idea, and the flowers were enough of a present from me. After a tepid protest, I let her take the check. I had less than $20 in my wallet.

It had been a miraculous day, and I took it as a divine sign, a positive, tangible signal that I was doing the right thing in my life. After that day, we talked more frequently on the phone, and Allie started confiding more personal things. I tried to be a good listener. I was especially encouraged by a telephone conversation we had the week after that lunch meeting.

I heard Allie say, *I seem to be doing all the talking.*
And I said, "I don't mind."
Well, what do young boys like you like to talk about?
I was silent.
Larry, that came out all wrong. I'm sorry.
"It's all right. We've got some differences, I know."
Like you're a boy and I'm a girl?
"That wasn't what I was thinking."
Ah, you mean that age thing, that difference?

"Wasn't that what you were thinking when you asked that condescending question?"

Let's get one thing straight, okay?

"Okay."

I may be a few years older and been around the block a few more times. But Larry, you have such an easy, caring, and mature way. You're amazing, so . . . She seemed to be struggling for the right word.

"Extraordinary?"

Yes! Extraordinary! You've got more personality and you're more interesting than any of the people I work with and any of my—

There was silence. I finally said, "What's the matter?"

When Tom and I split up, he got all our friends here in town. Sad how that happens, friends choosing sides. But it didn't surprise me, given the way my supposed *girlfriends would always give their husbands dirty looks when they caught them staring in my direction or talking with me for too long.* I heard her sigh. *But that's another story.*

"I've got time."

Not now. But having good friends, true friends, is critically important to good mental health. And I do so look forward to talking with you, Larry—not as a big sister or some learned old therapist. Just one good friend talking to another. In fact—

"What?"

Well, truth is, talking with you is about the best thing going on in my life just now. I heard another sigh, a long one this time.

"Yeah?"

Yes, and any difference in our ages is irrelevant to me.

Silence.

Larry?

"Yes?"

Do you believe me?

"I do."

Do you forgive me?

"I do."

Can you do something for me?

"Sure. What?"

Tell me another joke. Please make me laugh, okay?

"So, a duck walks into a bar." Silence.

And? What happens?

"Well, he's unconscious. It's a metal one hanging low that gets him right across the forehead."

My God, how I loved her laugh.

Allie also started talking about her marriage. It had been an ugly breakup. When he moved out, Tom had left her a nice bottle of wine with a note that read, "Put this between your legs to keep it cold." She had been going through one of those rough patches for several months, and it would be an understatement to say she was a little low on self-esteem. It didn't help when she found out that Tom had moved in with the young hairdresser he'd been dating. On the 5th of March, Allie filed for divorce. I told her I was confident that she was doing the right thing.

The next night, we had a marathon telephone conversation where she confided that her personal and professional lives were both "in shambles." On top of no longer having any girl friends in Beaumont, she had lost touch with most of her good friends from college. The ones she still communicated with were married, had started families, and were scattered across the country. She said that she felt unfulfilled in her work. She blamed Tom for convincing her to drop out of medical school in Dallas and give up on her dream of becoming a psychiatrist, so she could come back to Beaumont and marry him.

Since the separation from Tom, a lot of men had started hitting on her, including a married guy who was a friend of Tom's. Allie called it revolting how men automatically assumed that she was in a distraught and weakened emotional state. When translated, this meant that it should be easier to get into her pants. She said they had this notion that married women had gotten used to having regular sex, and when they were separated and weren't getting it, they became like a cat in heat prowling around for someone to scratch their itch.

She said that the two men she'd agreed to go out with over the past month were both losers. She joked about wanting to lend one of them a flashlight to help him find a coherent thought, and the other wouldn't stop calling her "Babe" and responded to every topic she brought up with a your-place-or-mine innuendo. She said it was maddening, and the thought of getting into the dating scene at her age in a redneck town like Beaumont was too depressing for words. As a result, she'd given up trying to meet men. She said her biological clock was ticking, and she worried if she'd ever have a chance to have children and raise them with a man she loved and respected.

When she whispered, "What's wrong with me?" and it seemed like she might start crying, I told her not to despair, that she'd surely find the right man—perhaps very soon. I thought about my father and the words he'd used to console me so long ago, and I told her not to focus on next week or next month, but for now, take things one day at a time. That struck a chord, and she must have said, "You're right" a dozen times. I got a lump in my throat near the end of our conversation when she said it was a godsend to have someone like me to talk to. I told her that's what friends are for and added that I was available at any time—day or night. She said, "I know," and then we hung up.

We started seeing each other after that, once or twice a week. It was never anything as official as a date where I went to her place to pick her up. We'd meet at the cinema, for example, each of us arriving in our own car. After the movie, we'd go somewhere quiet to critique the film over coffee or a drink or two. At some point, usually prior to 10:30, she would say she was tired. We always went home separately.

This had been going on for a few weeks when Allie called after work to ask if I could meet her at the Treehouse for a late supper. There was stress in her voice. When I got there, she was on her second drink, and she was unusually quiet as we ate. After the meal, we moved to a little booth in the bar, where she told me that she had met with Tom for a couple of hours that afternoon and had worked out the property settlement. Their divorce would be final within 30 days.

"I've read textbooks and study after study about the feelings people experience when they go through a divorce. They describe the emotions; they *dissect* them," she said, moving her two hands like they were cutting something with little knives. "All in a sterile, clinical way, and then they tell you exactly what to do so you can feel better about yourself or help someone else feel better, so it's: *Oh, no big deal. You're gonna be just fine.*" She took a deep breath. "Well, they are *sooo* full of shit, every last one of 'em," she said, her words slurred from the Scotch.

I wanted to say something, but I was afraid it would sound stupid or, worse, like one of those textbooks. So, I stayed quiet and just stared at her with an aching in my chest.

"There must be something terribly wrong with me," she said as she took another swig. "And nothing in some book is gonna help. *Nothin'!* I put so much into this marriage and now, you know, it all sunk in today. It's gone. Tom's gone. He doesn't love me anymore, and now I'm . . . *out there* again," she said with a sweeping gesture to the hinterlands. "How da ya just wash seven years down the drain and start over? Huh?"

I had to do something, say something. So, just like Sister Mary Margaret had done with me after Daniel's death, I leaned forward, gently cupped her face with my hands, and looked deep into her eyes. I said, "I can't possibly understand what you're going through. But you've got to believe me: There is nothing wrong with you, Allie. I've told you that before, remember?"

She nodded and I slowly removed my hands, allowing my fingers to tenderly brush across her cheeks.

"In fact," I said, "you're absolutely amazing, the way you care about people, how much fun it is to be around you. That is, when you're not wallowing in self-pity."

I swallowed hard. Saying that last part was a big chance, but I had to climb onto her level in this conversation. This was live and in person, not chitchat over the telephone line. I had to take charge and say something to get her attention, something she needed to hear as opposed to the Norman Vincent Peale clichés.

Allie looked up and squinted, trying to focus through the

alcohol. "Are you saying I'm wallering . . . I mean, wallowing—in self-pity? Is that what you said?"

I didn't take the bait. Instead, I asked, "When we walked into this bar, did you notice what happened?"

She shook her head.

I smiled at her and whispered, "Every pair of eyes in this place looked up. They looked at you. You're so beautiful, Allie, that you light up the room—*any room*—wherever you go. While you sat down, I looked around the bar at all of them watching you, and it made me smile, ear to ear like a raccoon. Do you know why?"

"Because you were the guy with the pretty girl."

"No. Wrong. I smiled because those poor people just saw a beautiful person on the outside, whereas I've had the privilege to get to know you on the inside. I smiled because they only saw your external beauty, but me, I've seen your internal beauty and it's amazing. It even outshines your physical appearance."

"When I'm not wallowing in self-pity, right?"

"Well," I said with arms raised, palms up. We both laughed.

"You just remember one thing and you'll be fine," I said.

"Yeah, what's that, Sigmund?"

"You remember that Tom is an idiot. You got that, kid?" My eyes were like lasers trained on hers, trying to look beyond them into her brain. "He may have been a great guy once upon a time, but he took a wrong turn out there. You are an amazing person, and *he* is an idiot to have left *you*. There's nothing wrong with you, Allie, so don't you be thinking and saying it, not ever again. It's annoying."

"Thank you," she said softly.

"And I'll be around as much as you'll let me, you know, to keep you in line."

She stared down at the golden liquid and ice cubes in her glass. Her voice was shaky as she said, "You know, the past few months have been like living in a pool of quicksand. I struggle but I can't get out. My parents are there, watching me. They stand on safe ground and keep shaking their heads, saying they can't understand how I let this happen, like I've made terrible choices and that's why I'm in this mess. My friends from work are also up there on the high ground. They're all shouting cliché tips like, 'Keep your head up.' They're acting concerned, but what they're really wondering is when I'll be able to get out of this hole and get focused on work again. And my old friends from school and the couples that Tom and I used to see all the time—well, they're nowhere. Most of them don't even know that I'm in quicksand." She looked up, into my eyes. "And then you came along, Larry. Do you know what you did?"

"No," I answered.

"You waded waist-deep into the quicksand—into *my* quicksand—and you stretched out your arm to me. That's what you did." Tears were welling up in her eyes, and as she said it, she leaned across the little table and kissed me on the cheek, right there in the bar like she didn't care if everyone could see.

I gave her an *Aw, shucks* shrug and a smile as she leaned back. All my feelings for her bubbled up into my throat, and I opened my mouth to tell her, to say the words. But all that came out was, "I . . ." I wanted to say it—*that word.* Every nerve in my body ached to be bold, to say it out loud. But I didn't. I couldn't risk spoiling this precious moment. *Just hold on,* my racing heart told me, and instead I said, "I'm just trying to help."

"I know." She paused and then repeated my words, "You're just trying to help."

Allie composed herself and then changed the subject. For the remainder of the evening, our conversation glided from one light topic to another. We talked and laughed, and when the waiter asked if she wanted another drink, she said, "No, I don't need it," and he took her glass. When we finally walked outside, it was almost midnight and a light rain was beginning to fall. She kissed me again on the cheek and gave me a long hug before we ran for our cars.

I sat in my Volkswagen as the red taillights of her car pulled away and then disappeared. I lingered for another 30 minutes in the parking lot to soak up the moment. I listened over and over to "Colour My World" by Chicago on my cassette stereo. I dreamed of our special moments together and let it color my world with hope—of loving her. I smelled the cedar-scented rain and tasted the drops as I stuck my head out the window and let them splatter softly on my face. And I said a silent prayer like my father had taught me, eyes closed with her beautiful face filling my mind and my soul.

We spent even more time together after that, seeing each other two or three nights a week and talking on the phone almost every day. I learned so much about her—that she was close with her parents, who lived in Corpus Christi, where she'd grown up. That she had a brother, eight years her junior, whom she adored and had been devoted to. Marty Shannon, with his fun-loving and irresponsible lifestyle, had reminded Allie of her brother, who'd turned hippie, dropped out of school, and left for San Francisco in 1968 in search of peace, free love, and other American myths. He'd been ostracized by their family, and Allie had recently called him, at my urging, to patch things up. She said they both cried on the phone and talked for over an hour in that first conversation. They were now in regular communication, and he had promised to come to Texas for a visit over the summer.

Allie could be serious, polished, and professional on the outside, but she was deeply caring, emotional, and fragile on the inside. She needed a confidant to be open and honest with, where she didn't have to worry about maintaining the facade. With her soon-to-be ex-husband out of the picture, I was thrilled to have the opportunity to fill that role, but my intuition told me to continue to go slow, be cautious—for now—about trying to get her to accept me in a more intimate capacity.

As spring came into bloom around us, I grew increasingly perplexed and disturbed by the ironic, yet inescapable fact that the closer I got to Allie, the more out of reach she seemed. The more I came to know Allie, the less I understood my feelings toward her. For example, a few months earlier, I had spent virtually all my waking hours fantasizing about a long, loving, and deeply passionate relationship with her. Now, it only crossed my mind about eight or ten times a day.

She had come to my apartment to drop off some of her record albums, so I could record the best songs onto cassettes for her. We talked for about ten minutes before she had to go. In bed that night, I couldn't remember what she had been wearing, the smell of her perfume, or whether she'd kissed my cheek before leaving. Did that mean that I no longer loved her? Was I taking her for granted? Subconsciously, was my perspective on our relationship evolving away from a romantic notion? Or was I suffering from the early stages of dementia?

I didn't know what to make of these changes, so I decided to try an experiment: We would see less of each other. With a little space and time alone, like my father gave my mother when she was emotional, Allie would see how lonely it was without me around and what an intricate part of her life I had become. She would reassess her feelings about me and conclude that I should play an expanded role in her future.

The first evening after I concocted this brilliant plan, Allie called to say we should go to a movie. I wanted desperately to see her that night, but I maintained my resolve and told her *no*. I said that I wanted to stay home and research some obscure income tax question and then hung up without any small talk. Five minutes later, the phone rang again. When I finally picked it up after the fourth ring, the sweetest voice in the world whispered, "*Pleeease.*" Sixty seconds later, I was in my car driving to meet her. On the way, I felt contempt for my weakness, for appearing so eager and available to her on a strictly platonic basis. But she gave me that gorgeous smile and a big hug at the cinema entrance, and she thanked me profusely for coming. In that instant, my absence-will-make-the-heart-grow-fonder strategy seemed silly and sophomoric, and it evaporated into the warm night.

Allie came over on a Saturday near the end of April to help paint my apartment. She wore a thin halter top with no bra, a very short pair of cutoffs, and pumps.

"What are you doing?" I said and pointed at her.

She looked down at herself. "This?"

"Yeah, *this.*"

"This top is old. Don't worry, it's okay if I get paint on it. And the cutoffs have a tear in the seam and the back pockets are ripped. They're practically falling apart." She laughed. "I'll never wear any of this again."

"Allie, you know I've got two young guys coming over, those grad school nerds I've been helping with advanced stats. You know that, right?"

"Yeah, you said somebody owed you a favor and would be here to help. So?"

"*So*, you can't dress like that."

Her eyebrows went up. "What?"

"Every time you bend over or reach up to paint, those guys are going to be all distracted—ogling at you."

"Ogling? Did you say *ogling*?"

"My God, Allie, don't you know what seeing someone like you—*looking like that*—does to a young kid?" I knew firsthand.

"Ogling?"

"Yes, *ogling*, and we'll never get finished."

She took a step toward me with a smile forming on her face. "Are you jealous?"

"No."

"Are you . . . *possessive*?" She stretched out the word as she rested a hand on her hip in what I think was intended as a sexy pose and added, "Do you want me all to yourself?" She slowly brought the other hand up and started twirling her hair with a finger.

"No, I just want to get this job finished—today, if that's okay."

She took another step forward, so she was only inches from me, and she arched her back. "Are you . . . *desirous*?"

I grabbed her arms. "That's enough, okay? Knock it off."

She stepped back. "For God's sake, I'm just fooling with you. What's your problem?"

I extended an index finger toward her face and said, "Look, I can be your lover or I can be your friend. But I can't be both. It'll tear me apart." I lowered my finger and then my head, and I said, "Make up your mind, your choice." There was a long, uncomfortable silence as I stared at her shoes.

Finally, she pushed me hard in the chest. The force of it caught me by surprise, and I fell backward onto the sofa.

"Men! I swear!"

That was it, all she said before she turned and stormed out the door. For the next 30 minutes, I tried to contemplate what she meant. Then Allie opened the door. She stepped in and put her hands on her hips. She had changed into baggy, bell-bottom jeans and a long-sleeved cotton shirt buttoned up to her neck. She cocked her head and gave me a quick *So, there!* nod.

I smiled. My friend had made her choice. She still looked incredibly sexy.

That night, she phoned and the first thing I heard her say was, *I didn't want to get into it with those guys around, but I'm so sorry for that little scene today.*

And I said, "It's okay. Don't worry about it."

No, please let me explain. I came over dressed inappropriately and acted silly, teasing you like that. It wasn't at all like me. But I've analyzed it, and I think I know why I did it.

"Really?"

Please understand, Larry: I got married young, and I don't think I've flirted with a man for a long, long time. Flirtation is an innate process that is a fundamental part of natural selection. It's—

"I know what flirting is."

I was unmindfully taking advantage of you today—and our beautiful friendship—to practice flirtation like that. I treated you like a test subject in a study, to gauge your reaction to various stimuli without regard for your feelings. I'm sorry for all the confusing signals—for dressing so provocatively and acting like some silly coed who makes eyes at you in biology class. Do you understand? Can you forgive me?

"That was *flirting*?"

Yes.

"You *are* out of practice."

My God, how I loved her laugh.

* * * * *

Allie called to say she had big news. It was the first of May, just a few days before I was to take the CPA exam. She had an interview for a staff psychologist position at Texas Children's Hospital, a large, prestigious institution in Houston. A sorority sister had told her about the opportunity, and Allie had applied. She said she hadn't mentioned it to me previously because she thought it was a long shot. But a hospital administrator had called to say that he liked her resume and wanted to arrange an immediate interview.

I was anxious and on edge. The unnerving thought that she might move away and leave me behind in Bumpkinland consumed me. I had trouble concentrating, and I'm sure it's why I only passed three of the four parts to the CPA exam. When I returned from Galveston, where I had gone to take the three-day exam, she told me she got the job. She would start to work in Houston on June 3rd.

Allie was ecstatic. She kept talking about starting over, how this would be "a new beginning" for her. I was shattered and descended into a deep, depressing funk. I tried not to show it around Allie, but she was too perceptive.

"What's wrong?" she asked. It was Saturday night, and we were finishing our dinner at the Treehouse.

She had called from Houston earlier that afternoon to tell me she had just put down a deposit on a spacious one-bedroom apartment overlooking Braes Bayou just a mile from the hospital. Allie said her sorority friend wanted her to spend the night with her and her husband in Houston, but Allie had declined. She said she wanted to get back to Beaumont to be with me for a celebration dinner.

I knew she was trying to make me feel better. I had volunteered to come with her to look at apartments, but she'd already arranged for her friend's assistance. I told her I'd be happy to just tag along, but she said it wasn't necessary. Deep down, I suspected that she didn't want to have to explain a 21-year-old guy to her old college friend.

"Nothing," I muttered in response to her question.

"Don't play hard to get. What's wrong?"

"Oh, I'm gonna miss you," I said in a voice that was entirely too whiney, but I didn't care. I'd said it and I was glad. Now we could talk about it.

"I'll miss you too, but I'm only a phone call away. Don't worry. Our friendship is strong enough to survive 90 miles, isn't it?"

"Maybe. Oh, I guess so, but—"

"Larry, look at me."

I did as she said.

"You were there for me when I desperately needed someone. You cared about me, and you helped pull me through the toughest time I've ever had in my life. I can't—*I won't*—just forget that."

I didn't like what she had said. I knew she meant well, but it all sounded so blasé, so patronizing.

"Allie," I blurted out, "I've been thinking about giving up on the master's degree. Why do I need that additional sheepskin anyway? I can go to work anytime at Arthur Andersen, and I'm tired of being poor. I'd be making a fortune—$12,000 a year—and I'd finally be—"

She shook her head. "Don't do this, Larry. You've got your own life. You just changed all your plans in January to stay here and get that MBA. Now, you need to think rationally, not like someone with a dependency disorder. You can't be following me around everywhere I—"

"Dependency disorder?" I glared at her. "Are you crazy? Weren't you the one just talking about desperately needing me?"

"Larry, please," she whispered. People in the restaurant were staring at us.

I didn't care about the other people. Like a madman, I said loudly, "What makes you think I'm doing this for you? Maybe I'm doing it for me. Did you ever think about that, Miss Dependency Disorder?"

"You keep your voice down or I'm leaving," she said firmly.

I knew she was serious, and the madman disappeared. I couldn't bear it if she left before I could explain it all. We sat in silence while the waiter cleared our plates. Then I apologized and she did likewise.

"Allie, please come over to my apartment. I want to tell you something, and I can't do it here with all these people around."

"La*rrrry*?" she said warily.

"Hey, it's not a *dependency* thing, and I'm not *flirting*, okay? I just need to talk."

"I'm sorry," she said. "If you need me, I'll be there."

We split the check and then left.

When we got to my apartment, Allie sat on the sofa while I went to the refrigerator and found the bottle of Boone's Farm Strawberry Hill that I'd been saving for a special occasion. I unscrewed the top and savored the robust, freshly pollinated bouquet as I poured us each a tall glass. When I joined her with the wine, I also carried a box of tissues.

Then I told her about the bullet I had sold to Daniel Carter, the one he shot into his brain. I tried to describe the colossal guilt that I had felt and how it had changed me. I told her how empty and void of any close relationships my life had been for nine years, until I reconnected with Marty and her. I confessed that the girlfriend story I'd told her was a lie. I told her that she was the first and only female that I'd ever had any sort of a relationship with. Then I told her how I ran out the back door just before Marty blew the top of his head off. If I had stayed with him to face the McCarthys—who knows? I described how I was still trying to cope with that question. I told her how I'd worked with Detective Stuart to get the McCarthys and how I thought Lefty McCarthy had killed me. How my last thought before I lost consciousness—on the floor there in my apartment—was that I was glad I wasn't dying a virgin, that I was thankful for that one special night with her.

I didn't whine about it and I didn't cry. It wasn't easy, but I was determined not to get emotional, just give her the facts—cold, analytical, straightforward, and without excuses—like my father would have done.

Allie didn't interrupt. She sat silently next to me—digesting my revelations, biting on her lower lip, and trying to keep her emotions in check. After a short while, she gave up and let the tears, one by one, emerge from her eyes and roll down her cheeks. She kept her hands clenched in her lap except when she was wiping her face or reaching for a fresh tissue.

When I finished, she slid over and reached for me with her arms outstretched. "Oh, Larry, this is a remarkable breakthrough, you poor—"

I pushed her away. "Allie, please. This is hard for me."

"Yes, I know it must be. You've been carrying these repressed feelings of—"

I interrupted again. "Yeah, I've got some baggage. I know that. But I didn't ask you here and tell you these things to get you all emotional, all wound up. *Please*, I don't want you to psychoanalyze me. And I don't want you to hug me or kiss me or do anything else, you know, *with me*."

"What do you want, then?"

"I just want to be your friend." I paused. "No, that's not correct. I want to be someone special in your life, now and in the future—your *really good friend*. I want to be completely and totally honest with you. I'm tired of keeping secrets. If you like me when you don't know everything about me, then it doesn't count. I want you to know these things I've done. I want you to know *the real me*, like I've come to know the real you. Don't you see? I've only had two special friendships in my life, and I've blown it with both of them. I don't want to blow it with you, but you have to know *everything*. You've been the one pleasant, beautiful thing through all of this, and I want you to see how special our relationship is." I hung my head and added, "At least, it is for me."

"It is for me too, Larry. It truly is," she said, "and I have even more admiration for you, and even more affection, knowing what you've been through." She shook her head. "My God, these secrets you've carried, what you've had to deal with."

I let her take my left hand, and she held it in her lap.

"I have to admit," I said, "there was a time after our little Christmas Eve encounter at your place when I fantasized about spending the rest of my life with you in, you know, a much more serious relationship. And I'm going to come out now and finally say it, okay? Are you ready?"

Her eyes opened wide, and she said, "I think so."

I took a deep breath. "I love you, Allie. I think I always have and always will. But it's different now, the way I see things and the way I feel about you. I know you so much better, and it's a different love. I've moved beyond that romantic stuff that never would have worked out between us, you know . . . you being so bossy and all."

"Hey, careful now," she said.

I gave her a smile and a shrug. "Didn't I say I was going to be truthful?"

"Well, you don't have to be *that truthful.*"

"Oh, yes, ma'am. Whatever you say, Kemosabe," I said, and we both laughed. But after a couple of seconds, I gave her my most serious look. "What I'm trying to say, Allie, is I love being your friend, your confidant, your *best Buddy*. Okay?"

She smiled. "I know. I understand. I love you too, Larry, the same way."

"That's all fine. I mean, it's great. But I'm afraid that I'll lose touch with you." Symbolically, I removed my hand from hers and continued, "We'll drift apart and I'll lose that closeness, that special friendship."

"That isn't going to happen," she said.

"I don't know about that. Making small talk over the phone is not the same as seeing each other—going to a movie, having dinner, hanging out, you know, and helping each other with whatever comes along."

"What are you saying?"

"I'm saying those 90 miles between Beaumont and Houston might as well be 90 thousand miles. You'll get wrapped up in your new job, make some new friends, maybe even meet some guy who will appreciate how wonderful you are. Well, I want to be there for that. I want to help you when you need an honest opinion—someone to tell you what you *need* to hear, not what they think you *want* to hear."

"And?" she asked, knowing what I was thinking.

"And, okay, I admit it. *I* need someone like that, especially right now."

She raised her eyebrows.

"I'm sorry," I said. "I don't need just *someone*. I need you, kid—as my friend. And if that's dependency, then I'm guilty as charged."

She smiled. "I'm sorry I used that word. I don't know what I was thinking," she said. "Mutual dependency and trust are integral parts of a healthy friendship." Then she raised her right hand. "And I pledge—to you, Larry Torrence—my everlasting friendship. I want to be that *really good friend*."

We embraced and I got a little emotional after that. I'd been holding it in, not knowing how she'd react when she heard my confession. I'd felt a tremendous sense of freedom in finally telling the truth, like throwing off a heavy weight that I'd been dragging around for years. And I felt a glorious relief in her acceptance of that truth, her acceptance of me for who I was.

While she was holding me, she kept whispering, "It wasn't your fault. You know that, right?"

I grunted like I agreed. She was being kind and I didn't want to argue with her, so I didn't say anything as she justified her opinion with some four-syllable clinical terms. But I must have drifted off because she pulled away from me. "Okay, what's wrong?" Allie asked.

"What?"

"I asked you what's wrong."

"Nothing," I said.

She put her hands on her hips. "C'mon, what's bothering you? You can tell me. I want to help."

So, I told her I was daydreaming about Daniel and Marty up in Heaven. It was something I'd been thinking about a lot recently. I explained that they were both kids, and Jesus was standing between them with a loving hand on each of their heads. After Jesus left, Daniel told Marty he'd show him around and introduce him to St. Peter. Only it wasn't really St. Peter that Daniel took him to meet. It was a distinguished-looking black man with gray hair and a long beard whose name was Peter.

Marty was surprised. He told Daniel that the man resembled the paintings and other depictions he'd seen of St. Peter, but he didn't recall that St. Peter was black. Daniel put his hands on his hips and said, "I can't believe you can be so ignorant sometimes. Those pictures you saw on Earth were a form of prejudice that we don't have up here. Let's get a Bible and I'll show you." Daniel was smiling as he walked away with Marty in tow.

Allie gave me an encouraging smile and reached over with a tissue to wipe my cheek.

"You know," I said, "I've just about convinced myself that we couldn't have saved Marty, no matter what. He was so far gone by the time we got involved. I lost the chance to save Marty when we were 13, and I didn't return his phone calls. But Daniel—my God, Allie, he was only 12 years old. I still can't understand what went wrong with Daniel."

I wondered why I hadn't said those words to Daniel, the words Allie had just spoken. He was my best friend, and I knew something was dreadfully wrong with him. Why didn't I say, "C'mon, what's bothering you, man? You can tell me. I want to help, bro."

What would he have told me? I guess I'll have to wait until I join Marty and him to get an answer to that question, but it doesn't stop me from asking it about a hundred times a day since Marty's death brought all the memories flooding back.

Allie maintained her position that I shouldn't blame myself. She tried to get me to talk more about my feelings. She was persistent and her shrink powers were formidable, but I'd had enough for one night. Allie could tell. We both knew there would be time to discuss these things again later, and she allowed our conversation to move out of the past and into the future. She talked about her new job and apartment. I said that I was sure it would be a wonderful new beginning for her. Then I told her I was serious about moving to Houston and beginning my CPA career. Her response surprised me.

She leaned close and held me with her captivating eyes. "You said that really good friends need to be honest and tell each other what they need to hear, remember?"

I nodded.

"In my personal *and* professional judgment, you shouldn't waste two more years in school in this hick town. You've already got enough smarts and moxie to be the best auditor that Arthur Andersen has ever seen. And for now, I think you need to be close to me just like I needed to be close to you over the past few months."

I nodded again, and she gave me a smile that filled the entire room.

"Besides," she said lightheartedly, throwing her arms in the air, "you know I'd miss you terribly."

I reached out to her.

"We'll have a great time together in Houston," she whispered into my ear as we embraced.

Moving out of Beaumont was the best thing that could have happened for Allie. She cut her hair as soon as she arrived in Houston, very short. I told her I wasn't particularly fond of it, but she didn't care. She wanted a new look to match this new beginning.

She helped me find a little apartment near the Astrodome, only a mile from her place. I took her to an Astros game in that magnificent stadium I had once feared would cave in. She wasn't interested at first, but I was persistent. Actually, to get her to go, I had to agree to go with her to the ballet, but it was okay, I guess. Allie's become an Astros fan. She checks the sports pages daily, and we commiserate over our cellar-dweller team just like Mrs. Shannon and I had done over the old Colt .45s.

Allie's new job, evaluating and helping young children in the hospital, was perfect for her. She's become good friends with several colleagues there—some nurses and another psychologist—and they go out after work sometimes. She joined a group focused on convincing states to ratify the Equal Rights Amendment and other women's causes.

She talked me into taking country-western dancing lessons

with her. She also took me shopping, and we splurged on some first-rate boots and hats. We go to Gilley's in Pasadena on most weekends and drink Lone Star beer and tear up the dance floor with the Texas two-step and the other kicker dances. The cowboys stare as I twirl Allie around, all of them waiting for a chance to ask her for a dance. It's a hoot to see her laughing and enjoying herself with no quicksand—just like in my prayers for her.

At the end of June, a week before my 22nd birthday, I went to Arthur Andersen's two-week audit training school in St. Charles, Illinois. The sprawling campus at St. Charles used to be St. Dominic College. The firm purchased the property when the college closed, and they turned it into a self-contained training and conference center complete with dormitory-style rooms, kitchens and classrooms.

Arthur Andersen was referred to as the Marines of public accounting, and St. Charles was its boot camp. All new audit staff from North America were required to attend before they could work on client audits, and the instructors were partners and managers in the firm who'd seen that movie, *The D.I.*, too many times. They had lots of rules for how audits are supposed to be conducted and documented. Most of my colleagues bitched about how rigid and controlled everything was and how there was no tolerance for errors, but it didn't bother me. I felt right at home.

I was up late every night to complete the assignments that were due the next morning, and we put in a full day on Saturday. It was grueling because they wanted you to feel the pressure of having to complete audits under tight deadlines. But I made time most nights to call Allie, to hear about her new job (she loved it), and to tell her what a ball-buster this training school was (she knew I loved it). On my birthday, she had a box of chocolates delivered to my dorm room along with a nice card. I got razzed by the other guys on the floor, but I didn't care. They were all jealous because they didn't have a special friend like I did, like I knew I'd always have—at last.

* * * * *

PART TWO: BEST FRIENDS 357

I started working on this manuscript a couple of months ago, shortly after I told Allie the truth about Daniel and Marty and everything else. It was her idea. She made me dig out the private journal she'd persuaded me to write in 1965—that I hadn't opened in over nine years—and the poem I'd written. She wanted me to reflect on what transpired back then and everything that's happened since that time. She said that I needed to write it all down, all over again from the beginning, and bring my story up to the present time. She even bought me an IBM Selectric typewriter. It was amazing. After using it for a couple of months, I couldn't imagine how Twain, Fitzgerald, Hemingway, and all the great writers from the past were able to produce those classic works without an electric typewriter and a large bottle of Liquid Paper correction fluid.

Allie is a big believer in writing down all the details about your actions and the emotions you feel in a candid and honest manner. It's like going to confession, where you tell the truth about what a weak and worthless person you've been, and then you're supposed to feel cleansed. I was afraid it would make me feel depressed, but she was persistent. She was confident that I would be able to cope in a mature adult fashion with my youthful mistakes and shortcomings and how they had traumatized me, if I just confronted them—head-on.

She told me a story about Rembrandt, the great Dutch painter. In his youth, Rembrandt was commissioned to paint "The Prodigal Son." He had recently married and it was a happy time in his life. He painted the son in a tavern, laughing while hoisting a glass of beer with a woman sitting on his lap. The son's clothes are elegant and colorful, and he's enjoying the inheritance he prematurely coaxed from his father, as in Jesus' parable. Thirty years later, after Rembrandt's wife and three of their four children had died and his house and belongings had been sold at auction to pay his debts, he painted "The Prodigal Son" again. In this portrayal, the son has returned home in torn, ragged garments. He's fallen to his knees with arms lifted in entreaty, and you can't see his face because his head is buried in his father's body. Allie was sure that, like Rembrandt's changing view of "The Prodigal Son," time would give me a different perspective.

As usual, Allie was right, except she missed one important detail. I knew that I could never fully come to terms with those events and my actions until I did one more thing. Like that Prodigal Son, I had to return home to seek my father's forgiveness.

Chapter 31
DAD

My father got sick during my second week at the Arthur Andersen training school in Illinois. He got an infection in his lungs that turned into a bad case of pneumonia. It was extremely dangerous for him, given the weakened condition of his pulmonary system from all the cigarettes and the asbestosis. Mom took him to St. Elizabeth Hospital, and when his condition worsened, they put him in the intensive care unit.

As soon as I got back to Houston and unpacked, I drove to Beaumont. When I got to the hospital, I found my mother drinking coffee in the cafeteria, right where she had said she'd be. Her eyes clouded up as soon as she saw me. We had a long hug while she kept saying how much she loved me and how good it was that I was finally there. To calm her down, I talked about the training school, the weather, and other inconsequential things like that. I told her a stupid joke I'd recently heard. It wasn't all that funny, but Mom laughed out loud. Now we could have a real conversation.

"You look tired, Mom. Are you taking care of yourself? You don't want Dad and me to get all worried, do you?"

"Oh, you know, I'm trying to be brave about all this."

"I know you are. How's he doing—and give it to me straight, okay?"

"Not great."

"What does that mean?"

"The doctor says he expects your father to pull through this, but there's no guarantee. They have to knock out the infection, and the next couple of days, well, they're going to be crucial."

"And how are you holding up, Mom—seriously?"

"I'm just fine. Don't you spend one second worrying about me, dear."

She didn't look fine. Her eyes were bloodshot and swollen. The dark circles underneath them and the way she slouched in her chair told me that she was exhausted. It heightened my own concern and guilt for not flying back sooner.

Mom wasn't wearing makeup, and the wrinkles were more prominent in her face. The gray that had begun to sneak into her hair last year was overtaking it now. It was a strange feeling to be young and in the prime of life, noticing how your parents' features were changing with middle age. It was like looking into a mirror at what I'll go through someday. That's what made it so eerie.

Mom also had lost some weight. I made a comment about it and she blushed.

"Why don't you go up and visit with your father?" she said. "I know he'll be so glad to see you."

"Are you coming?"

"No, not just yet. I'll give you boys a little time to yourselves first. He's on the fourth floor, the room closest to the nurses' station—404."

As I stood to leave, she reached into one of the pockets of her baggy dress and removed her rosary, the beautiful one Dad had given her on her 40th birthday. She took one of the small beads between her thumb and index finger, lowered her head, and began silently moving her lips in prayer.

In the intensive care unit, they only allowed two hours of visitation in the morning and another two hours in the afternoon. When I got to my father's little room, we were already an hour into the afternoon session. Dad was lying in bed listening to Uncle Johnny. He had flown down from Detroit the previous morning. Back in 1970, Uncle Johnny and my Aunt Dottie had moved to Flint, Michigan, a booming city up north, where he'd gotten a much more secure job as a welder in a big auto plant.

When I reached out my hand to Uncle Johnny, he ignored it and wrapped his arms around me in a bear hug. Uncle Johnny was a hugger. He hugged everybody; it came natural for him.

When I shook Dad's hand, his grip was weak. It wasn't at all like my father. At the same time, Uncle Johnny asked about my flight and then my drive, and I responded politely.

"Uncle Johnny," I said before he could ask another question, "I hope you won't think this rude, but visiting time will be over soon. Would you mind if I spent some time alone with my dad?"

"Of course not. You go right ahead."

"Thanks. I hope I'm not breaking anything up."

"Not at all. We'll have plenty of time later," he said as he picked up a tattered brown satchel. "Besides, I wanta get 'round to some of the plants and give 'em my resume. I was just telling your dad 'bout how GM keeps cutting back production and now they're talkin' 'bout installing robots on the line. *Can you believe that?* Like some science-fiction movie. No way, right? Anyway, Dottie and me are thinkin' 'bout packing up the kids and movin' back to Beaumont . . . or maybe to Houston. The oil business down here is booming after the Arabs pulled that embargo crap. What do you think, college boy?"

"Well, you know what they say?" I said.

"No, what?"

"You know—about timing? About it being the best of times and the worst of times, about timing being everything. Remember?"

He nodded. "Yeah, right, but—"

I didn't let him finish. "Always remember, *this is your life*," I said like some old-sage, TV announcer, "And whatever *you*, John Gallagher, believe is correct, I'm sure if you proceed in a timely fashion with unquestioning purpose along a truly contrarian path, it will turn out—given time—to be precisely the right thing to do—*at the time*, of course."

He looked puzzled.

"I can get my old notebook so you can write all that down if you'd like," I said with a small grin.

"Touché, kid," he said, closing his eyes and nodding his head to tell me he remembered.

"Hey, I'm just playing around, Uncle Johnny. I'm sorry. I didn't—"

"No, it's okay. I deserved that," he said. "Had it comin' for a long time." Then he looked at Dad and said, "*Adios, amigo.* Hang in there."

"10/4," Dad replied.

As he closed the door, he shook his finger at me, but he also gave me a big smile. I was glad he wasn't sore about my smartass payback, and I made a mental note to have a serious conversation with my Uncle Johnny before he left town.

Dad and I made some small talk, and I tried to smile as much as possible as I stood facing him. I had anticipated the worst, that he would be all shriveled and lying on his deathbed. But he didn't look all that bad, considering the ominous white intravenous tube running into his left hand and the green oxygen tubes flaring into his nostrils. He was in good spirits and pleased to see me. His voice was steady and calm—like always—but raspy from so much coughing. All he wanted to talk about was me—how *I* was doing, for Chrissake. But I finally was able to pry out of him that he thought the worst was over and he'd be going home in a day or two. I was highly skeptical.

"I almost forgot," I said. "I brought you a card." It was one of those humorous Snoopy cards with a get-well-soon message. He chuckled and then had to cough, making a scratchy yet squishy sound like a bicycle braking on wet gravel. He opened the small envelope I'd put inside the card and removed three crisp five-dollar bills.

"It's the money I owe you from ruining—"

"I know what it's for," he interrupted. "Thank you."

As he placed the card, envelopes, and cash on a little table, I sat on the edge of his bed. His breathing was labored, and his face was thin and gaunt with a slightly bluish tint. I wanted to reach out and hold his hand in mine like he had done in our family room when I was 12, when he assured me that he wouldn't let any harm come to me from all the people en route to our house. But I couldn't bring myself to do it. We had a relationship that had evolved over the years based on respect, discipline, and adherence to rules, not intimacy.

"Dad?"

"Yes?"

"I need to tell you something."

"You don't need to do that, Son."

"Do what?"

"Make some big confession here 'cause you think I'm dyin' or something. Well, I'm not dyin'. I'm getting better."

"But I need to tell you something. It's been bothering me for a long time."

He turned his head and looked out the big glass window in the door. Out there, nurses hurried to check on critically ill patients, and family members gathered outside patient rooms. They spoke in hushed, anxious voices, no doubt discussing when, or if, their loved ones would be rejoining them in the outside world that seemed so far removed from this frightening place.

My father stared out that window like he couldn't bear to look at me. "Don't do it. I already know," he said.

"You don't know about this."

"I do," he said softly to the window.

"Well, what is it, then?"

After a few seconds, he shifted his gaze back to me. A strange grin had overtaken his face and it scared me at first. "Okay," he said, "you're gonna tell me the truth 'bout that hole that got blow'd into the carpet of the station wagon when we let you borrow it that Fourth of July, back when you'd just turned 16. How the firecracker didn't come from some mysterious guys who threw it through an open window into the car, you know, like you told us. You now wanta confess that you were cruising 'round in my car throwin' firecrackers out the window at lord knows what. How you lit one but accidentally dropped it onto the floorboard on the passenger side where it blew up and caught the carpet on fire."

"What?" I couldn't believe it. "Where are you getting all this—?"

"Fathers learn to read their sons—that is, if they stay close and keep their antenna up. That's why—"

"But you said you believed me. You made me write out a full description of the guys who threw that firecracker into the car."

"I asked for that description, but I never said I believed you. That's what your mother said."

"So, you think I lied?"

He ignored my question. "Did it scare you?" He laughed. "Did it make a lotta smoke?"

I shrugged. "A little," I said. What the hell? He was acting like he didn't care, and it seemed like a million years ago, so I asked, "But how did you know?"

"I just did," he said lightly and then let out three deep, barking coughs before he could continue. "Besides, I did a lot of foolish things when I was a boy. All young men do. You see, that's why you don't need to do this confession thing."

I was unnerved and tried to cover it up by being sarcastic and patronizing. "Okay, so you're a regular Sherlock Holmes *and* Sigmund Freud—all rolled into one," I said. "I get it. But that's not what I want to tell you about." My tone changed. "This is serious, Dad."

"Larry, don't do this. I told you, I already know."

I gave him an annoyed look that said, *Hey, smart guy, you don't know about this. This is something really important, okay?*

He shook his head, inhaled deeply from the oxygen tubes, and then let out a slow raspy sigh. "Okay, I'll tell you," he said. "You want to confess 'bout that last semester of your senior year in high school, how you—"

"That's not it," I interrupted, but he ignored me.

"—used to tell us you needed the car on weekends 'cause you had a date to take out some mystery girl—that you never wanted to talk 'bout, by the way. No details. But what you really wanted the car for was to drive to Louisiana to buy booze, since the drinking age is only 18 over there, and liquor stores in those Louisiana border towns will sell to anyone old enough to make a fist with their money and put it up on the counter. How you used to stash the bottles in your room. And—oh, this is the best part—how you used to supplement your stash by sneaking liquor from *my* bottles."

My eyes were wide with indignation. "Look," I said, "I may have put a few extra miles on the car some weekends, but what's this about taking booze from your bottles?"

Dad laughed and it made him cough again. I patted his back and gave him some tissues from a box by his bed. He spit something into the tissues and regained his breath. "Just 'cause you poured water into my vodka and gin bottles so they'd be at the same level, do you think that kept me from figuring out what you were doing?"

"I don't know what you're talking about," I said. "Besides, even if I did, vodka's not supposed to have any taste. Nobody can tell if there's a little water mixed in. That is, I mean, if there was a little water mixed in—which there wasn't! No one could tell."

He continued to stare at me without answering.

"Isn't that right?" I asked.

He smiled, then shook his head. "I suspected that you had a little business goin' at the time, collecting money from those derelicts in your senior class, then using my gas to go over to Louisiana to buy liquor for them—making a profit in the process."

He was enjoying these revelations of my indiscretions as a young entrepreneur. His eyes narrowed as he looked at me, straight through my eyes into my mind and soul, as only my father could do. I swallowed hard and tried to think of words to say to defend my enterprising actions. But before I could speak, he nodded at me and continued.

"I prayed it was just a teenage thing that you'd grow outta. I wanted to say something 'bout the underage alcohol." He paused to catch his breath. "But I figured it'd come out all hypocritical, you know, comin' from me."

He was right. I knew it all when I was 17, and I yearned at the time to have a relationship with my fellow graduating seniors, even one as pedestrian as their booze supplier. I would not have welcomed his advice or criticism back then, particularly in this area.

"I decided instead to trust in your character," he said, "that you wouldn't push things too far. Of course, I kept an eye out to make sure you didn't get outta control."

"Do you think I ever got out of control?" I asked.

"Not really, 'cept you came close once."

"When?"

"When you went off to college, that first semester. But I was able to get you straightened out."

"That's not the way I remember it."

"That's fine. You remember it any way you want," he said in a grating whisper. He cleared his throat and his voice was a little stronger. "But you did develop a good plan for your future that semester. And you did stop all the nonsense that was pulling down your grades. Right?"

"Maybe," I reluctantly conceded.

"So, I'm just glad we had this opportunity to talk and clear the air 'bout all that stuff. Now, if you don't mind, I'd like to—"

"Wait, that's not what I wanted to tell you about."

Anger flashed into his face. "Don't you think I know that? Can't you see what I'm trying to tell you? Why can't you just drop it?" He coughed and then refilled his lungs with a gurgling sound, sucking deeply from the green tubes, all the while assessing my reaction.

What's he saying? He couldn't know about that, I thought. *Could he?* All I could do was stare at him.

"I wonder where your mother is," he said. "Why don't you go check—?"

"No way. Tell me what you think you know."

"I swear, you may have a college degree, but you can still be dense as bricks when it comes to picking up on things." He spit into a tissue and then stared up at me with a sad face. "Can't you see I'm tired? I don't wanta talk 'bout this."

"You have to tell me," I said firmly.

After a long pause, he gave in. His voice was matter-of-fact. "I know what *Buddy* did."

I stood up, my toes curling in my shoes. My mind was racing yet not going anywhere. I gave him a disbelieving look, but it was weak. *He knows. My God, somehow, he knows.*

"You don't know about this," I said without conviction.

"I told you, I do," he said. "I don't know *why* you did it, but *I know what you did*—back then." He looked down at the IV tube draining into his hand.

"But how?"

"Do you really wanta do this?"

"Yes, I have to," I said numbly.

He coughed to clear his throat once more, and he exhaled slowly, trying to relax. "That police officer said Daniel shot himself with a single .38 caliber bullet that somehow mysteriously got into his father's gun. Well, I didn't buy his theory on how it got there. I couldn't see Dr. Carter, or any father for that matter, being so careless that he left a live round in a gun that he didn't keep under lock and key. I could tell there was something more to the story, something that you knew and wanted to get off your chest . . . but you couldn't. You acted so strange that night, what with lyin' to Allie 'bout the last time you saw Daniel, askin' me to pray for you in the car, havin' those bad dreams. I knew we had .38 caliber shells in the house, and I just put two and two together."

"What do you mean, me lying to Allie?"

He didn't speak. Instead, he shook his head and gave me that smug look again, the one that said he couldn't believe I thought I could ever hide anything from him.

After a few seconds of silence, he added, "When I checked, there was one bullet missing from my box of shells."

I was stunned. "But nobody counts bullets," I said.

"That .38 was a new gun that I bought just before that trouble with Mr. Washington—for protection, to keep in the trailer. I kept meaning to go to a practice range, but the bottom line is that I'd never fired that pistol. I loaded six shells out of a box of 20 into the gun that night I got all worked up. I checked in the cabinet on the morning after you got so scared from that dream." He paused. "The gun was still fully loaded, but I only found 13 shells in the box." He added softly, "I musta counted 'em a dozen times."

"But if you knew, then why, why didn't you say something, you know, to me?"

"I couldn't."

"*What*? What do you mean, you couldn't?"

"Don't you see? You have to appreciate that I didn't have a clue why—and I still don't know—why on earth you gave that boy a live round of ammunition."

"I didn't just give him—"

He put his hand up for me to stop as he cleared his throat again. "Hold on a second. Let me finish this point," he said. "If I woulda forced the issue and made you break down and tell me what I already knew, well, then we woulda had to go tell the authorities."

"Wait a minute, are you saying that—?"

"I'm saying," he interrupted, "if I'd heard you say outright that you gave that boy a bullet that he used to shoot himself . . . and you knew that I knew what you did, then we'd've been forced to go to the police."

"Why?"

"*Why*? 'Cause that's the *required* procedure in the circumstances. What kinda lesson would I be teaching if I didn't make you do the right thing? And at that point, the good Lord only knows what woulda happened—your school, the police, the Carter family knowing where that bullet came from, all the other repercussions. It woulda got all outta control."

"But I lived in Hell all those years."

"And I didn't?" he shot back at me.

"But you could've helped me deal with it. That was your job, your responsibility."

"My job, young man, was to provide for you and your mother, and my responsibility was to teach you right from wrong and try to set a good example for you, so you'd see how a man should behave." His voice was strained and he was getting agitated. He coughed several times into a tissue before he could continue. "Yes, if you'd told me everything, I coulda tried to help you deal with it all back then, but *only* after we'd followed the procedures required by law and by a civilized world.

Only after you told the authorities and made a full, truthful statement. *Only* after—"

"Are you saying that you couldn't bend those goddamn rules just once, for your own son's sake? That you wouldn't have been able to just keep it in the family? Is that what you're telling me? *Is it?*"

He turned his head and gazed out the window. The hissing from his oxygen tubes was the only sound in the room. When he finally looked back at me, his voice was barely audible as he said, "We tried to raise you as best we could, your mom and me. I thought that givin' you rules—clear boundaries that you live your life within—I thought that was the best way to teach you values that would serve you well when you became a man, like you are now. And what good are rules and values if you just disregard 'em when it suits your purpose or when the goin' gets tough?"

"I just wish I could have talked to you about it—back when I was a kid."

"I'm sorry, Son. But, if you'd told me, then that woulda involved consequences. It woulda opened a messy can of worms."

"Yeah, I can see how *you* would think that way," I said with a sneer.

"You gotta understand, I didn't know why you did it, what part you played in that boy's death. I still don't." It was an invitation.

I slumped back down on his bed. This time, however, I reached beyond my inhibitions and took his hand in mine. It was cold and I thought I felt it trembling slightly. His eyes told me he was afraid after all these years that he would now learn the truth and that the truth would be ugly.

"He paid me $20, Dad. I never had a red cent to my name before that, and Daniel Carter gave me 20 bucks for swiping one lousy bullet. He wouldn't ever be serious and tell me what he wanted it for. Maybe I didn't care. I wanted that money. I'd ignored all the other signs Daniel gave us that he was sick, and I guess I ignored this one too. Besides, he got me all twisted up about doing it as a way to break the rules just once, you know, *your* rules."

He gave me a cold stare, but it had no intensity. Behind his eyes I saw doubt, uncertainty. A *Did I do the right thing?* sign hung on his brow. I could read it. I could read *him*, I suddenly realized, just like he'd been able to read me over all these years. And I felt a deep sorrow and was ashamed of myself for injuring him with my words.

"Or, I don't know, Dad, maybe just rules in general. Daniel called me Mr. Goody Goody, and I guess he got under my skin. I'm sure that was his plan."

When he didn't respond, I continued, "I don't know anymore. It was a long time ago, but it sure screwed up my life. Then, when I was about to graduate from college, about to go to work, and finally get on with a semi-normal life, Marty comes along." I shook my head.

He continued to look at me but didn't speak. So, we sat there in silence once more, my father with all his tubes, hacking cough, and cold hands, and his only son with a hollow ache in the pit of my stomach and tears forming in my eyes.

Suddenly, with his right hand, my father made the sign of the cross over his weakened, recumbent body and closed his eyes. The muscles in his face tightened, and I heard him inhale deeply through the green tubes as though he was trying to draw the Holy Spirit into his receptive body.

At first, it frightened me. "Dad?" I asked as a cold chill passed through me.

He didn't respond, but his rhythmic breathing returned, and I instinctively knew he was in no immediate danger. As I looked at him, my free hand rose to my forehead, and like him, I also opened myself with the sign of the cross. The chill was replaced by a warmth which permeated my entire body. After 30 seconds passed, each of us deep in his own prayer-vision, he crossed himself again and opened his eyes. I had been staring at him, concentrating on him the entire time, and now he watched me cross myself to end my prayer of hope and thanksgiving—for him.

"Amen," I said as I leaned forward. I rested my weight on my left elbow and gently cupped the back of his head. I continued to hold his left hand with my right. "It's okay," I said, his face close to mine. "I was in a pretty bad place for a long time, but I made it through okay. I come from pretty good stock, you know." Then I added, "I love you, Dad."

"I love you too, Son, with all my heart," he whispered hoarsely. The pressure from his cold hand intensified as he added, "And do you know what else?"

I tensed, staring into his face. His forehead tightened and there was a puffiness in his eyes. Words were difficult, but he smiled and said, "I also like you." He was choking from the sickness deep in his lungs as well as the emotion, but he added in a booming voice, "I like you a lot!"

"I like you too, Dad," I said. That's when I lost control, and he reached up with both arms and drew me to his thin body and all his tubes.

After a minute, when I was once again the master of my own emotions, I sat up and said, "Dad?"

"Yes, Son?"

"You know, it's probably better if we don't tell Mom all this stuff about Daniel and everything that happened back then. Don't you agree?"

At that moment, the door opened, and Mom walked into the room. She leaned over to place her purse on the floor beside a chair.

My father winked at me with his left eye just like Marty used to. "What's it worth to you?" he whispered.

Mom straightened up and saw us sitting together, holding hands on the bed. She looked surprised. "What are you boys laughing about?"

The pneumonia slowly cleared up, and when Dad was finally released from the hospital, they told him to take it easy for a while. He did—for about two days. Then he went back to work. The doctor said it was quicker than he would have liked, but he said that my father was an extraordinary man. I agreed with him.

That was a couple of months ago. I fear that Dad's respiratory system will continue to deteriorate over the coming years, but neither he nor my mother are willing to talk seriously about it with me. I haven't pressed them, although I call regularly to chastise him about his smoking and make certain he's taking his medication and using those bronchial inhalers the doctor prescribed.

My parents seem to have adjusted to my move to Houston. They refer to it as "the Big City." They were pleased when I told them that I'd recently started going to church again, even though it wasn't a Roman Catholic Church. This girl that I work with—she had just started at the firm, like me, and she's a University of Texas graduate and a fox, just like Allie—insisted that I go with her to an Episcopal Church in Houston where she and her parents were members. It was because I started telling her some personal things late one night, including how I had drifted from the Catholic Church and felt lost in my relationship with God. A good friend had told me long ago when we were both kids that women love it when you open up and tell them real personal stuff, but this time it was true.

I've been giving it some thought, and I might convert to become an Episcopalian. Episcopalians call themselves "Catholics" and are similar to Roman Catholics in their liturgical style, but they seem more laid back and not as judgmental. Allie thinks I should do it. She knows me better than anyone and hangs out a lot with my new friend and me.

And if I do convert my religious affiliation, don't think it's because of that new friend, the girl I was referring to. Just because we're together so much, that doesn't mean anything. It seems like everywhere we go, there's always people—complete strangers—staring at us and telling us that we're such a cute couple. I tell them, "No way! You've got us all wrong." Arthur Andersen has a strict rule that prohibits their professional staff from dating one another or dating client personnel. You can get in big trouble if you get caught breaking that rule.

* * * * *

I've been incredibly busy at work, and I recently did something stupid that made my father angry. Our staff had been working long hours to complete the audit for a big Fortune 500 company, an energy-services conglomerate based in Houston. The company had closed several complex transactions just before their fiscal year-end. As a result, their earnings were going to be better than Wall Street was expecting.

Every 30 minutes we'd get word that their CFO was losing his patience with us and couldn't understand what was taking so long. He was anxious for us to finish the audit and bless the financial results, so they could get the good news out and get their stock price up. Then our audit partner on the account would call and want a detailed status report from each of us like a little kid constantly asking, "Are we there yet?" He also was quick to remind us that auditors who couldn't complete assignments on a timely basis didn't advance within the firm.

I was the rookie, the least experienced auditor on our team. But it seemed obvious to me that we could be a lot more efficient if they would just leave us alone and let us go about systematically verifying the revenues and expenses and the various documents supporting all the significant transactions for the year. That way, the CFO and our audit partner, who were big buddies, could be confident that everything was properly recorded in the financial report that our firm would be certifying.

But I guess that's not the way it works, and things were insanely hectic and hurried for our audit team. Workpapers and client documents were strewn everywhere when the phone rang in the conference room we had dubbed our audit war room. The guy who answered the phone shouted above the din, "Hey, Torrence, it's your mother!" A chuckle came from another of my colleagues who was totaling a column of numbers on a ten-key adding machine.

"Oh, my God," I moaned. I looked at the watch on my wrist. I hadn't slept in a day and a half and had a dozen points on my mind that all had to be buttoned up in the next 24 hours. "Tell her I can't talk now. Ask what she wants and take a message, okay?"

Fifteen minutes later, the war room phone rang again, and the same person answered it. He nodded and said, "Uh-huh. Just a minute," and then cupped his hand over the voice piece so the caller couldn't hear. "Larry," he said sheepishly, "it's a guy with a deep voice who says he's your father. He says he needs to talk to you—right now."

Why am I not surprised? I thought as I locked my fingers behind a very tired neck and squeezed my cheeks with two forearms. I took a deep breath, then released the vice on my face as I exhaled and leaned forward to accept the telephone.

"Yes, sir?" I said, trying to sound chipper.

As usual, the voice was firm but calm. *Son, we need to get something straight—a rule. Do I have your attention?*

"Yes, I'm listening." The pace of work in the war room had slowed. The other five sets of ears in the room had all perked up.

Dad spoke slowly, methodically. *Your mom and I know that you're busy at work, so we try not to bother you there unless it's something important. If I call and you are extremely busy, you may have someone tell me that you'll call me later. I probably won't be impressed with your manners, but I'll understand. But anytime your mother calls, no matter where you are or what you are doing, you will take her call. You will not have someone she doesn't know say, 'He's too busy for you, so please leave a message.' Do you understand?*

"Yes, sir."

Good, now call your mother as soon as we hang up. She's still at work, and she needs to ask you 'bout something.

"I will."

And by the way, that's a good rule to follow with your wife, when you get married, Son. It's worked for me for 23 years. Women are funny 'bout stuff like that, and you have to be more sensitive.

"I agree," I said. I removed my glasses, closed my eyes, and rubbed my forehead in fatigue and shame.

And, Larry?

"Yes, sir?"

That's not a bad rule to follow when a very special gal like Allie calls you at work. Given the way you two feel 'bout each other, I'm sure she'd appreciate—

"What?" I exclaimed into the phone as I stood and turned my back to the big conference table. "How did you know about that?" I demanded. I felt my colleagues' stares as the work behind me slowed even further.

I heard him chuckle, then he said, *Like most everything you do, I just know. It's not that hard if you keep your antenna up.*

"Tell me what you think you know."

Listen, I know you're busy now, so why don't you call me when you have a free moment? We can discuss it some more, you know, when you're not so tied up.

"I'd like to discuss it now," I said.

Oh, I couldn't possibly take up any more of your precious time—

"Dad," I interrupted. "Please tell me why you said that."

Well, Allie's a wonderful gal, quite a few years older, but I suppose that's your business. Listen, if you need someone to talk with, we'd be glad to listen. That is, if you ever have the time.

"Dad?"

Speak up a little, Larry, I can barely hear you.

"Dad, she's just a really good friend—a special friend like you taught me, remember? She's someone I can talk to about anything, have fun with, and just be myself around—but as a friend, that's all." My words were the only sound in the war room. They bounced off the wall I was facing and ricocheted through the room for everyone to hear.

That's what I figured. I told your mom as much, that you two were most likely just friends. But she's worried 'bout you over in the Big City. Listen, you call her right now. Tell her you're sorry for your rudeness a minute ago and set up a time you can call her at home and have a nice long chat.

"I will."

Right now, okay?

"Okay, right now. I got it!"

There was silence, and I sensed that our conversation had

ended, that he was going to hang up before I could tell him.

"Dad?" I whispered in a panic, afraid it was too late, that he was gone.

Yes?

"Thank you. You know, for everything."

You're welcome.

"And Dad?"

Yes?

I didn't care if they heard me in the war room. I had never said it before on the telephone, but a powerful sensation deep inside had taken over. I had to tell him what he already knew. I said, "I love you, Dad."

He replied immediately. *I love you too, Son, with all my heart.*

I hung up the phone and walked briskly out of the room, holding my glasses in one hand and rubbing my moist eyes with the back of my other hand, cursing myself for having so little control over my emotions. Behind me, I could hear the decibel level increasing in the war room. The busybodies back there were probably talking about me, but I didn't care. I had to find a more private phone. I had to call my mother.

>Two mistakes that I can never repair;
>Forgive me, friends—accept this, my confession;
>My youth's been a mix of regret and despair
>Alone, at the outskirts of redemption.
>
>So, bless me, Father; there's no more to say,
>Except I'm sorry for each transgression,
>And with God's good grace along my way
>I'll find the hallowed halls of redemption.
>
>*- Lawrence J. Torrence, 1974*

THE END

POSTSCRIPT

I'm doing well . . . I suppose. But there's something nagging at me like a relentless drumbeat pounding over and over in my mind. It's those words Daniel said, "I'm leavin' now, Jackie, but you gonna be just fine. Buddy, he'll take care of you." She was the gravy, such a beautiful, trusting child, and I can't stop wondering what she's like, all grown up. I know that I owe her (and her family) an explanation. I know that the pounding in my head won't stop until I find her, look into her eyes, tell her the truth about her brother, and ask for her forgiveness.

But that's another story.

AUTHOR'S NOTE

This novel and the characters and events described in it are fictional. Unfortunately, the tragedy of suicide by adolescents and young adults that is portrayed herein, including the toll that it takes on family members and young friends, is all too real.

When my daughter was 12, a friend and classmate of hers took his life. The young boy's sudden demise came as a great shock to everyone who knew him. To help my confused daughter cope with her grief and make sense out of a senseless act, to get her to stop blaming herself for not being a better friend, I had to crawl inside her skin. I went to parent meetings at her school and listened closely to the counselors they brought in, and I tried desperately to understand my daughter's innermost emotions, to feel her adolescent pain. That process led to this fictional story.

Someone once asked the legendary Hank Williams, who couldn't read sheet music and had limited formal education, how he came up with all those great songs. His answer was something along the lines, "I just pick up the pen. It's God who moves it." I know that's what I experienced writing this novel. It's been a long journey, along which I've been steadily driven and inspired by forces I cannot fully comprehend—to craft this story and ultimately have it published.

I hope that readers find it entertaining but, most importantly, find it enlightening. I hope they will reflect on how the pressures on our youth and the suicide rate among young people have increased at an alarming rate since the Sixties and Seventies, when this story takes place. During 2020, about

AUTHOR'S NOTE

6,650 Americans ages 10–24 died by their own hand, one every 80 minutes. Suicide is now the second leading cause of death for this age group.*

Mental health professionals cite many reasons for the increase in suicide rates among our young people over the past several decades. However, they generally agree that the steady decline in family unity during this period is one of the major factors. As Allie Masterson, the child psychologist character in this story, noted, suicidal adolescents typically feel misunderstood, especially by their parents (or parent), and believe they cannot effectively communicate with their guardian(s). And so, in today's digital era, they often turn to social media and inappropriate websites for behavioral guidance and reinforcement of their self-worth, instead of opening up to Mom, Dad, an adult family member, a teacher, or a friend.

In this story, I've portrayed situations that can lead young people to feelings of hopelessness and suicidal acts, contrasted against the support and inner strength that can be provided by engaged and loving parents and good friends. If reading this story motivates a family member or friend to reach out to a young person they're concerned for, or if it inspires an at-risk youngster to seek a caring ear or to call the 988 Lifeline (or 800-273-8255), my goal in writing this book will have been fulfilled.

*According to statistics provided by Centers for Disease Control and Prevention.

Made in the USA
Las Vegas, NV
15 March 2023